THE GENERATIVE INTERPRETATION OF DIALECT

A STUDY OF MODERN GREEK PHONOLOGY

BRIAN NEWTON

Professor of Linguistics,
Simon Fraser University

CAMBRIDGE
at the University Press · 1972

Published by the Syndics of the Cambridge University Press
Bentley House, 200 Euston Road, London NW1 2DB
American Branch: 32 East 57th Street, New York, N.Y. 10022

Library of Congress Catalogue Card Number: 72–187080

ISBN: 0 521 084970

Printed in Great Britain
at the University Printing House, Cambridge
(Brooke Crutchley, University Printer)

Contents

Map

Tables and figures

Preface

Most of the ideas presented in this book will be found somewhere or the other in the works listed in the bibliography; I also rely heavily on them for data although my numerous wanderings in Greece have taken me to all major dialect areas.

My main thanks must go to the hundreds of 'informants' in the villages of mainland Greece and the islands who have never failed to answer with patience and care the strange questions of a strange *turístas*, and also to my colleagues in Athens and Saloniki who have put their intimate knowledge of modern Greek linguistics at my disposal, especially N. Andriotis, N. Conomis, S. Karatzas, V. Phoris and A. I. Thavoris. I am grateful to the University of Cape Town for allowing me a sabbatical leave in 1963 for field work in Greece and to the Canada Council, who made possible by their award of a Leave Fellowship a second year of data-collection in 1968–9. The President's Research Fund, Simon Fraser University, assisted me with typing costs. Certain sections of chapters 3, 6 and 7 contain material previously published in *Lingua*, *Journal of Linguistics*, *Canadian Journal of Linguistics* and *Language* and I am grateful to the publishers of these journals for allowing me to use it.

B. N.

Vancouver
Canada
August 1971

Special symbols used

θ A voiceless dental fricative as in English *thigh.*

δ A voiced dental fricative as in English *thy.*

x A voiceless velar fricative as in Scottish *loch*, German *Buch.*

γ A voiced velar fricative as in Spanish *fuego.*

č A voiceless palatal[1] affricate as in English *chin.*

ǰ A voiced palatal affricate as in English *gin.*

t^s A voiceless dental affricate as in English *bits.*

d^z A voiced dental affricate as in English *bids.*

š A voiceless palatal sibilant as in English *ship.*

ž A voiced palatal sibilant as in English *pleasure.*

ŋ A velar nasal as in English *sing.*

r̥ A voiceless trill as in a whispered Scottish pronunciation of *row.*

n′ A palatal nasal as in French *montagne.*

l′ A palatal lateral as in Italian *gli.*

s′ A voiceless slightly palatal sibilant between [s] and [š].

z′ A voiced slightly palatal sibilant between [z] and [ž].

k′ A voiceless palatal stop as in English *cute.*

g′ A voiced palatal stop as in English *regular.*

x′ A voiceless palatal fricative as in German *Ich.*

γ′ A voiced palatal fricative, somewhat as the second segment of English *view* or the final one of French *travail.*
A prime may also be used after other symbols to indicate the palatalized (y-coloured) consonants found in some Thessalian and Macedonian dialects.

N A cover symbol for any nasal.

[1] 'Palatal' is used throughout to include [č, ǰ, š, ž], which are phonetically palato-alveolar; similarly 'dental' is used of the alveolar sounds [t^s, d^z, s, z].

P A cover symbol for [p] or [b].
T A cover symbol for [t] or [d].
K A cover symbol for [k] or [g].
ä A low front vowel as in English *cat* (ordinary Greek [a] being more central as in French *la*).
ü A high front round vowel as in French *tu*.
ö A mid front round vowel as in French *œuf*.

Diagonals are used to enclose the 'underlying forms' normally common to all dialects, square brackets the phonetic forms specific to individual dialects. Thus 'underlying' /xéri/ 'hand' is pronounced [x′éri] in Athens, [x′ér] in the north, [šéri] in Crete and Cyprus.

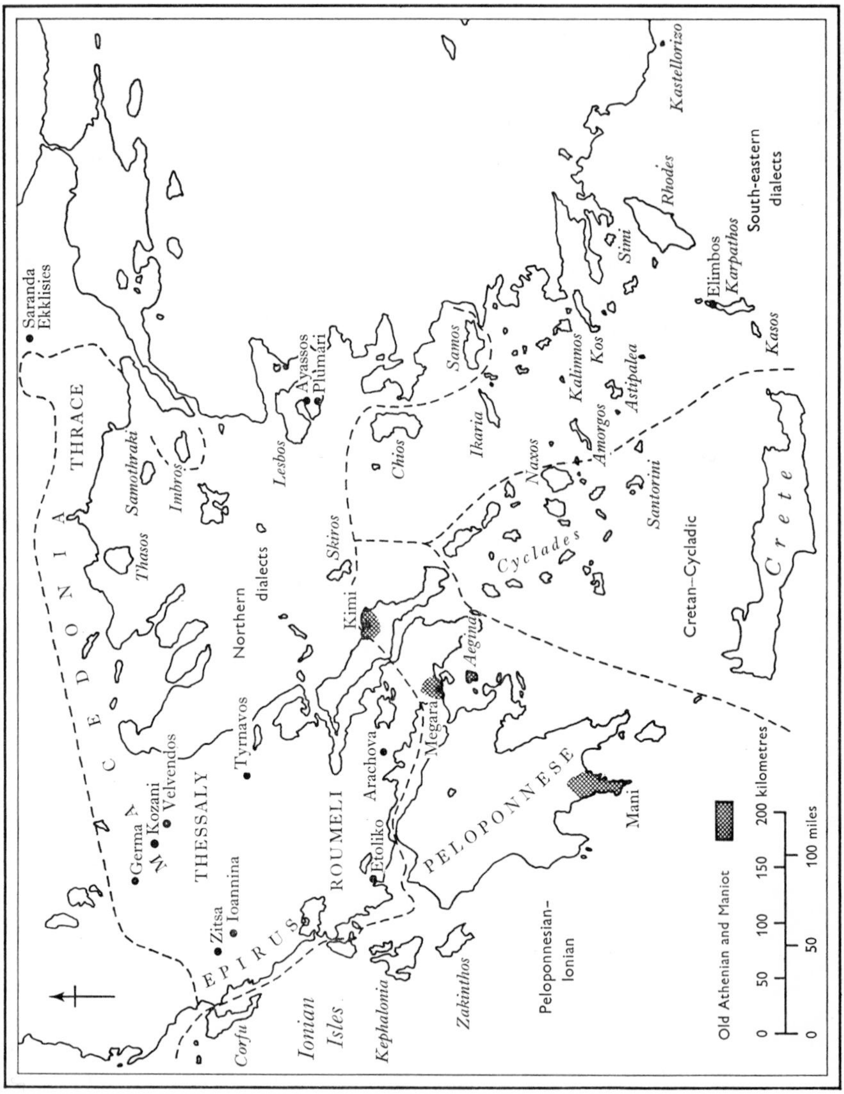

MACEDONIA
THRACE
THESSALY
ROUMELI
EPIRUS
PELOPONNESE
Saranda Ekklisies
Germa
Kozani
Velvendos
Tyrnavos
Zitsa
Ioannina
Etoliko
Arachova
Megara
Kimi
Ayassos
Plumari
Mani
Elimbos
Samothraki
Imbros
Thasos
Lesbos
Skiros
Chios
Samos
Ikaria
Naxos
Amorgos
Astipalea
Kalimnos
Kos
Simi
Rhodes
Karpathos
Kasos
Kastellorizo
Santorini
Cyclades
Crete
Aegina
Corfu
Ionian Isles
Kephalonia
Zakinthos
Northern dialects
Cretan–Cycladic
South-eastern dialects
Peloponnesian–Ionian
Old Athenian and Maniot
0 50 100 150 200 kilometres
0 50 100 miles

1 *Introduction*

1.0 The first chapter begins by stating the central aim of this book (the establishment of a descriptive framework for the study of modern Greek dialects) and 1.2 seeks to justify briefly the interpretation of dialectal variation as the outcome of historical changes acting on an originally uniform language rather than as a conglomeration of static self-contained phonological systems. The next two sections describe the sounds of the various dialects in terms of the usual articulatory features and 1.5 lists the segments (phonemes) which can be shown to underlie (or provide the historical source for) these sounds. Section 1.6 presents a rough classification of the 'core' dialects, whose phonological structures are studied in this book (i.e. all except those of southern Italy, Tsakonia and Asia Minor). Readers with some knowledge of linguistics will doubtless wish to proceed immediately to chapter 2.

1.1 Aims

Ancient Greek παιδία, pronounced something like [paydía] (with the accent realized as a rise in pitch), and meaning 'young children' or 'young slaves', persists in modern standard Greek as [peδyá] (or better [peδγʹá], with a voiced palatal fricative rather than a glide). Its accent is now represented by increased loudness ('dynamic stress') and its meaning is 'children, lads, folks'. This is a fairly commonplace piece of information, familiar to many readers of this book. But why should anyone be interested in it? Among other things it tells us something about the way a certain word has changed in sound, and an investigation of this and other items enables us to formulate the general rules which correlate ancient and modern sound systems. But sound change itself may be studied for a variety of reasons. There are at least three possible motivations, and the sort of data we select for examination as well as the method of description we employ will be largely determined by our particular goal:

(*a*) We may be interested in accounting for all the changes which are observed to have affected the sound structure of Greek over the period for which documentary evidence is available or which is accessible to the methods of internal and comparative reconstruction. This is an important and, particularly in the case of Greek, rich and rewarding field. This book is not concerned, however, with the history of Greek as such.

(*b*) We may wish to seek an explanation for the phonological (morphophonemic) alternations of a language or dialect at a given stage of its evolution. As was observed by the great historical linguists of the last century, sound change (specifically, 'conditional merger') often has the effect of introducing 'irregularity' into a language. The Latin morpheme meaning 'flower' had two shapes, *flos* (in the nominative singular) and *flor* (in the other forms of its paradigm), and it is easy to establish that the reason for this 'biallomorphy' lies in a sound change which replaced *s* by *r* intervocalically in the pre-classical period; so that while, e.g., *flos* remained with a final sibilant, *flosem* went to *florem*. This alternation between *s* and *r* occurs throughout classical Latin (cf. *genus*:*generis*, *est*:*erat*, *mus*:*muris*) and is clearly an important phonological feature of the language. The possibility of studying morphophonemic alternation from a synchronic (descriptive) point of view provides one of the main justifications for modern 'generative' phonology. It is important to notice that while some changes leave a mark on the language in the form of alternations, not all do. Furthermore, changes which do leave alternations do not do so in every morpheme affected by them. The fronting of Latin *ū* to French *u* has left no trace in the modern language and there is no evidence within classical Latin itself to suggest that the *r* of *ara* 'altar' was once *s*; it is true that we know from comparative evidence that it was indeed *s* (cf. Umbrian *asa*), but this information cannot be recovered by internal reconstruction and is accordingly irrelevant to a generative phonology of classical Latin (it could form no part of the Roman speaker's linguistic 'competence'). The study of morphophonemic alternation therefore ranges over such data as are available to the native speaker and is not concerned with phenomena accessible only to the historian or dialectologist. Clearly the generative phonologist's 'rules' will to a large extent recapitulate some of the language's history, and aims (*a*) and (*b*) may lead to very similar types of activity (although in strictly generative studies considerations of simplicity and naturalness may take precedence over the faithful reproduction of known historical fact). Again the purpose of this book is not to describe the generative phonology of modern Greek as such; rather it is orientated towards a reconstruction of the actual sequence of events which led to the dialectal differentiation of the modern language, and it does not attempt to handle alternations which are common to all dialects. Furthermore there is no explicit discussion of 'morpheme structure' (the principles which determine the set of possible 'underlying forms', or sound sequences in the structures from which the morphemes of the modern dialects are derived by the application of sound changes).

(*c*) We may wish to account for the interdialectal variation which characterizes a language at a particular stage. Dialects arise because many sound changes fail to diffuse over a whole speech community, so that the study of dialects and the study of a language's history are intimately connected; furthermore dialectal variation may involve differences in patterns of alternation (Umbrian lacked the *s/r* alternation of Latin). Closely linked as the methods and results associated with these three approaches are, our selection of data will be largely determined in accordance with our particular interest. The present book sets out to make a modest contribution towards the achievement of this third goal, that is, to suggest a framework for the study of dialectal variation in modern Greek.

To clarify the relation of choice of goal to data selection let us again consider [peδyá]. The most obvious historical changes affecting ancient [paydía] have been as follows:

(1) The diphthong [ay] has developed to [e]. This has not resulted in any obvious alternation pattern and the change has affected all dialects. This means that the change from [ay] to [e] is of no relevance to the functioning of the modern language, so that only a historian of Greek would wish to consider it.

(2) Ancient [d] is now continued as the fricative [δ]. Now this change was inhibited by a preceding nasal (e.g. ancient [ándres] 'men' has [d], never [δ], in all modern dialects), so that the possibility of [d]:[δ] alternation arose. Does it occur? I think we can say that it occurs marginally in the case of the word for 'ten'. Ancient [déka] goes to modern [δéka] but [héndeka] 'eleven' is represented by [éndeka]. It is doubtful, though, whether there is much point in setting up a rule '[d] goes to [δ] except after a nasal', although if such cases were much more frequent it might be worth while. In any case all dialects agree in this matter and even if alternation were regular it would belong to generative phonology rather than to the topic of this book.

(3) Ancient [i] before a vowel goes to [y] and any stress borne by it

is shifted forward. This development has had a far-reaching effect on the structure of the language. [peδyá] matches the singular [peδí] and illustrates the common rule that neuters in stressed [í] have a plural in [yá]. Thus the 'biallomorphy' of the stem (the alternation between [peδí] and [peδy]) has a simple explanation in terms of a particular historical development. A description of modern Greek which incorporates the change in the form of a 'rule' will clearly be more revealing than one which merely repeats the facts. However, from our point of view the rule is important, not because it accounts for alternation of this type, but because not all dialects have undergone it. Thus in Megara (on the isthmus of Corinth) and in Zakinthos we find [peδía], which means that these dialects are distinguished by not possessing that part of the rule of 'glide formation' which converts stressed [í] to [y] before vowels. In the island of Karpathos we observe that the word is pronounced [peía], which means that not only did the above change fail to occur but the [δ] dropped. Again we are confronted not with an isolated phenomenon but with the effect of a change which dropped the intervocalic voiced fricatives [v], [δ] and [γ] over a wide area. Just as the replacement of [í] by [y] has resulted in alternation so has the loss of voiced fricatives. Consider a dialect which underwent 'glide formation' and then 'voiced fricative deletion'. Its [peδía] would first go to [peδyá], and then when the fricative was later lost from the singular [peδí] the plural would remain unaffected because of the protection afforded by the [y]. The resultant [peí]:[peδyá] type of alternation is found in various Dodecanesian dialects.

I shall be concerned then with establishing the rules which account for dialectal variation, and shall give general indications of their areal extent; incidental reference will be made to the types of alternation induced by the rules where appropriate.

1.2 General approach

In discussing various dialectal forms of the word for 'children' I referred to the occurrence of sound changes (or, looking at the matter from a synchronic angle, 'rules') and it is clear that a description of dialectal variation will involve a specification of the changes operative in each area. It is equally clear that in illustrating the effects of a given change or series of changes on a particular word we shall require a suitable starting point. In this instance there would be no gain in starting with, say, [paydía], for the monophthongization of [ay] and the fricativization of [d] are common to all dialects. In fact it turns out that we do not need to go further back than [peδía] to account for all the dialectal forms of the word in terms of phonological processes. In general I shall not delve any further back into the history of Greek than is necessary to illustrate the operation of the rules required for the purposes of the book. In accordance with common practice I shall refer to the starting point as the 'underlying form' and enclose its transcription in diagonals (e.g. /peδía/).[1] Square brackets are used to indicate the phonetic form of the word, i.e. the broad phonetic transcription of the word as it appears in a particular dialect. When reference has to be made to a form intermediate between the underlying and phonetic representations square brackets will also be used, but this should not cause any confusion. It should be noted that just as it is important to select an appropriate cut-off point in working backwards from a given pronunciation, so we must stop at a reasonable point in the other direction; there are clearly many phonetic peculiarities of dialects which must be ignored in a general survey of this kind (if indeed they are known!). In general, differences which cannot be expressed in terms of the distinctive phonological features mentioned in 1.3 and 1.4 will not be mentioned. For example, the retroflexion of /l/ in the Sphakia area of Crete, or the differences in the points of articulation of palatalized /s/, the lesser or greater degree of fronting in /a/ and many similar points of divergence belong to the detailed investigation of specific dialects.

Because dialects arise from an originally more or less uniform language it is possible to show that they can for the most part be described in terms of a common set of underlying forms; variation is introduced by the phonological processes which operate on these forms. Not only may certain processes be completely absent from a given set of dialects, or differ somewhat in character from one dialect to the other; we also find instances where two dialects have the same underlying forms and share a common set of rules, but differ in the order in which they apply the rules. While this is a commonplace of dialectology, readers new to linguistics might appreciate an illustration from modern Greek of what is involved here.

[1] Because the most appropriate starting point may vary according to the purpose in hand the same word may be shown in more than one way; in particular verbs may be unstressed and marked for vowel length or stressed and not so marked. Single symbols enclosed in diagonals indicate underlying segments or epenthetic elements such as /γ/ which are acted on by subsequent rules.

In all modern dialects there is a prohibition against a sequence of two voiceless fricatives (other than [sf]). Where such a sequence would be expected we find instead a sequence of fricative + stop (with certain qualifications not relevant to the present discussion). Thus while underlying /skotóθike/ 'he was killed' goes to [skotóθik'e] in, e.g., a Peloponnesian dialect, /γráfθike/ 'it was written' and /kurázθike/ 'he was tired' go to [γráftik'e] and [kurástik'e]. There is in other cases no evidence in the form of alternations to indicate whether a sequence such as [sk] originates in earlier /sx/ or /sk/; [sk'ílos] 'dog', for instance, reflects an earlier /sk/, while [sk'ízo] 'I tear' may be regarded as coming from /sx/. We can therefore claim for all dialects the (rough) rule that any voiceless obstruent following a voiceless fricative will be a stop. Let this be labelled the rule of 'manner dissimilation'. Now we noted in the last section that [i] converts to [y] before a vowel. This [y] usually then goes to [x'] (a palatal voiceless fricative as in German *ich*) after a voiceless consonant or to [γ'] (the voiced counterpart of this) after a voiced consonant. Thus /mátia/ 'eyes' goes first to [mátya], then this to [mátx'a], [δóndia] 'teeth' (from underlying /δóntia/) to [δóndya], then [δóndγ'a]. Consider now a word such as /ráfia/ 'shelves'; this will go by 'glide formation' to [ráfya] and by the present rule ('consonantality') to [ráfx'a]. However [fx'] from original /fx/ is subject to manner dissimilation (e.g. /efxí/ 'blessing' becomes [efx'í] by 'palatalization', then efk'í]), and the question which naturally poses itself is whether this [fx'] from /fi/ undergoes manner dissimilation. The answer is that it does indeed go to [fk'] by manner dissimilation in some dialects, yielding e.g. [ráfk'a]. The simplest way to describe this difference is to say that in some dialects manner dissimilation precedes consonantality, while in others the rules are transposed:

(1)	ráfia	efxí
Glide formation	ráfya	
Palatalization		efx'í
Manner dissimilation		**efk'í**
Consonantality	**ráfx'a**	

(2)	ráfia	efxí
Glide formation	ráfya	
Palatalization		efx'í
Consonantality	ráfx'a	
Manner dissimilation	**ráfk'a**	**efk'í**

Even where dialects agree in having undergone a given pair of rules in the same order it is often important to specify this order. We saw, for instance, that some dialects have [peí] but plural [peδyá]. Clearly the [í] of the plural went to [y] before the loss of voiced fricatives occurred, for if the contrary had been the case the process which deleted the [δ] of [peδí] would also have deleted that of [peδía]:

(3)	peδí	peδía
Voiced fricative deletion	**peí**	peía
Glide formation		***peyá**

As far as I am aware such a dialect does not in fact exist.[1]

It is important to notice that in accounting for dialectal variation in terms of ordered rules acting on underlying forms I am presenting the facts in so far as they are recoverable by internal reconstruction (based on alternation in a single dialect) or cross-dialectal comparison, not as they may be deduced, in certain favourable instances, from extant documentation. The justification for this is partly that the history of only very few dialects is reasonably well attested (e.g. Cretan, Cypriot) but more particularly that I am concerned essentially with exhibiting the nature of the differences between dialects as these differences represent a synchronic reality. Thus, while the 'rules' we shall require reflect in general historical processes, and their ordering recapitulates the actual temporal sequence of events, there may very well be discrepancies between historical fact and synchronic description. One obvious illustration is provided by the account just given of the difference between dialects with [ráfx'a], [efk'í], which were said to apply manner dissimilation and consonantality in that order, and those in which the order is reversed, yielding [ráfk'a], [efk'í]. For it is perfectly possible, and indeed likely, that dialects of the last type went through the [ráfx'a], [efk'í] stage and then at some later time manner dissimilation reoccurred:

(4)	ráfia	efxí
Glide formation	ráfya	
Palatalization		efx'í
Manner dissimilation		**efk'í**
Consonantality	ráfx'a	
Manner dissimilation	**ráfk'a**	

[1] The asterisk is used throughout to indicate an incorrect 'output', not a reconstructed form.

The crucial point to notice, however, is that the question of whether derivation (4) or (2) represents the true historical development is irrelevant to a statement of the present-day realities of the language. These are more naturally represented by derivation (2), which has the virtue of relative simplicity. Then again, while historical processes are extended in time, the picture imposed on our minds by 'derivations' tends to be that of instantaneous changes; yet still a third historical account of a [ráfk'a], [efk'í] dialect might assume the action of manner dissimilation over a long period, enclosing, so to speak, that of consonantality at both ends. In fact there are occasional cases where the relevant historical processes were so spaced in relation to one another that the conventional 'derivation' cannot easily be made to work.[1] For the most part, though, what I shall have to say can be interpreted either as recoverable history or synchronic description. Most linguists would probably accept that the two approaches are not as incompatible as they once seemed.

1.3 The consonants of modern Greek

Although it would certainly be possible to describe the sound structure of modern Greek dialects in terms of unanalysed sounds (or 'phonemes' or 'segments'), only by using a classificatory scheme of some sort can we make fairly simple and straightforward statements; this is largely because historical sound changes act in general not on individual sounds but on classes of sounds. For instance, at some stage a change must have occurred whereby [mp] was replaced by [mb], [nt] by [nd] and [ŋk] (as in English *sink*) by [ŋg]. Rather than list the individual changes we prefer to regard them as instances of a single change which brought about the voicing of stops after nasals; or, looking at the matter from a purely descriptive point of view, we can state that in modern Greek stops are always voiced after nasals. I shall follow the usual custom of describing sounds in terms of their articulation and try as far as possible to avoid technical terms which do not at the time of writing have general currency outside linguistic journals. The only term which may puzzle readers lacking direct acquaintance with linguistics is 'strident'; I shall use this to describe the sibilant sounds such as [s] and [č] (as in *church*) which contrast (by being 'noisier') with their non-strident counterparts as follows:[2]

[1] The topic is discussed, with examples from modern Greek, in Newton, 'Ordering Paradoxes in Phonology', *Journal of Linguistics* 7 (1971), 31–53.

[2] 'Strident' is not used in this book of [f] and [v], although they are labio-dental in Greek. In some languages [f] is said to contrast with a bilabial fricative (similar to the sound made when blowing out a candle) as 'strident' versus 'nonstrident' ('mellow').

(1) The strident counterpart of [t] is [t^s] as in German *Zimmer*; that is, it is an affricate similar to the final cluster of English *bits* but pronounced more rapidly as a unit segment. We may note here that in some dialects the affricate [t^s] contrasts with the sequence [ts]. Thus in parts of Lesbos we find [ét^sa] 'so' but [métsa] 'I got drunk'.

(2) The strident counterpart of [d] is [d^z] as in Italian *mezzo*; it is simply [t^s] voiced and accordingly similar to the final cluster of English *bids*.

(3) If [t^s] is pronounced a little further back we get [č], a sound very similar to the *ch* of English *chin* or the *c* of Italian *cento*. It is in contrast with [k′], which shares with it a palatal point of articulation but lacks stridency. Again certain dialects have a contrast between the affricate [č] and the sequence [tš] (this may be compared loosely to the *ch* of *why choose* versus the *t sh* of *white shoes*).

(4) The voiced counterpart of [č] is [ǰ] as in Italian *gente*, English *Jim*. Its non-strident counterpart is [g′].

(5) [s] and [z] are strident in contrast to [θ] (as in *thin*) and [δ] (as in *this*). Pronounced further back they become [š] and [ž] as in French *chien*, *Jean*, English *she*, *measure*.

The palatal sounds of modern Greek are represented by a prime (′) in the case of the non-stridents and by an inverted circumflex (ˇ) in the case of the stridents. The former consist of [k′], [g′], [x′] and [γ′]. [k′] and [g′] are usually thought of as fronted counterparts of [k] and [g] and resemble the initial sounds of English *keep*, *geyser* (compared to those of *call*, *gaunt*). Phonetically they might equally well be described as backed [t] and [d] and indeed in one dialect (that of Plumari, Lesbos) [k′] and [g′] arise from [t] and [d] before [i] (cf. [afk′í] for αὐτή 'her'). [x′] is similar to the sound of *ch* in German *ich* and is again conveniently thought of as a fronted [x] (this latter as in English *loch*, German *ach*). [x′] when voiced gives [γ′], just as [x] when voiced gives [γ]. [γ′] is closely related to the glide [y] from which it differs in having audible fricativity. If the reader starts from [peδyá] 'children' and attempts to narrow the gap between his tongue and palate in pronouncing the [y], he will get [γ′].

The consonants of modern Greek are displayed in Table 1 in terms of the features we shall be needing. The voiceless stops [p, t, k′, k] and their voiced correlates [b, d, g′, g] are described as 'noncontinuous'. The affricates [t^s, č, d^z, ǰ] are also 'noncontinuous', and are distinguished from the stops in being 'strident'. The fricatives are 'continuous'. Stops, affricates and fricatives constitute the 'obstruent' system. Obstruents and nasals are 'true consonants' (consonantal, nonvocalic), while the liquids are consonantal, vocalic. The four points of articulation are 'labial', 'dental', 'palatal', 'velar'. As in English, [p b] are bilabial while [f v] are labiodental. [m] is also bilabial except in the learned clusters [mf] and [mv], when it becomes labiodental by assimilation. It would be possible to describe the four points of articulation in terms of combinations of plus and minus values of two features, according to a common practice (i.e. by treating 'dental' and 'palatal' as central versus peripheral and 'labial' and 'dental' as front versus back) but there seems to be no clear advantage in departing from the familiar four-term system in a description of modern Greek dialects.

TABLE 1. *The consonants of modern Greek dialects*

Cont.	Voiced	Stri.	Lab.	Dent.	Pal.	Vel.
			Obstruent			
−	−	−	p	t	k′	k
−	+	−	b	d	g′	g
+	−	−	f	θ	x′	x
+	+	−	v	δ	γ′	γ
−	−	+		t͡s	č	
−	+	+		d͡z	ǰ	
+	−	+		s	š	
+	+	+		z	ž	
			Nasal			
+	+	−	m	n	n′	ŋ
			Liquid			
+	+	−		r/l	l′	

In addition to the true consonants modern Greek dialects possess the liquids [l] and [r], as well as a palatal variant of the former [l′] (resembling the *gl* of Italian *gli*, or the *ll* of Castilian Spanish). I shall follow the usual practice of treating liquids as consonantal and vocalic (while the true consonants are consonantal and non-vocalic). The [l] and [r] share a dental point of articulation and differ in that [l] is lateral; the normal replacement of [l] by [r] before true consonants can then be described as 'delateralization'; for example standard [aδelfós] 'brother' appears as [aδerfós] in the dialects. Palatality is viewed above as a point of articulation. It may be mentioned at this point that in parts of north-eastern Greece a plain: palatal contrast may characterize all the consonants (e.g.

[kát] 'below' versus [kát′] 'something') and for this group of dialects we must regard palatality not as a point of articulation along the labial–velar dimension but as a special feature of 'sharpness'.

1.4 The vowels and glides of modern Greek

Most dialects possess a five-vowel system of a very common type:

i				u
	e		o	
		a		

That is, we have three degrees of height and, for vowels other than the low [a], a distinction between front and back. [i] and [u] are described as high and non-low, [e] and [o] as non-high and non-low, and [a] as non-high and low. [i] and [e] differ from [u] and [o] in being front as opposed to back. In Thessaly, Macedonia and Thrace we find in addition an [ü] as in French *tu*, an [ö] as in French *neuf* and, most important, an [ä] which differs from [a] in being more fronted; it resembles the vowel of southern English *had* versus that of *hard*, or, perhaps better, the [æ] of Russian [p′æt′] 'five' versus the [a] of [sat] 'garden'. To describe these dialects we shall need to recognize a feature 'roundness' so that while [u] and [o] are round, back, [ü] and [ö] are round, front. Although it is only in these dialects that a back [a] contrasts with a front [ä] it is still highly convenient to describe the phonetically central [a] of most dialects as back. For instance, palatalization of [k] and [x] occurs everywhere before [i] and [e] but not [a], so that it is useful to have a label for the first two ('front'), which will distinguish them from [a].

While vowels are vocalic, non-consonantal, glides are non-vocalic, non-consonantal. All dialects have the high front glide [y] (as in English *yacht*) and many have a high back glide [w].

The vowels and glides of modern Greek may be tabulated as in Table 2.

TABLE 2. *The vowels and glides of modern Greek dialects*

	i	e	o	a	u	ü	ö	ä	y	w
Consonantal	–	–	–	–	–	–	–	–	–	–
Vocalic	+	+	+	+	+	+	+	+	–	–
High	+	–	–	–	+	+	–	–	+	+
Low	–	–	–	+	–	–	–	+	–	–
Front	+	+	–	–	–	+	+	+	+	–
Round	–	–	+	–	+	+	+	–	–	+

1.5 Underlying segments

The features we require in order to classify the actual sounds of Greek can be used to describe the historical development of the language (or, looking at it synchronically, the underlying phonology). There is one important exception. Ancient Greek had a distinction between long and short vowels which disappeared in the straightforward sense in the post-classical period, so that no modern dialect contrasts long and short vowels. However, the ancient length contrast played a crucial role in accent placement. The modern stress continues in general the ancient accent, but because of the loss of length contrast in the vowels is superficially erratic in its behaviour. In particular the ancient accent could not go further back than the penultimate syllable if the last vowel was long, so that while ἄνθρωπος was stressed on the first syllable, a shift occurred in the genitive: ἀνθρώπου. To make the shift from modern [ánθropos] to [anθrópu] more intelligible it is useful to consider the underlying form of [anθrópu] to be /ánθropū/, so that the stress shift becomes predictable. We shall not be much concerned with stress shift so that there will not normally be any need to distinguish in underlying structure between long and short vowels. However, a deeper study of modern Greek phonology than is attempted in this book would certainly require a feature 'length' in the vowels. But not only did ancient Greek contrast long and short vowels; it also had long and short consonants. ἄλη 'wandering' differed from ἄλλη 'other' (fem. sing.) only in having a shorter consonant. South-eastern dialects, as we shall see in 1.6, retain this distinction, so that in describing them we must refer constantly to consonantal 'length'; furthermore, even in other dialects 'long' consonants are required in underlying structure. τὸν νόμο 'the law' (acc.), for instance, must have an intermediate form [tonnómo], which is reduced to [tonómo] by the process we shall call 'degemination'.

We shall find in the course of our investigation that some of the vowels and consonants which occur in modern dialects can be accounted for by supposing them to represent clusters of underlying segments. Thus [b], [d] and [g] can be shown to derive from /mp/, /nt/, /nk/; the northern [ǻ] comes from /éa/. In other cases we have simply variants of other sounds. The palatal sounds, for instance, are in general merely velar sounds fronted through the influence of a following front vowel or glide, and the glides themselves derive from /i/, /u/ or, in the case of [y], sometimes from /γ/. It might be useful to conclude this section by listing the underlying segments which we shall be requiring (see Table 3). It will be obvious that the underlying consonants are considerably less numerous than the total phonetic consonants required for all dialects and it is also largely true that they are fewer than those needed for any individual dialect. The underlying vowels, however, include /ü/, which represents ancient υ and οι; while in most dialects its reflex is [i], as is that of /i/, in Old Athenian we find that it goes to [u], thus coalescing with the reflex of /u/. In addition to the segments listed we also require a stress and the feature of 'length'.

TABLE 3. *The underlying segments of modern Greek*

p	t		k	i	ü	u
f	θ	s	x	e		o
v	δ	z	γ		a	
m	n					
	l					
	r					

1.6 The classification of Greek dialects

We do not find in modern Greek, any more than we do in, say, Italian or German, a determinate number of sharply defined dialects. What we do find is a linguistic continuum criss-crossed in all directions by a vast number of isoglosses marking the geographical limits of the different phonological features (and, of course, grammatical and lexical phenomena as well). Nevertheless it is highly convenient to have available a rough classificatory scheme, and in the case of modern Greek, provided we are willing to accept some degree of inaccuracy and arbitrariness, we may think of the core dialects which form the subject of this book as falling into five basic groups:

(1) *Peloponnesian–Ionian.* This set comprises the dialects spoken in the Ionian Isles (Corfu, Kephalonia, Zakinthos and various smaller islands) and in the Peloponnese apart from Mani and Tsakonia. In Mani, the central and most barren of the three peninsulas projecting towards the Cretan sea, a dialect is spoken (by the few hundred remaining inhabitants) which bears striking resemblances to Old Athenian, and which may for practical purposes be regarded as a variety of it. Tsakonian is idiosyncratic and isolated and is usually claimed by the numerous scholars who have investigated it to derive not from the Hellenistic κοινή, the probable

source of all other dialects, but from ancient Doric. It is still spoken in a handful of villages on the seaward slopes of Mount Parnon in the east, although not any longer in Leonidion, the only large community in the area, and there is little doubt that it will soon be obsolete. Peloponnesian and Ionian dialects have played a crucial role in the evolution of what Greek scholars nowadays term the 'modern Greek common language', ἡ Νεοελληνικὴ κοινή, so that Peloponnesian dialects in particular differ only marginally from 'educated Athenian'. Doubtless because of this, Peloponnesian–Ionian has received disappointingly little attention from Greek scholars and apparently none whatever from foreigners.

(2) *Northern Greek.* Characteristically 'northern' dialects are spoken not only throughout the mainland north of Attica and in northern Euboea, but on the islands of the northern Aegean; these latter include Thasos, Samothraki, Limnos and Lesbos, and a northern dialect was previously spoken on the island of Imbros, now a Turkish possession. The island of Samos has a typical northern dialect, in spite of the fact that Chios, between it and Lesbos, belongs linguistically to the south-eastern complex; it appears that Samos was devastated and repopulated from the north in the fifteenth century (Sigalas 1949). In spite of the vast geographical extension of the northern dialects, the relatively recent inclusion of northern Greece within the national boundaries of the modern state has prevented them from making any significant contribution to the standard language. It may be added that where the various minority languages such as Arumanian, Macedonian and Turkish have yielded to Greek, it has in general been to the standard form. The dialect of Saloniki differs hardly at all from that of Athens, and such differences as are observable affect trivial points of vocabulary and grammar rather than phonology (e.g. ἤμασταν 'we were' for Athenian ἤμαστε, ἔρχονταν 'he was coming' for ἐρχότανε, νὰ σὲ πῶ 'let me tell you' for νὰ σοῦ πῶ).

(3) *Old Athenian.* Modern Athenian, as was noted above, is based on Peloponnesian–Ionian. But before the War of Independence Athens was an insignificant village whose Greek inhabitants spoke a dialect, 'Old Athenian', which survives still among the older generation of Megara and various villages near Kimi on the east coast of central Euboea. It was also spoken at the beginning of the present century in Aegina, although my enquiries on the island suggest that it has been completely supplanted

there by modern Athenian. It was previously thought that the Kimi dialects reflect an immigration to the region from Athens in 1688, but Karatzas (1940) has produced powerful evidence that Old Athenian was originally spoken over a continuous area which included Attica and southern Euboea; in particular he has shown that the Greek dialects spoken in the villages near Karystos in S. Euboea share important features with that of the Kimi region, and that the Greek elements incorporated in the Albanian presently spoken in S. Euboea betray an Old Athenian source. My own observations indicate that the Greek which has largely replaced Albanian in S. Euboea appears to be standard with various features typical of nearby islands (e.g. ἦρχα for ἦρθα 'I came'). Mani, in spite of its remoteness from Attica and Euboea, has a dialect which shares so many crucial features with Old Athenian that we may regard it as a species of the latter with little risk of distortion. The Maniot colony in Cargese (Corsica) had a handful of Greek speakers at mid-century but its dialect has been carefully studied by Blanken (1951). Our knowledge of pre-Kingdom Athenian is nugatory and based on various documents gleaned by Kambouroglous from the point of view of lexicon; for Megara, Kimi and Mani we are much better off (see Bibliography).

(4) *Cretan.* Because of the fairly regular pattern of revolt followed by mass exodus, Cretans under the Turcocracy established themselves throughout the nearby islands (Cyclades), and upper Naxos in particular has been shown by recent Greek publications to have a dialect virtually indistinguishable from Cretan; Ikaria also shows strong Cretan influence. The other islands of the Cycladic group such as Santorini, Siphnos, Mikonos have received only desultory attention from Greek scholars, but the general features of their dialects are reasonably well known.

(5) *South-eastern dialects.* These are spoken in Chios, the Dodecanese (including Kalimnos, Kos, Astipalea, Simi, Karpathos and Rhodes) and Cyprus. Kastellorizo, a tiny island off Turkey between Rhodes and Cyprus, has an unmistakeably south-eastern dialect but with various peculiarities such as the use of [e] for forms of the definite article elsewhere distinct. Livisi, and probably Halicarnassos, on the mainland, seem to have belonged to the south-eastern group (rather than that which included Pontic and Cappadocian). The most carefully described dialect of this group is Chian (Pernot 1907).

The above grouping will now be briefly justified by listing the phonological phenomena which determine it.

(1) *High vowel loss and raising.* These rules define the limits of the northern dialects. High vowel loss involves the dropping of unstressed /i/ and /u/. Thus /kutí/ 'box' becomes [ktí] and /piθári/ 'jar', [pθár]. The rule I shall refer to as 'raising' converts unstressed /e/ and /o/ to [i] and [u] respectively. For example, /fénete/ 'it appears' goes to [féniti] and /kotópulo/ 'chicken' to [kutóplu].

(2) *Softening.* In Cretan, Old Athenian, and south-eastern dialects one or more of the velar consonants /k/, /x/ and /γ/ is 'softened' before a front vowel or glide to [č], [š], [ž] respectively (this output being subsequently 'depalatalized' to [tˢ], [s], [z] in some dialects). Thus /kerós/ 'weather' is heard as [čerós] in Crete and Cyprus, and as [tˢerós] in Megara and Rhodes. /xéri/ 'hand' is [šéri] in Crete and Cyprus, [séri] in Rhodes. In Crete /γí/ 'earth' appears as [ží].

(3) *Degemination.* This reduces 'geminate' (long) consonants to their simple counterparts, and is operative in almost, but not quite all dialects outside the south-eastern group. Thus while /θálassa/ 'sea', /γrámma/ 'letter' are [θálasa], [γráma] throughout the mainland and in Crete, yet Chian, Rhodian and Cypriot have [θálassa], [γrámma].

(4) *Glide formation.* Unstressed [i] converts to the glide [y] before a vowel in all dialects. In most dialects stressed [í] also goes to [y] before a vowel and its stress is shifted forward. But in Old Athenian this does not occur, so that while /peδía/ 'children', /filía/ 'kisses' are realized almost everywhere as [peδyá], [filyá] (or some subsequent development of these, such as [peδγ'á], [fil'á]), Old Athenian shows [peδía], [filía].

(5) [u] *for* /ü/. Many words which in ancient Greek had υ or οι, pronounced as [ü] in the medieval period, and nowadays in most dialects as [i], are found with [u] in Old Athenian. Thus common [ksílo] 'wood', [k'il'á] 'belly' (ancient ξῦλον, κοιλία) are matched by Megarian [ksúlo], [tˢulía].

(6) *Voiced fricative deletion.* In south-eastern dialects there is a regular loss of the voiced fricatives (/v/, /δ/, /γ/) in intervocalic position. Thus

common [láδi] 'oil', [fóvos] 'fear', [máγos] 'magician' appear there as [láin], [fóos], [máos].

(7) *Final nasal deletion.* In most dialects an inherited word-final nasal is lost except in certain forms of the article and verb, and of adjectives when in prevocalic position. But this loss has not affected most south-eastern dialects, so that while ancient τὸ καλὸν παιδίον is usually continued as [tokalópeδí] 'the good child', south-eastern dialects have rather [tokalómbeín] (/np/ going to [mb] by 'postnasal voicing' and 'nasal assimilation').

(8) *Manner dissimilation.* Details aside, manner dissimilation has the effect of imposing the pattern fricative + stop on any sequence of two obstruents. Thus ancient ἑπτά 'seven' goes to [eftá] and εὐχή to [efk'í] 'blessing'. A sequence of voiced fricatives is, however, permissible in most dialects (cf. [avγó] 'egg', [ravδí] 'rod'). In south-eastern dialects they too are subject to manner dissimilation, the last items appearing as [avgón], [ravdín].

(9) */γ/ epenthesis in verbs.* In Cretan, Old Athenian and south-eastern dialects a [γ] is inserted between the [ev] of verbs in [évo] (-εύω) and a vowel-initial ending. Thus, for Peloponnesian–Ionian [δulévo], northern [δlévu] 'I work' we find [δulévγo].

TABLE 4. *The distribution of some important features in Peloponnesian, northern, Old Athenian, Cretan and south-eastern dialects*

	P	N	OA	C	SE
High vowels lost, mid ones raised		+			
[í] remains before vowel			+		
[u] replaces /ü/			+		
Softening occurs			+	+	+
/γ/ in -εύω verbs			+	+	+
Long consonants remain					+
/v, δ, γ/ lost intervocalically					+
Final [n] remains					+
[vγ] > [vg] etc.					+

It is interesting that although northern dialects differ as a group from the others only in the possession of the rules of high vowel loss and raising, yet most scholars, Greek and foreign, no matter what system of classification they favour, almost invariably insist on the primacy of the division between 'northern' and 'southern'; this might seem strange, considering that more isoglosses divide south-eastern dialects from the rest than separate northern from southern. The traditional view does, however, correspond to the impression of native speakers: an Athenian will normally claim northern dialects to be more difficult to understand than south-eastern. There appear to be two main reasons for this. (*a*) The northern rules have some effect on practically every word in the language, the only immune forms being those with no instance of unstressed [i] [u], [o] or [e]. The other rules affect at most a small minority of items in any given stretch of speech. (*b*) Perhaps more important, high vowel loss occurs relatively early on in the rule sequence associated with an individual northern dialect. In particular it is succeeded by several of the rules which operate in all dialects on primary clusters. Underlying /simpáθise/ 'he liked', realized elsewhere as [simbáθise] or [sibáθise], might in the north take the shape [zbátsi]; yet this arises by applying to the output of high vowel loss and raising ([smpáθsi]) rules which are perfectly normal in the south. /mp/ goes to [b] widely, as in Crete, [s] is everywhere voiced before a voiced consonant, and [θs] always undergoes manner dissimilation (cf. standard [káts͡e] 'sit down!' for /káθise/). In explaining popular intuitions on the subject of dialectal divergence, it is clear that we must do much more than simply count the isoglosses.

2 *Vowel Sequences*

2.0 In the present chapter we consider the phonological processes which act on vowel sequences in the underlying forms, while chapter 3 examines the development of secondary vowel sequences arising from the loss of consonants. But first we raise certain questions relating to the sources of modern Greek [u]; while most occurrences go back to the ancient diphthong ου, in Old Athenian υ and οι provide a source for it (2.1) and it arises from [o] by raising (2.2) or (allegedly) from [i] by rounding (2.3). After listing the main sources of primary hiatus (2.4), we describe in turn the various means by which the dialects eliminate vowel sequences. The sequence /éa/, for instance, normally goes by height dissimilation to [ía] (2.6) and this by glide formation to [yá] (2.7), and where a vowel sequence escapes these processes contraction usually takes place (2.8), sometimes preceded by fronting to yield [ä] or [e] for /éa/ (2.9). Finally surviving sequences may be eliminated by the insertion of /γ/ (2.10), the replacement of -εύω in verbs by -εύγω being a special case (2.11).

2.1 Underlying /ü/

It is thought that ancient υ and οι collapsed into the high front round vowel [ü] (as in French *tu*) relatively early on in the present era and that this pronunciation persisted until about the tenth century, when it was unrounded to [i] in most dialects. Thus the words ξῦλα 'wood' (pl.) and μοῖρα 'fate' went through the stages [ksǘla], [móyra], then [ksǘla], [mǘra], and finally [ksíla], [míra]. However, there are two important classes of exception to the general principle that ancient υ and οι go to [i] in modern Greek.

(*a*) There are several words with ancient υ which appear universally in modern dialects with [u]. There is no reason to assume for this group an underlying vowel other than /u/, although a description aiming at a correlation of demotic and katharevusa doublets might seek to justify /ü/ as the source on the ground that a demotic form with [u] occasionally has a cognate of learned origin with [i]. Thus [fúska] 'bubble, balloon' from ancient φύσκη has a cognate [físka] which (in spite of its meaning 'chock full') may originate in the normal modern reading pronunciation of its ancient etymon. The vernacular pronunciation of the ancient name Κύμη is [kúmi], although [k'ími] appears to be ousting it. The main items in the present category are κουλλός 'maimed', κουλλούρι 'round sesame-coated bread', μουστάκι 'moustache', σκουτιά 'clothes', στουππί 'taw, drunk', τουλούπα 'swaddling bands', φούχτα 'handful' (if in fact from πύκτη).

(*b*) In the dialects of Megara, Aegina, the Kimi area and pre-Kingdom Athens (the 'Old Athenian' complex), as well as in Mani, many, but by no means all cases of ancient υ and οι went to [u].[1] From the point of view of the modern distribution of [i] and [u] we may therefore set up three groups of words, the first comprising items with [u] everywhere (e.g. ποῦ 'where?'), the second those with [i] everywhere (e.g. φίλος 'friend'), and the third, items in which Old Athenian and Maniot [u] answers to [i] elsewhere (e.g. ξῦλο 'wood'). On this basis alone a case could be made for setting up for the sake of the last category an underlying /ü/, which would be backed in all positions to [u] in some dialects and unrounded to [i] in others. However, the strongest argument for assuming an underlying /ü/ is provided by the phenomenon of palatalization in Old Athenian–Maniot. Palatalization is the fronting of the velar segments /k/, /x/ and /γ/ to [k'], [x'] and [γ'] respectively and is conditioned in most dialects only by a following front vowel (e.g. /ke/ 'and' > [k'e]). But in Old Athenian palatalization occurs not only before front vowels but before [u] in precisely those items which have [i] in other dialects. Corresponding, for instance, to normal [x'íno] 'I pour' Megarian has [x'úno] and for [yinéka] 'woman' (the [y] arising via [γ']) it has [yunéka]; common Greek [k'il'á] 'belly' is matched by [t̑ulía] ([k'] being softened in Megarian to [t̑]). Historically, we must suppose that palatalization occurred in Old Athenian when medieval [ü] still remained a front vowel, as otherwise the modern pronunciations of the above items would be *[xúno], *[γunéka], *[kulía]. Furthermore, when Old Athenian agrees with other dialects in having [u] for ancient ύ, palatalization does not occur (cf. [kúmi], not *[k'úmi]), which implies that group (*a*) items underwent the conversion of ancient υ to [u] before

[1] The islands of Skiros (Phavis 1909) and Kithnos (Koukoules 1923) have numerous forms with [u] from /ü/ for which borrowing from Old Athenian may be suspected.

palatalization took place.[1] Setting up underlying /ü/ for group (*b*) items, therefore, we may derive χύνω, γυναίκα and κοιλιά in Megarian as follows:

(1)	xǘno	γünéka	külía
Palatalization	x'ǘno	γ'ünéka	k'ülía
Backing	**x'úno**	γ'unéka	k'ulía
Softening			čulía
Depalatalization			**ʦulía**
Consonantality		**yunéka**	

The last three rules will be described in detail later (see chapter 5) but we shall have occasion to refer to them quite frequently before then. Briefly, the softening rule converts [k'] to its strident counterpart [č] and, in some dialects, [x'] to [š], or even (as in Cretan) [γ'] to [ž]. Dialects with the depalatalization rule shift any [č], [š] or [ž] to [ʦ], [s] or [z] respectively. The last rule has among its general effects the replacement of [γ'] by [y] except after a consonant. After a voiced consonant both it and [y] are realized as [γ'], and as [x'] after a voiceless one.

In Mani (and Cargese) we find the same backing of /ü/ but softening occurs in its fullest form, so that χοῖρος 'pig', γύρω 'round', κοιμᾶμαι 'I sleep' develop as follows:

(2)	xǘros	γǘro	kümáme
Palatalization	x'ǘros	γ'ǘro	k'ümáme
Backing	x'úros	γ'úro	k'umáme
Softening	**šúros**	**žúro**	**čumáme**

There seems to be no obvious way of stating the conditions under which ancient υ and οι went to [u] in Old Athenian. Among the many words which always have [i] are δάχτυλο 'finger', βυʒί 'breast', πολύ 'very', φύλλο 'leaf', ἄνοιξη 'spring', νύχτα 'night'; the only useful generalization is that final occurrences of υ or οι are reflected by [i] (e.g. βράδυ 'evening', ἄνθρωποι 'men'). It may be added that at the present day standard pronunciations with [i] are rapidly ousting the truly dialectal forms. As early as 1911 Phavis noted the virtual obsolescence of [u] pronunciations in the villages around Kimi. He cites, for instance, [síka] for σῦκα 'figs' (but [suʦéa] 'fig-tree', [sukófilla] 'fig-leaves' and

[1] The item κιούπι 'barrel', if related to the ancient root κυπ- ,would constitute an exception (see Chatzidakis 1907: 295). However, Andriotis (1967, *sub voce*) is almost certainly correct in associating it with Turkish *küp*.

[sukás] 'a kind of mushroom'). In Megara today [síka] has replaced the [súka] cited by Chatzidakis (1916), although [suťéa] and [sukófila] survive. There are slight variations in the distribution of [u] forms in the subdialects of Old Athenian, but the forms most frequently appearing with [u] for [i] elsewhere are as follows (the Megarian pronunciation is given):

γυναίκα	'woman'	[yunéka]
γυρεύω	'I seek'	[yurévγo]
γύρω	'round'	[yúro]
ʒυγός	'yoke'	[zuγós]
θυγατέρα	'daughter'	[θuγatéra] (Kimi)
κοιλιά	'belly'	[ťulía]
κοιμᾶμαι	'I sleep'	[ťumáme]
κοιτάʒω	'I look'	[ťutázo]
κοίτη	'nest'	[ťúti]
κύκλος	'ring'	[ťúklos]
κυλῶ	'I flow'	[ťuláo]
Κυριακή	'Sunday'	[ťury'aťí]
μυρτιά	'myrtle'	[murtéa]
ξύδι	'vinegar'	[ksúδi]
ξῦλο	'wood'	[ksúlo]
ξυνός	'sour'	[ksunós]
σῦκο	'fig'	[súko]
συννεφιά	'cloud'	[suγnefía]
συγγενής	'relative'	[sug'enís]
συνηθίʒω	'I am accustomed'	[suniθáo]
συρτάρι	'drawer'	[surtári]
σχοινί	'rope'	[sťuní]
σχοινιά	'lentisk'	[sťunía]
τυραννῶ	'I torment'	[turaγnáo]
χοῖρος	'pig'	[x'úros]
ψυχρός	'cold'	[psuxrós]
ψυχή	'soul'	[psux'í]

Certain words which show [u] for common Greek [i] in Old Athenian and Maniot are also found sporadically in the Peloponnese outside Mani in this form. [trúpa] 'hole', for instance, is widespread, and [ax'ura] 'hay', [súro] 'I pull', [sk'ulí] 'dog' also occur. While [k'il'á] is normal throughout the Peloponnese for κοιλιά 'belly', [prok'úli] 'paunch' was cited to me at Dimitsana in Arcadia and κολύμπι 'swimming' is pronounced [kolúmbi] in Laconia according to Koukoules (1908). In such cases borrowing from Old Athenian is doubtless to be suspected.

Finally there are a few items which resist classification. βούτυρο 'butter' appears as [vúturo] not only in Old Athenian but in Chios and Cyprus; σκύβω 'I stoop' is frequently found with [u], especially in the Peloponnese (as [zγúfto]) and the Ionian Isles. ἐσύ 'thou' commonly has [u] in insular dialects (cf. Cypriot [esú(ni)]) and also in Megarian. ξυρίζω 'I shave' has [u] almost everywhere and should perhaps be placed in our group (*a*). A particularly puzzling item is μύτη 'nose', which appears as [mútti] in at least Chios, Ikaria, Rhodes and Cyprus in the south east, but also as [múti] in an island (Othones) off Corfu;[1] yet it is not recorded with [u] in the literature on Old Athenian and Maniot and was unknown to my Megarian informants. A similar situation holds for Chian and Cypriot [múya] 'fly' (common [míγa]). The initial labial in these last two items might suggest the recent rounding of an [i] (see 2.3), perhaps originally affecting unstressed allomorphs as in [muttás] (feminine [mutté]) 'long-nosed person'.

It is sometimes supposed that Old Athenian forms with palatal + [u] sequences imply an earlier [yu] rather than [u].[2] But the spellings such as χιούνω favoured by Greek scholars who have described Old Athenian must not be thought to support this view as the insertion of an iota is simply a common means of indicating palatality before back vowels. Furthermore, if medieval [ü] went first to [yu] in [xǘno], the [y] then palatalizing the [x] and dropping (and [xy] normally does go to [x']), one might reasonably ask why [yu] did not occur after consonants other than the velars. Why, for instance, did [murtéa] 'myrtle' not yield modern *[myurtéa]? The comparisons often made with Tsakonian are of doubtful relevance. In Tsakonian [u] occurs for practically all cases of ancient υ and οι and is preceded by [y] not after velars but after dentals. Furthermore any assumption of wholesale borrowing from Tsakonian must face the fact that Old Athenian has [u] for [i] in words which do not occur in Tsakonian (e.g. [sťúlos] 'dog', [ťulía] 'belly', but Tsakonian [kúe], [fúkha]).

[1] See Λεξικογραφικὸν Δελτίον (1963), p. 157.

[2] Shipp (1965) presents a recent account on these lines.

2.2 Back vowel raising

A considerable number of words with ο or ω in ancient Greek appear with [u] in modern dialects. Common examples are κουδούνι 'bell', κουφός 'deaf', κουμπί 'button', κουκκί 'bean', πουλῶ 'I sell', σκουριά 'rust'. The general (historical) rule, as normally given, is that unstressed [o] (whether from ancient ο or ω) is raised to [u] in the environment adjacent to a velar or labial consonant. The question which concerns us is whether it is worth while to recognize this raising of the mid back vowel [o] as a synchronic rule of modern Greek either on the basis of morphophonemic alternations induced by it or of dialectal variation.

Because only unstressed [o] was raised in the appropriate consonantal environment, the strict application of the rule as formulated above would be expected to yield alternations between [ó] and unstressed [u]. We would have, for instance, [puló] 'I sell', but *[pólisa] 'I sold'. However, in this and similar cases the [u] has been generalized, so that we in fact find [púlisa] and so on. Alternation is found to a small extent between certain pairs of derivationally related forms. The adjective [kók'inos] 'red' is related to ancient κόκκος 'berry', and this latter now appears as [kuk'í] 'bean' (from a diminutive κοκκίον). [aγóri] 'boy' is etymologically related to [áγuros] 'unripe' (cf. ancient ἄωρος). But within the vernacular dialects such pairs are quite rare, and probably not thought of by native speakers as related in any case. Only a decision to take cognizance of items of katharevusa origin could justify the assumption of a raising rule on synchronic grounds. It would then be possible to explain the relation of [skolikoiδítis] 'appendicitis' to vernacular [skulík'i] 'worm' by deriving the latter from /skolíki/; [kopilasía] 'rowing' could similarly be related to [kupí] 'oar', [zóni] 'zone, belt' to [zunári] 'belt', [traγoδía] 'tragedy' to [traγúδi] 'song'. In these last instances the first member of each pair lacks a demotic form. If we consider learned forms which are merely katharevusa counterparts of demotic items, and naturally recognized by Greek speakers as such, then doublets may be found very easily. πωλεῖται 'for sale', for example, is merely [pul'éte] dressed up as ancient Greek, and ὑποκάμισο 'shirt' is a 'translation' of [pukámiso]. It certainly seems quite reasonable to include some knowledge of katharevusa in the native speaker's linguistic competence; however, in this book we shall not consider the learned language unless the rules which link it to demotic also play a role in dialectal variation. In this case the core dialects all apply the rule under consideration, although it appears that in Asia Minor the original [o] sound remained in various words such as [koδóni] 'bell'.

If a rule raising an underlying /o/ to [u] in the neighbourhood of a labial or velar consonant were incorporated into our phonological description of Greek, it would be important to distinguish it carefully from the normal northern raising rule which converts the front and back mid vowels to [i] and [u] respectively in unstressed position. If the rule '/o/ > [u]' is included, it must be made to take effect before high vowel loss and (normal) raising. Consider, for instance, the northern forms of πουλῶ 'I sell', πολύ 'very' and πουλί 'bird' assuming underlying /poláo/, /polí/, /pulí/:

(3)	poláo	polí	pulí
/o/ > [u]	puláo		
High vowel loss	pláo		**plí**
Raising	**pláu**	**pulí**	

It will be seen that πολύ represents an exception to the special rule raising /o/ to [u], for if /polí/ followed this rule then the output [pulí] would have gone to *[plí] by high vowel loss just as original /pulí/ did. The net effect of the ordering illustrated in derivation (3) is to ensure that [u] from ancient ο or ω does not behave differently in northern dialects from underlying /u/ (usually from ancient ου).

In short, considerations neither of morphophonemic alternation nor of interdialectal comparison justify us in treating the replacement of ancient ο and ω by [u] adjacent to labial or velar consonants as anything more than a fact of the history of Greek. We shall therefore ignore it in future discussion, and treat words such as πουλῶ as having underlying /u/.

The Peloponnesian pronunciation of standard Athenian ἀπάνω 'above', κάτω 'below' and χάμω 'on the ground' as [apánu], [kátu] and [xámu] is difficult. It is not clear how locative adverbs with stressed οῦ (ἀλλοῦ 'elsewhere', ποῦ 'where?') can have provided the analogy claimed by Chatzidakis (1907: 309). Northern dialects have [pán], [kát] ('on the ground' is expressed by καταγῆς), so that whatever the historical origin of the change, we must posit for the whole mainland underlying /apánu/, /kátu/, /xámu/.

2.3 Rounding

There is evidence that the front vowel [e] tends in many dialects to convert to [o] when unstressed and preceded or followed by one of the labial consonants (/p/, /f/ or /v/). Thus, for standard [yefíri] 'bridge', [yemízo] 'I fill', [perpató] 'I walk', [revíθi] 'chick-pea' we commonly find [yofíri], [yomízo], [porpató], [rovíθi]. The south-eastern dialects and Cretan may be particularly prone to this rounding; mainland [kremíδi] is [krommín] in Cyprus and [psóma] is Cretan for [pséma] 'lie' (although the vowel is stressed). In Chios we even find [krováti] 'bed' for the usual [kreváti], and [čofáli] 'head' for [k'efáli]. The last case and that of [yofíri] show that if a rounding rule is set up, it must follow palatalization. Consider, for example, the Maniot reflex of an underlying /γefíri/ 'bridge', and the Chian form of /kefáli/ 'head':

(4)	γefíri	kefáli
Palatalization	γ'efíri	k'efáli
Rounding	γ'ofíri	k'ofáli
Softening	**žofíri**	**čofáli**

Although the relative ordering of the last two rules is indifferent, palatalization must clearly precede rounding, as otherwise we would obtain *[γofíri], *[kofáli].

In northern dialects we find the pronunciation [yufír], which implies that rounding precedes the northern raising of mid vowels to high. Combining this constraint with the last one, we arrive at the following derivation:

(5)	γefíri
Palatalization	γ'efíri
Rounding	γ'ofíri
High vowel loss	γ'ofír
Raising	γ'ufír
Consonantality	**yufír**

In establishing the order rounding – raising we assumed that rounding affects only [e], not [i]; if raising preceded, its output [γ'ifíri] would go to [γ'ufíri] only provided that rounding affected [i] as well as [e]. Now there do indeed appear to be a few words in which an earlier [i] from ι or η has gone to [u]. [zulévo] 'I envy' (ancient ζηλεύω) and [supx'á] 'cuttle-fish' (σηπία) are general, and others such as [purnári] 'holmoak', [susámi] 'sesame' (commonly [prinári], [sisámi]) are restricted to particular areas. The verbal ending which has replaced ancient -όμην (imperfect passive first singular) is [ómuna] in the Peloponnese and Ionian Isles, while [umun] is characteristic of insular dialects. However, it is quite uncertain what phonological processes underlie these and similar cases. Chatzidakis (1907: 292) revives the suggestion of Psicharis that the [u] in such words arose by epenthesis after the original [i] had been lost, but it is not clear why the [i] should have been deleted nor is there any evidence that forms such as *[zlévo] ever occurred. However, [u] does occur as a 'svarabhakti' vowel to break up original consonant clusters: dialectal [munúxos] 'eunuch' appears to have arisen from εὐνοῦχος via [vnúxos] and [mnúxos], and ancient ἰγδίον 'mortar' is usually [γuδí]. It is difficult to regard the rounding of [i] as an instance of a general rule rounding non-low vowels; not only are the conditions of [i] rounding quite obscure but it is impossible to determine general principles of ordering.[1] Northern dialects, for instance, which palatalize [s] and [z] to [š] and [ž] before [i] have [zúlipsa] 'I envied' and not *[žúlipsa], which implies the order rounding – palatalization (of sibilants); Megarian [t͡šútrinos] 'yellow' for [k'ítrinos] points to the opposite order.

In conclusion, we may claim some justification for setting up a rule of rounding which converts unstressed [e] to [o] in the environment adjacent to labial consonant. The rule affects certain words in various dialects but does not appear to induce morphophonemic alternation. Any rounding of [i] is better regarded as of purely historical interest, and even then does not appear to have systematic status within the phonological framework of modern Greek.[2]

2.4 The sources of primary hiatus

In the underlying structures to which our phonological rules apply, cases of primary hiatus (i.e. vowel sequences) are quite rare. The

[1] The conditions usually cited are too wide to constitute 'rules' on any natural interpretation of that over-worked word. Psaltis (1905: 31), for instance, claims that [i] goes to [u] 'adjacent to palatal, velar, or labial'.

[2] The form [ómorfos] 'beautiful' is often stated to have arisen by anticipatory rounding from [émorfos] (ancient εὔμορφος), as is [ovriós] 'Jew' from Ἑβραῖος, but initial vowels frequently shift as a result of contraction with a preceding article and 'false division'. Thus [orpízo] 'I expect' seems to have arisen from ἐλπίζω via constructions such as τὸ ἐλπίζω, which contracts to [torpízo] (see 2.8). [ókso] 'outside' is alleged to result by vowel assimilation from ἔξω.

diphthongs of classical Attic were αι, οι, αυ, ευ and the first two of these were early reduced to [e] and [ü], while the last two went to [av], [ev] before voiced consonant or vowel, elsewhere to [af], [ef] (cf. αὐτός > [aftós] 'he', εὐαγγέλιον > [evaŋg'élio] 'bible'). These monophthongization processes have left no synchronic mark on the language. The underlying vowel sequences of modern Greek usually continue ancient sequences (ἀκούω 'I hear', τρία 'three', θεία 'aunt'), although some have arisen since the classical period by internal borrowing (ἀγαπάει 'he loves', see below), or borrowing from foreign languages. Most of these are eliminated in true demotic by conversion of one of their terms to a glide (θεία > [θyá], ἀγαπάει > [aγapáy]), by contraction, especially across word boundaries (τὰ ἀδέρφια > [taδérfya] 'the brothers and sisters'), or, where neither of these processes applies, by the insertion of [γ] or [y] ([akúγo] 'I hear' in many dialects). First let us list the main sources of primary hiatus in modern Greek.

(*a*) Feminine nouns in -ία, -έα, -εία, -εια. Examples are /omorfía/ 'beauty', /miléa/ 'apple tree', /δulía/ 'work', /alíθia/ 'truth'.

(*b*) Masculine nouns in -έας (usually classical -εύς), e.g. /voréas/ 'north wind', /vasiléas/ 'king'.

(*c*) Plurals of neuters in -ι or -ί (classical -ιον, -ίον according as the previous vowel was short or long). Thus, /póδia/ 'feet', /peδía/ 'children'.

(*d*) Neuter singulars in -ιο and -ίο (or -εῖο). Examples are /stixío/ 'ghost' (στοιχειό), /sxolío/ 'school', /siníθio/ 'habit'. These are often of the same origin as (*c*), but have failed through learned influence to go to -ι, -ί (note δωμάτιον > [δomátio] 'room' but ὀμμάτιον > [máti] 'eye').

(*e*) Adjectives in -αῖος, -ιος, -ιάρης, e.g. /paléos/ 'ancient' (but classical παλαιός), /vunísios/ 'mountain dwelling', /saliáris/ 'dribbling'.

(*f*) Verb forms constructed from a vowel-final stem. Typical in this group are /akúo/ 'I hear', /kéo/ 'I burn', /lúo/ 'I wash', /ptéo/ 'I am to blame'. To these we may add forms such as /káika/ 'I was burnt' and /kaiménos/ 'wretched' (usually said to have replaced in this sense /kamménos/ 'burnt' on the analogy of κάηκα).

(*g*) Verb stems in -ιαʒ- and -ειων- as in /miázo/ 'I resemble', /telióno/ 'I finish'.

(*h*) Miscellaneous items such as /aetós/ 'eagle', /eortí/ 'holiday', /iatrós/ 'doctor', /leontári/ 'lion', /tría/ 'three', /aiδóni/ 'nightingale'.

(*i*) Apart from these cases of inherited hiatus, new instances have arisen within the paradigms of oxytone verbs by processes of internal borrowing. In particular verbs of the large ἀγαπάω class have in mainland dialects developed a new set of present singular endings -άω, -άεις (rarely), -άει by suffixing on to their stems the normal barytone endings -ω, -εις, -ει (while insular dialects retain the old contracted forms ἀγαπῶ, -ᾶς, -ᾶ). Secondly the imperfect of μπορῶ 'I can' and the small number of verbs in its class (on the mainland often only θαρρῶ 'I believe' and ʒῶ 'I live') is formed in most mainland dialects and in some insular ones by suffixing -α, -ες, -ε to a stem -ει-, giving, for example, μπόρεια, μπόρειες, μπόρειε, μπορείαμε, μπορείατε, μπορείανε.

(*j*) Foreign borrowings, especially Turkish ones, often show a sequence of two vowels in their spelling. These include γαϊτάνι 'braid', καϊμάκι 'cream', καϊσί 'apricot', μαϊντανός 'parsley', τσάϊ 'tea', γαϊδούρι 'donkey'.

The above list seems to exhaust the possibilities for most dialects. However, for northern Greek and Mani some process of 'diphthongization' is occasionally mentioned in the literature. The question is discussed briefly at this point for the sake of completeness, but the facts are obscure and of little relevance to the overall picture, so that the section may be omitted without loss.

2.5 Alleged diphthongization in modern Greek

It was claimed by Foy (1879: 88) that καημένος 'wretched' and Epirot ἀϊτάρι 'spouse', ξαϊκουστός 'renowned' (standard ταίρι < ἑταίριον, ἐξακουστός) result from a diphthongization of [a] to [ay] comparable to that which yielded medieval French *clair* from *clarus*, but this particular hypothesis must surely be rejected; not only is the evidence minimal, but the few examples adduced involve unstressed position. More recently Phavis (1951) has explained the occurrence of [yé] for [é] in the dialect of Chalkidiki (Macedonia) on the basis of the stronger stress usually claimed for northern dialects. He believes that forms such as [yékama] 'I did', [yéxu] 'I have' imply the sequence [é] > [ḗ] > [yé]; in support of this he mentions a pronunciation [wó] for [ó] in Kozani and other parts of Macedonia. If the phenomenon is in fact of purely phonological nature then we must posit a diphthongization rule with very limited geographical extension, prefixing on to stressed mid vowels a homorganic glide. This is perhaps preferable to postulating with Papadopoulos (1923) a blending in forms such as [yékama] of the normal ἐ- augment and the so-called 'temporal' augment ἠ- which is found regularly in Cretan and various insular dialects and specifically to certain verbs in the north (e.g. [ífira] ἔφερα 'I brought'). It is difficult to see how such a blending could have been generalized to all cases of [é].

I know of no evidence for the assertion in Deffner (1871: 40), repeated by Foy, that parasitic [y] occurs before palatal obstruents, giving pronunciations such as [peδáyk′i] 'child'. However, in Mani a [y] is epenthesized before sequences of dental or [r] as first term and [y] as second. My own notes, based on a very brief stay in Mani, have [póyδa] for πόδια 'feet', [máyta] for μάτια 'eyes', [šeyra] for χέρια 'hands', but this suggests some sort of metathesis rather than diphthongization. Published data on the matter are not as clear as one would wish; Mirambel (1929) appears to ignore the question and most later discussions revolve round the factual point of whether the dental is palatalized or not (see Vagiakakos 1953; Patriarcheas 1939).

2.6 Height dissimilation

It will be noted from the examples cited in 2.4 that most instances of primary hiatus involve final /éa/, /éas/, /ía/, and it is the development of these sequences which is usually taken as the basis of the classification of dialects into those which replace them by [yá], [yás], [yá] (the vast majority) and those which do not (Old Athenian, Zakinthian, Karpathian). Practically all published discussions deal with the replacement of the initial vowels of these sequences by [y] under the rubric 'synizesis', but the conversion of [e] to [y] actually involves two stages, raising to [i] and then glide formation. For purposes of interdialectal comparison also, it is convenient to postulate a rule of 'height dissimilation' in addition to that of 'glide formation' (synizesis proper). Consider, for example, the derivation of ἀπιδιά 'pear tree' and παιδιά 'children' in a typical Peloponnesian dialect:

(6)	apiδéa	peδía
Height dissimilation	apiδía	
Glide formation	apiδyá	peδyá
Consonantality	**apiδγ′á**	**peδγ′á**

The rule of height dissimilation in this case acts on [é] to convert it to [í] before [a], but can be shown to be of more general nature. First of all it covers cases of [é] before [o]. Thus /roméos/ 'Greek', /paléos/

'ancient' go in Peloponnesian dialects to [romn'ós], [pal'ós], which imply an intermediate stage [romíos], [palíos]:

(7)	roméos	paléos
Height dissimilation	romíos	palíos
Glide formation	romyós	palyós
Palatalization		pal'yós
Postpalatal yod deletion		**pal'ós**
Consonantality	**romn'ós**	

Secondly, cases of unstressed [e] are also affected. Thus /leontári/ 'lion' goes through [liondári] to [lyondári] and finally [l'ondári] (or [l'odári]). Thirdly the conditioning environment may precede. /aetós/ 'eagle' goes in most dialects to [aytós], which suggests an intermediate [aitós]. Finally [o] is raised to [u] before or after [a], although the evidence for this is derived from the study of secondary hiatus (e.g. /róγa/ 'grape' > [róa] > [rúa] in various dialects, see 3.1). We may therefore state the rule of height dissimilation in its most general form as follows:

> **Height dissimilation:** (*a*) [e] > [i] in the environment adjacent to [a] or [o], and (*b*) [o] > [u] in the environment adjacent to [a].

This has the effect of specifying as high all non-low vowels when adjacent to non-high vowel, except that when both are mid [e] and not [o] is raised. It does not apply to geminate sequences of [e] or [o], but there is no need to mention this if we place the contraction rule before height dissimilation.

2.7 Glide formation

Glide formation has the effect of converting a high vowel to its corresponding glide before and after a vowel. That is, [i] > [y] and [u] > [w]. Again, the evidence that the rule of glide formation has this degree of generality is provided by a study of secondary hiatus (see 3.1). It is important to notice that the order of the words 'before and after' represents the way the rule is applied when both vowels are high. For example, we have in θὰ πιεῖτε 'you will drink' an underlying /píite/, and by stating first what happens to a high vowel before another vowel we ensure that this goes to the correct [pyíte] and not *[píyte].

The case of [peδía] > [peδyá] illustrates an important feature of the rule of glide formation: any stress carried by a high vowel acted on by the rule is transferred to the vowel of the conditioning environment. Thus, an /aí/ goes to [áy] and an [ía] to [yá], and similarly for other sequences. We are now in a position to frame our rule:[1]

Glide formation: A high vowel converts to its corresponding glide in the environment before and after a vowel, any stress which it bears being transferred to this vowel.

A few examples should suffice to illustrate this important rule. They represent pronunciations characteristic of Peloponnesian dialects.

βοήθα	'help!'	/voíθa/	[vóyθa]
τὸ εἶδα	'I saw it'	/toíδa/	[tóyδa]
τὰ εἶδα	'I saw them'	/taíδa/	[táyδa]
ἀγαπάει	'he loves'	/aγapái/	[aγapáy]
στοιχειό	'ghost'	/stixío/	[stixyó] > [stix'ó]
μιά	'one' (fem.)	/mía/	[myá] > [mn'á]
ἥλιος	'sun'	/ílios/	[ílyos] > [íl'os]
αὐτιά	'ears'	/aftía/	[aftyá] > [aftx'á]
δύο	'two'	/δío/	[δyó] > [δγ'ó]
ἀγγειό	'pot'	/ankío/	[aŋgyó] > [aŋg'ó]
ἀηδόνι	'nightingale'	/aiδóni/	[ayδóni]

The development of the [y] which arises from /i/ between consonant and vowel (as in /δío/) varies considerably according to dialect, and is dealt with in chapter 6. The relation of glide formation to height dissimilation may be further illustrated by presenting typical derivations for ἀιτός 'eagle', ἐλιά 'olive', βασιλιάς 'king', νιός 'young man':

(8)	aetós	eléa	vasiléas	néos
Height dissimilation	aitós	elía	vasilías	níos
Glide formation	**aytós**	elyá	vasilyás	nyós
Palatalization		el'yá	vasil'yás	n'yós
Postpalatal yod deletion		**el'a**	**vasil'as**	**n'ós**

The discussion thus far has been based on the Peloponnesian complex of dialects, but when we turn elsewhere we find various departures from the above pattern. All dialects with the exceptions noted in (*c*) below agree in applying height dissimilation and glide formation to unstressed /e/ and /i/; that is, all dialects convert these to [y]. Thus /eortí/ 'holiday',

[1] In those dialects which have [múype] for μοῦ εἶπε the rule would have to be modified slightly (see 2.8).

/iatrós/ 'doctor', for instance, never retain the front vowels of their first syllables. The first usually goes to [yortí] in the south ([žortí] in Crete) and [yurtí] in the north; /iatrós/ yields [žatrós] in Crete, elsewhere [yatrós]. It is when we consider the behaviour of stressed /é/ and /í/ that distinctions must be made between dialects. There are four cases:

(*a*) Neither height dissimilation nor glide formation apply. This is the case in all Old Athenian dialects, and in the dialect of Elimbos, an isolated village in northern Karpathos. In these dialects underlying /miléa/ 'apple tree', /vasiléas/ 'king', /peδía/ 'children' are pronounced [miléa], [vasiléas], [peδía] (Elimbos [peía]). However, standardizing pronunciations with [yá] are common, especially in the Kimi region and Mani.

(*b*) Height dissimilation applies, but glide formation affects only cases where the [í] is preceded by one of the palatalizing consonants ([k, x, γ, n, l]). This situation is found in Zakinthos (Ionian Isles). Consider the derivations required in order to account for the Zakinthian forms of μηλιά 'apple tree', καρυδιά 'walnut tree', φιλιά 'kisses', καρδιά 'heart':

(9)	miléa	kariδéa	filía	**karδía**
Height dissimilation	milía	**kariδía**		
Glide formation	milyá		filyá	
Palatalization	mil'yá		fil'yá	
Postpalatal yod deletion	**mil'á**		**fil'á**	

It is interesting that this failure of glide formation after non-palatalizing consonants is not found elsewhere in the Ionian Isles, although the neighbours of the Zakinthians on the mainland and Kephalonia apparently regard the trait as a fit subject for parody (cf. the Kephalonian merchants' call [avánti peδía] 'roll up, lads!' cited by Lorendzatos 1904).

(*c*) In Thessaly, Macedonia and Thrace, as well as in western Crete and Ikaria, the sequence /éa/ contracts to [ā́] (then going in the last two islands to [é]) before height dissimilation can take effect, but in Crete and Ikaria both it and glide formation act regularly otherwise. Thus in Thessaly we get for the items of derivation (9) above [milā́], [karδā́], [fl'á], [karδγ'á]. In this latter dialect there is some evidence that unstressed /e/ does not go to [y] before vowels (see 2.9).

(*d*) In standard Athenian neither height dissimilation nor glide formation occurs after a sequence of consonant + /r/. Common examples include [ávrio] 'tomorrow', [tría] 'three', [kréas] 'meat', [prióni] 'saw', [kriári] 'ram', [xréos] 'debt', [δákria] 'tears'. It is not clear where the vernacular basis for this pronunciation lies. Peloponnesian dialects, the usual source for standard phenomena, appear to prefer [ávrγ'o], [trγ'á], [krγ'ás], and so on, as do many northern dialects. Insular forms such as [kriás], [kriyás], [krikás] imply, as we shall see in 6.5, intermediate forms with [y]. In some northern dialects epenthetic [y] destroys the hiatus but even there a previous occurrence of glide formation is required to account for the stress shift in, e.g. [kriyás] (see 2.10). Corfu follows the Athenian pattern and perhaps provided its source.

Before we turn to various questions of ordering, it may be pointed out that within paradigms height dissimilation and glide formation are to a large extent prevented from inducing morphophonemic alternation by the action of analogical generalization. Usually a [y] produced by these rules is generalized to those members of the paradigm which do not meet the appropriate input conditions. For example, the plural of /miléa/ 'apple tree' is /milées/ and this would normally contract to [milés]. It does so, however, only in those dialects in which the singular contracts to [milǽ] or [milé]. Where a singular /éa/ becomes [ía], as in Zakinthian, the plural follows ([kariδía], [kariδíes]); where glide formation occurs as well a singular [mil'á] will be pluralized as [mil'és].

We turn now to the position of glide formation within the rule sequence. We have already seen that the rule of glide formation is 'fed' by that of height dissimilation. That is, the action of height dissimilation on /éa/ creates a sequence [ía] which fulfils the input conditions for glide formation. Thus /kariδéa/ 'walnut tree' goes by height dissimilation to [kariδía], and this by glide formation to [kariδyá]. If the rules were transposed (if historically glide formation had ceased to operate when height dissimilation began to take effect), while original /i/ in a word such as /peδía/ 'children' would go to [y], the [i] arising by the later height dissimilation would no longer be synizesized, so that we would get [peδyá] but [kariδía]. There appear to be no dialects in which this is the case.

In addition, crucial ordering constraints exist between glide formation and (*a*) high vowel loss, (*b*) palatalization, (*c*) stress placement and (*d*) enclisis. These are now examined.

(*a*) *Glide formation and high vowel loss.* It is at least simpler to suppose that in northern dialects glide formation preceded the dropping of unstressed /i/ and /u/. Consider, for instance, the derivations for πόδι 'foot' and its plural πόδια in a northern dialect:

(10)	póδi	póδia
Glide formation		**póδya**
High vowel loss	**póδ**	

If high vowel loss had applied historically before glide formation its appropriate conditions would have excluded position before and after vowel, i.e. precisely the environments in which /i/ later went to [y]. It is more plausible to assume that glide formation came first, so that high vowel loss then applied to any remaining [i] without restriction. Because glide formation precedes high vowel loss, and this precedes raising, we would naturally expect glide formation to precede raising by transitivity. There is indeed independent but limited evidence that this is so. If we assume for northern [miydán′] 'village square' (cf. Turkish *meydan*) the underlying structure /meidáni/, then the derivation presumably runs thus:

(11)	meidáni
Glide formation	meydáni
Palatalization	meydán′i
High vowel loss	meydán′
Raising	**miydán′**

If raising applied before glide formation /meidáni/ would have gone to [miidáni] and this then to *[myidáni].

(*b*) *Glide formation and palatalization.* As will be shown in 5.2, if [e] triggers palatalization in a given dialect so does [i], but the converse does not necessarily hold. Thus, while the velar consonants are palatalized to [k′], [x′], [γ′] in all dialects by both front vowels, /s/ goes to [š] in, e.g., certain Lesbian and Epirot dialects only before primary /i/, not /e/. What about the palatalizing effect of [y]? If we consider the word παιδάκια 'small children' in a typical Peloponnesian dialect, it is clear that two derivational orders are possible:

(12)	peδákia		peδákia
Palatalization	peδák′ia	*Glide formation*	peδákya
Glide formation	peδák′ya	*Palatalization*	peδák′ya
Postpalatal yod deletion	**peδák′a**	*Postpalatal yod deletion*	**peδák′a**

In this instance there seems to be no obvious reason for selecting the order palatalization – glide formation over its converse. It might be thought that the first ordering above has the virtue of notational economy, for we need specify the palatalizing environment as 'before [i] and [e]' alone; but in actual fact an analysis in terms of component features would make it simpler to include [y] with [i] and [e] ('front, non-consonantal segments') than to exclude it (and require the additional specification 'vocalic'). Where a particular palatalization is conditioned by /i/ but not /e/, it is again a matter of indifference whether we think of glide formation as preceding or following palatalization, provided both follow height dissimilation. This may be shown by considering the derivation of κερασιά 'cherry tree', βρύσες 'springs', νησί 'island' and νησία 'islands' in the dialect of Ayassos (Lesbos):

(13)	keraséa	vríses	nisí	nisía
Height dissimilation	kerasía			
Glide formation	kerasyá			nisyá
Palatalization	k′erašyá		n′iší	n′išyá
Postpalatal yod deletion	k′erašá			n′išá
High vowel loss			**n′ší**	**n′šá**
Raising	k′irašá	**vrísis**		
Softening	**čirašá**			

It would not affect the outcome whether we placed glide formation and palatalization in the above order or transposed them, as long as we framed the relevant section of the palatalization rule to specify the conditioning environment for sibilants as 'high, front, non-consonantal' ([i] and [y]).

In spite of this, there do seem to be dialects in which [y], but not [i], triggers a palatalization, in which case we are obliged to allow glide formation to act first. In Cypriot, for instance, /s/ is palatalized to [š] only before [y], never [i]. Thus, while /nisí/ 'island' is realized as [nisí], its plural /nisía/ is phonetically [nišá]. If we wish to subsume the various palatalization phenomena under one rule, then clearly the specific reference to [y] implied by the Cypriot form of the rule is only possible once glide formation has created [y]. Compare with (13) the derivation of 'cherry tree', 'island' and 'islands' in Cypriot:

(14)	keraséa	**nisí**	nisía
Height dissimilation	kerasía		
Glide formation	kerasyá		nisyá

Palatalization	k′erašyá	nišyá
Postpalatal yod deletion	k′erašá	**nišá**
Softening	**čerašá**	

As we shall see in chapter 5, there are probably numerous dialects which distinguish the output of /ní/ (νύφη 'bride') from that of /nií/ (γονιοί 'parents') as [ní] versus [n′í]. Here again, we must assume that glide formation precedes palatalization.

While various dialects appear to apply glide formation before palatalization (or, strictly speaking, certain types of palatalization), that of Zakinthos might be claimed to require the prior application of palatalization. In derivation (9) above we employed the order glide formation – palatalization, but it could be argued that this is counter-intuitive for the dialect. It will be remembered that in Zakinthos glide formation occurs only after the palatalizing consonants [k, x, γ, n, l]. Now the order adopted in (9) entails the specification of this set of segments twice in the course of the derivation, once in order to state the restriction on glide formation and once to identify the input to palatalization. If we reverse the order the input to the glide formation rule is simply stated as 'after palatal consonant'. The descriptive simplicity of this ordering reflects its intrinsic historical plausibility.

(*c*) *Glide formation and stress shift.* As we saw earlier (1.5) the ancient Greek accent was not permitted to fall further back than the penultimate syllable of the word if the final vowel was long; more generally, attributing a length of two moras to final long vowels, it could not occur earlier than the third mora from the end of a word. Modern Greek, while it has eliminated the length distinctions in the vowel system and replaced the pitch accent by expiratory stress, has yet in general not shifted stresses from the position of the ancient accent. Thus we saw that the ancient predictable ἄνθρωπος:ἀνθρώπου accentual shift is continued by the superficially unpredictable shift from [ánθropos] to [anθrópu]. It was suggested that by recognizing an underlying length feature in the vowels we can retain the 'three mora rule'.[1] Thus the stress of [ánθropos] shifts forward one syllable before the genitive termination /ū/ for the same reason that we find [éγrapsa] 'I wrote' but [γrápsame] 'we wrote'. Now the rules of stress placement are of ancient origin while glide formation

[1] The term 'three mora rule' applies to ancient Greek only if we treat all vowels except final longs as of one mora. Thus the second vowel of ἄνθρωπος would have to represent a single mora. However, the *length* of accented penultimate vowels was relevant to the acute : circumflex selection.

is relatively recent, so that we might expect any stress placement rule to precede glide formation in a phonological description based on the concept of ordered rules. Indeed this turns out to be the case. Consider, for example ποδιοῦ, the genitive of πόδι 'foot':

(15)	póδiū
Stress placement	poδíū
Vowel shortening	poδíu
Glide formation	poδyú
Consonantality	**poδγ′ú**

It is clear that the rule of stress shift, which transfers on to the vowel three moras from the end any earlier stress, should precede glide formation. For a glide is non-syllabic and cannot represent a mora, so that if glide formation acted before stress placement we would get [póδyū], and then by vowel shortening and consonantality *[póδγ′u]. Another example concerns the verb system. The stress on most verb forms is placed in ancient Greek at the earliest point permitted by the three mora rule, and this is reflected in the modern language. Now in many modern dialects the imperfect of oxytone verbs of the μπορῶ 'I can' class shows the singular endings -εια, -ειες, -ειε (see 2.4). Thus 'he was walking' occurs in such dialects as [perpátye], or by consonantality [perpátx′e] (Cretan [perpáθx′e]). The stress can be accounted for by setting up the following derivation:

(16)	perpatie
Stress placement	perpátie
Glide formation	perpátye
Consonantality	**perpátx′e**

That such forms went historically through a stage with [i] is shown by the fact that many mainland dialects insert [γ] or [y] between it and the following vowel, thus eliminating the hiatus by consonantal epenthesis rather than by glide formation. Thus in the Peloponnese we find [bóriγa] 'I was able' (see 2.10). If in the case of /perpatie/ glide formation preceded, its output [perpatye] would then acquire an incorrect stress on the [per]. Similarly if we assume that the [y] in the item [γáyδaros] 'donkey' (a word for which no convincing etymology appears to have been offered) has its source in an /i/ (rather than in a /y/ specific to borrowings) it might appear that the underlying form would be /γáiδaros/ in violation of the three mora rule. This is not so, however, for a /γaíδaros/ would yield the same result; remember that an /i/ acted on by glide formation shifts its stress on to the adjacent vowel.

However, there does appear to be one important class of exceptions to the principle that stress placement precedes glide formation, that of the verbs in -ιάζω, -ιάνω, -ειώνω. Consider μοιάζω 'I resemble'. In the imperfect of this we find [émyaza] 'I resembled'. Assuming for this an underlying /emiaza/, stress placement would yield [emíaza] and this would then go by glide formation to *[emyáza] if we applied these rules in the normal order. Presumably what happened here was that the present–imperfect stress alternation of forms such as [vázo]:[évaza] 'I put:I was putting' was generalized to verbs of the [myázo] type. It is easy to show that this is equivalent to applying glide formation before stress placement throughout the paradigm. Thus /emiaza/ goes by glide formation to [emyaza] and this by stress placement to [émyaza].

(*d*) *Glide formation and enclisis.* Postposed monosyllabic personal pronouns (με, μου, τον, του, etc.) are themselves unstressed but induce stress on the final syllable of any preceding noun, verb or adjective which has proparoxytone (antepenultimate) stress. Thus while φέρε τον 'bring him!' and ὁ φίλος μου 'my friend' appear as [fér(e)ton], [ofílozmu], σκότωσέ τον 'kill him!', τὸ ἄλογό μου 'my horse' are [skótoséton], [táloγómu], the only exception known to me in the core dialects being Cypriot, which does not have an enclisis rule ([skótoseton], [táloγomu]).[1] Now if, as is the case, 'my barrel' is [tovarélimu] from /to+varéli+mu/, how does its plural /ta+varélia+mu/ behave? If we place enclitic stress immediately we get [tavaréliámu], which would go by glide formation and subsequent rules to *[tavarél'ámu]. In fact, however, we always find [tavarél'amu], which implies the order glide formation – enclisis. Similarly ἔννοιά σου 'be careful!' is always stressed as in [én'asu], never *[én'ásu], which the prior occurrence of enclisis would produce. As a simple illustration of this relation, let us consider ἡ ὑπηρέτριά σου 'your servant' and τὰ ἀγόρια σου 'your boys' in a dialect in which glide formation is impeded after /tr/:

(17)	i+ipirétria+'su	ta+aγória+'su
Glide formation		ta+aγórya+'su
Enclisis	i+ipirétriá+su	ta+aγórya+su

This will now go to [iipirétriásu] and [taγórγ'asu].

[1] Published studies of Pontic and Cappadocian often imply a similar lack of enclisis (see, e.g., Andriotis 1948: 24 for Pharasa but cf. Dawkins 1916: 24).

It remains to point out that the rule of glide formation, besides failing to affect stressed [í] in Old Athenian, Zakinthian and Karpathian, also fails to affect both stressed [í] and unstressed [i] in a large number of words which are of learned rather than strictly inherited origin. Thus 'school' is [sxolío] in standardizing idiolects, although true dialectal [skol'ó] is not by any means unknown outside the towns. In many words glide formation is unknown: μουσεῖο 'museum', θυσία 'sacrifice', οἰκονομία 'economy', ἐργαλεῖο 'tool' (but [arɣal'ó] 'loom'). It may be noted that height dissimilation and glide formation (in dialects which have both) apply or fail to apply as a pair; thus ἰδέα 'idea', παρέα 'company' are always [iδéa], [paréa], μηλιά 'apple tree' (/miléa/) always [mil'á]. Where glide formation fails this will, of course, often have implications for the various phenomena of stress placement and enclisis. We may note, for instance, that τέλειωσε 'it's finished' may be pronounced either as [tél'ose], with glide formation followed by stress placement, or as [telíose], which implies failure of glide formation but the normal action of stress placement. To illustrate the effect of glide formation failure on enclisis, we may compare (τὰ) παραμύθια σου 'your tales', which follows the normal rules, to (ἡ) προμήθειά σου 'your supply', which involves a 'learned' element:

(18)	paramíθia + 'su	promíθia + 'su
Glide formation	paramíθya + 'su	(fails)
Enclisis	paramíθya + su	promíθiá + su

While we always find [paramíθx'asu] but [promíθiásu], some words may or may not undergo glide formation. Thus ἡ βοήθειά σου 'your help' is usually [ivoíθx'asu] or [ivóyθx'asu] in rural Peloponnese, but [ivoíθiásu] is common in urban idiolects.

It might be worth while to display the ordering constraints discussed above in the form of a diagram (see Figure 1). To the rules mentioned in this section, we add that of voiced fricative deletion (see derivation (3) of 1.2), and also incorporate the comment of 2.6 that height dissimilation does not have to be specified so as to exclude sequences of like vowels if contraction precedes it.

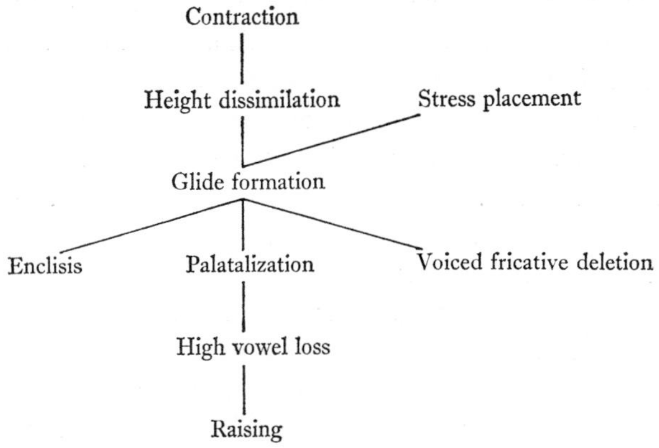

Figure 1. The position of glide formation within the normal rule sequence

2.8 Contraction

Ancient Greek contraction processes have left various synchronic marks on the language. For instance, a complete account of the accentual system of modern Greek might wish to account for certain stress phenomena in the oxytone verbs by referring to the ancient, uncontracted forms which at a level of analysis 'deeper' than that required in this book might be held to underlie the modern paradigm. The reason why [aγápa] 'love!' bears paroxytone stress in spite of the principle that verbs are stressed as far back as the three mora rule allows is that it arises by contraction from /aγapae/, which is stressed by the normal rule. Similarly [aγapá] 'he loves' (in insular dialects) derives from /aγapaī/, which yields [aγapáī] then [aγapái] according to the rules of stress placement and vowel shortening. As a final example we may take the stress shift from a feminine singular noun such as [xóra] 'country, main town of island' to [xorón] in the genitive plural. Noting first that the genitive plural ending contains a long /ō/ (cf. [ánθropos] but gen. pl. [anθrópon] from /ánθropōn/) we may wish to treat [xorón] as deriving from /xóraōn/, in which case our account would recapitulate the ancient sequence of stress shift followed by contraction of /a/ and /ō/.

Because such vowel sequences as survived contraction normally undergo height dissimilation and glide formation in most modern dialects, contraction of underlying vowel sequences within words is of relatively small importance as a productive phonological process. There is some evidence, however, that sequences of like vowels undergo contraction word-medially. Thus the sequence /ées/, which occurs in the plural of feminine nouns in /éa/ (as ἐλιά 'olive', Old Athenian [eléa]) contracts to [és] in those dialects in which /éa/ goes to [ấ] or [é] (see 2.9); otherwise we find [elíes] or [el'és] according as the singular goes to [elía] or [el'á]. Other cases of like vowels in succession are rare. Ancient ζῶον 'animal' often occurs as [zó] (plural [zá]) 'donkey' but this is a fact of etymology rather than of synchronic phonology. The expression [θému] 'my God!' certainly represents a contraction of /θeé + mu/ but it is unclear whether this pronunciation is truly inherited, as some dialects have this in conjunction with [θyós] for /θeós/ (nom.), in which case one might expect analogy to yield *[θyé] just as [pal'ós] for /paléos/ 'ancient' leads to [pal'és] for /palées/ in the feminine plural form, or as the vocative of /roméos/ > [romyós] 'Greek' is [romyé].

Sequences of different vowels within words rarely undergo contraction rather than height dissimilation and glide formation, and where they do, the rules are probably of doubtful synchronic validity. It is customary in the literature to cite [θóδoros] 'Theodorus' and similar names in Θεο-, together with [xrostó] 'I owe', which goes back to χρεωστῶ, and [θoró] 'I see' (θεωρῶ). Similarly βοηθῶ 'I help' contracts to [vuθó] in Crete and various other islands ([voθú] in Skiros) and ἀιτός 'eagle' sometimes turns up as [atós] rather than the common [aytós]; /máis/ 'May' is [más] in the Dodecanese. Apart from isolated cases such as these, contraction is characteristic of certain members of the paradigms of verbs such as καίω 'I burn', ἀκούω 'I hear' with vowel-final stems, as well as of τρώγω 'I eat', λέγω 'I say', θέλω 'I wish' and others, which drop their medial consonant (e.g. [akús] < /akúīs/, [léme] < /léγome/). But these 'semi-contracted' verbs conjugate differently according to dialect in ways which suggest conflicting analogical pulls rather than the distribution of phonological rules, so that their treatment belongs rather to the study of verb morphology (see Koutsoudas 1962).

Discussion of the above phenomena usually takes place within the framework of the 'hierarchy of dominance' which we owe originally to Chatzidakis. Its basic concept is that the vowels of modern Greek can be placed on a scale such that the surviving vowel of a sequence of two is that which occurs first in the series /a o u e i/. Reference to the above data will show that this works well enough within words, although in the case of the verb forms it is difficult to sort out morphological from phonological factors. /akúete/ 'you hear' becomes [akúte] in agreement with the hierarchy of dominance. /lé(γ)une/ 'they say' goes to [léne] in violation of it. Is this because stress overrides the normal contraction rule or is it a matter of paradigmatic pressure? If the latter, why not explain [akúte] the same way?

Before we consider the sandhi phenomena which provide the most cogent evidence for Chatzidakis' rule, let us first note that the hierarchy of dominance involves more general principles than the simple listing /a o u e i/ might suggest. In fact back vowels dominate front ones and low vowels dominate higher ones; if we apply these principles in this order we shall obtain the correct result. The rule may therefore be summarized as follows:

Contraction: (*a*) A vowel is deleted in the environment adjacent to an identical vowel. (*b*) A front vowel is deleted in the environment adjacent to a back vowel. (*c*) A vowel is deleted in the environment adjacent to a lower vowel. (*d*) Any stress carried by the deleted vowel is transferred to the survivor.

By no means all cases of hiatus across word boundary are resolved by contraction. Indeed contraction is regular only in the following groups of cases:

(*a*) A form of the definite article with the shape CV (i.e. τό, τοῦ, τά) precedes a noun beginning with the same vowel or one which dominates that of the article:

τὰ ἀδέρφια	'the brothers and sisters'	[taδerfx'a]
τοῦ ἀδερφοῦ	'of the brother'	[taδerfú]
τοῦ ὀρφανοῦ	'of the orphan'	[torfanú]
τὸ ἄλλο	'the other'	[tálo]

When the article contains the dominant vowel contraction does not occur; thus τὰ ὄνειρα 'the dreams' [taónira]. It is true that historically this restriction has not always been observed; indeed unrestricted contraction has been a rich source of restructuring of nouns. Thus τὰ ἐρίφια 'the kids' appears to have contracted to [tarífx'a] at one stage; this was then analysed as the output of /ta+arífia/ or /ta+rífia/, whence dialectal ἀρίφια, ρίφια. Similarly 'orphans' appears in the dialects as [arfaná], implying a similar process. Because such developments have resulted in the replacement of the underlying forms ('restructuring') they belong rather to the history of Greek. Examples are numerous and interested readers may be referred to Chatzidakis (1905: 211 ff.).

(*b*) A personal pronoun of CV shape precedes a verb. In this case contraction is usual irrespective of whether the dominant vowel belongs to the first or second element. The pronouns affected are the accusatives μέ, σέ, τό, τά, and (outside north-eastern Greece, where they are replaced by the accusative forms) the datives μοῦ, σοῦ, τοῦ:

μοῦ ἔδωσε	'he gave me'	[múδose]
τὰ ἔφερε	'he brought them'	[táfere]
σοῦ εἶπα	'I told you'	[súpa]
σοῦ ἄρεσε;	'did you like it?'	[sárese]
τὸ ἤξερα	'I knew it'	[tóksera]

(*c*) The particles θά, νά or the conjunction πού (or adverb ποῦ) precede a verb. Again contraction is not sensitive to the position of the dominant vowel:

ποῦ εἶναι;	'where is he?'	[púne]
θὰ ἔλεγα	'I would say'	[θáleγa]
νὰ ἤξερες	'if only you knew'	[nákseres]

It is sometimes claimed (following Chatzidakis) that the hierarchy of dominance shifts from /a o u e i/ to /a o e u i/ in northern Greek; this is equivalent to transposing parts (*b*) and (*c*) of the contraction rule as it was formulated above. However, the evidence adduced is usually based on the relative construction; in some northern dialects (e.g. Samothraki, Thessaly) we get [aftósapéx'] for αὐτὸς ποὺ ἔχει 'he who has'. However, it may be observed that the relative pronoun underlying such phrases, /apu/, undergoes high vowel loss at least before consonants, so that /apu+péfti/ 'who falls' becomes [appéfti]. While high vowel loss does not normally occur before vowels (see derivation (10) above) we may here have a generalization of the preconsonantal [ap] form. If in fact dialects with a general rule contracting /ue/ to [e] occurred, we would expect to find *[pémenes] for /pú+émenes/ 'where were you staying?', *[téleγa] for /tu éleγa/ 'I was telling him', and so on, but these forms do not apparently occur. There is, however, one widespread departure from the rule as stated above. In Mani, parts of Crete, Cyprus, Epirus, Thrace and doubtless elsewhere, the sequence /u/+/e/ goes to [o]. Thus ποὺ ἔρχεται 'who comes' appears as [pórx'ete] rather than [púrx'ete]. It may also be added that some speakers fail regularly to apply the contraction rule across word boundaries in cases where others would apply it. It is true of Cypriot, and perhaps the other dialects of the south-eastern group which do not normally prepose object pronouns in positive declarative sentence (e.g. ἔδωκε μου 'he gave me'), that when the pronoun is preposed, as in negative sentences, it does not participate in contraction. Thus δὲν μοῦ ἔδωκε 'he did not give me' is in Cypriot [émmuéδok'e].

One of the most interesting problems raised by contraction is that of its relation to raising in northern dialects; the question of the relative ordering of these rules has never, as far as I am aware, been discussed, and it is unfortunate that published data are insufficiently detailed to permit more than a few tentative remarks. First of all, it may be noticed that not all sequences involving underlying mid vowels are sensitive to the choice of order. Thus the sequences /o/+/á/ and /o/+/ó/ (as in τὸ ἄλογο 'the horse',τὸ ὄνειρο 'the dream' will lead to [á], [ó], irrespective of whether raising or contraction occurs first. /to+áloγo/, for instance, would go by raising to [tu+áluγu], and this by contraction to [táluγu]; alternatively we might get the same output by applying contraction to yield [táloγo], and then raising. A sequence of /o/+/é/, as in σοῦ τὸ ἔδωσα 'I gave it to you' provides crucial evidence in a dialect which contracts underlying /u/+/é/ to [ú]. If in such a dialect raising applies first we shall get [ué] and this will go to [ú] by contraction;[1] the converse order will yield [ó]. However, many northern dialects have [ó] for /u/+/é/, in which case either order will yield [ó]. The sequences which are in fact crucial for the determination of the position of contraction in respect to raising are /e/+/á/ (as in μὲ ἄρεσε 'it pleased me') and /o/+/í/ (as in τὸ εἶπε 'he said it'). Consider the derivations of these phrases in a northern dialect which applies the rules in the order raising–contraction:

(19)	to+ípe	me+árese
Raising	tu+ípi	mi+árisi
Contraction	**túpi**	**miárisi**

We are assuming here that contraction will not act on the sequence [i]+[á] on the ground that it does not appear to affect primary /i/ in this position (τί ἄφησες; 'what did you leave?' [tiáfises]). The converse order would lead to the following result:

(20)	to+ípe	me+árese
Contraction	tópe	márese
Raising	**tópi**	**márisi**

Now such data as are available suggest that in fact raising precedes contraction in the case of items with an /o/+/í/ sequence, but that in the

[1] I have found [stúδosa] only in Thasos.

case of /e/ + /á/ the rules are transposed. Thus in Velvendos and at various other points for which I have data we find [túpi] 'he said it', [túx'i] 'he had it' (from /to + íxe/) but [márisi], [máfisi], etc.[1] In Tyrnavos it appears from Tzartzanos that /me + árese/ yields [mä́risi], with the front low vowel originating as elsewhere in the area from sequences of /e/ + /a/; this clearly implies the prior occurrence of contraction, although in Tyrnavos /o/ + /í/ is realized as [ú]. It is difficult to come to any firm conclusion in view of the paucity of data, but one hypothesis suggests itself. In a dialect such as that of Tyrnavos I would propose that contraction occurred in two stages. First those sequences were affected which consisted only of non-high vowels; a later extension of the rule took in sequences containing high vowels. These two stages were separated by the raising rule:

(21)	to + ípe	me + árese
Contraction ([a, e, o])		mä́rese
Raising	tu + ípi	**mä́risi**
Contraction (*unrestricted*)	**túpi**	

There is another reason, quite unconnected with the northern phenomena just discussed, for supposing that contraction took place in two stages, the first not involving [i]. It is that a large number of dialects, including those of Crete and the Ionian Isles, do not apply contraction to sequences with [i]. Thus while μοῦ ἔλεγε 'he was telling me', τὰ ἔφερα 'I brought them', τὸ ἔγραψα 'I wrote it' appear as [múleye], [táfere], [tóɣrapsa], μοῦ εἶπε 'he told me', τὰ εἶδε 'he saw them', τὸ εἶδε 'he saw it' are [múype], [táyδe], [tóyδe]. In this case we may postulate a contraction rule for all sequences other than those with [i], these latter then undergoing glide formation:

(22)	ta + éfere	ta + íδe	mu + ípe
Contraction	**táfere**		
Glide formation		**táyδe**	**múype**

2.9 Contraction in the north east and in Crete

In the dialects of Thessaly, Macedonia and Thrace a low front vowel [ä] occurs in contrast with [a]. Thus we find [krä́ta] 'meats' for /kréata/ versus [kráta] 'hold' for /kráta/. Furthermore, front round [ö] and [ü]

[1] In dialects which use μοῦ, σοῦ in a dative function, [máfisi] (μὲ ἄφησε) but not [márisi] (μοῦ ἄρεσε) would be relevant.

are found in at least parts of Macedonia and Thessaly. Let us first consider the case of [ä], for which the facts are relatively clear. Typical data are as follows:

/apiδéa/	'pear tree'	[abδä́]
/apiδées/	'pear trees'	[abδés]
/miléa/	'apple tree'	[milä́]
/milía/	'speech'	[mil'á]
/milá/	'he speaks'	[milá]
/traγía/	'goats'	[trayä́] (Tyrnavos [traä́])
/rolóγia/	'watches'	[rulóyä] (Tyrnavos [rulóä])
/vraδía/	'evening'	[vraδγ'á]
/xeréa/	'handful'	[x'irä́]
/xoría/	'villages'	[xurγ'á]

The general principle seems clear enough: [ä] derives from /ea/, or from /a/ after a sequence of vowel + /γi/. One possible reconstruction of the sequence of events might be as follows for μηλιά 'apple tree', μιλιά 'speech', τραγιά 'goats':

(23)	miléa	milía	traγía
Glide formation		milyá	traγyá
Palatalization		mil'yá	traγ'yá
Postpalatal yod deletion		**mil'á**	traγ'á
Consonantality			trayá
Fronting	miléä		trayä́
Contraction	**milä́**		
Intervocalic yod deletion			**traä́**

That [milä́] went through a [miléä] stage is supported by the remark of Chatzidakis (1905: 344) that in Ikaria, whose dialect has various features of Cretan origin, [miléä], [eléä] were heard at the turn of the century for Cretan [milé], [elé] (although my observations indicate that these latter pronunciations are now current). Further evidence from northern Greek itself that vowels may undergo progressive assimilation in respect of frontness is provided by a phenomenon reported by Andriotis (1939: 198) for Samothraki. There [u] is fronted to [ü] when immediately preceded by [e] or [i]. Thus /γéros/ 'old man' develops to [yéus] (with the loss of intervocalic [r] characteristic of the dialect of Samothraki, as well as normal northern raising) and then [yéüs].

One point worth noting in derivation (23) is that the /l/ of /miléa/ does not at any point come into contact with a following [i] or [y], so that the degree of palatalization which it shows in the output [milä́] is that associated with the position before [e]. The /l/ of /milía/, on the other hand, acquires the fully palatal pronunciation normally induced by [y] once glide formation yields [milyá]. Similarly for /n/: in most dialects /n/ is palatalized fully to [n′] only before [y], so that while /panía/ 'sails' will go in the present group of dialects to [pan′á], /ennéa/ 'nine' will become rather [enä́].[1]

It might also be observed that by placing the consonantality rule before fronting and contraction, we are able to state the conditions for fronting in a straightforward way: [a] > [ä] after any front non-consonantal segment (i.e. after [i], [e] or [y]). If fronting occurred first we would have to confine its conditioning environment to position after [e]. Consider, for example, the derivations for ἀπιδιά 'pear tree', παιδιά 'children' in the dialect of Velvendos:

(24)	apiδéa	peδía
Glide formation		peδyá
Consonantality		peδγ′á
Fronting	apiδéä	
Contraction	apiδä́	
High vowel loss	apδä́	
Raising		**piδγ′á**
Voice assimilation	**abδä́**	

If fronting occurred before consonantality we would have to ensure that it did not affect /peδía/.

Reference to the contraction rule formulated in 2.8 (p. 43) will suggest that the conversion of [eä] to [ä] constitutes a straightforward instance of principles (*c*) and (*d*). That is, the [e] is deleted in the environment of the lower vowel [ä] and any stress carried by it goes on to the [ä].

The position with regard to [u] and [o] is far from clear. Boundonas (1892: 32) implies that in Velvendos /eo/ and /eu/ develop in a parallel manner to /ea/, i.e. they go to [ö] and [ü] (with, according to him, a [y] onset). The data in Tzartzanos (1909) also provide evidence that in

[1] I owe this information to N. Andriotis (oral communication) for Thrace and to V. Phoris for Kozani (Macedonia). The pronunciations given also correspond to my data on Velvendos, although Boundonas (1892: 32) appears to have heard a [y] before all occurrences of [ä]. The statement in Tombaidis (1967: 13) that [ä] arises from [ya] in Thasos is unsupported by his own data, which imply an underlying /ea/ in all cases.

Tyrnavos not only does /eo/ go to [ö], but that [o] and [u] are rounded after [y] just as [a] is:

/koréos/	'bug'	[korö́s]
/γiomízo/	'I fill'	[yümízu]
/panaγiótis/	'Panayotis'	[panaö́ts]

However, it appears that not all cases of /eo/ go to [ö]. Tzartzanos cites [pal'ós] 'ancient' from /paléos/, and my own enquiries failed to turn up a single instance of [ö] < [eo] for Velvendos (/koréos/ being given as [kurγ'ós]). Typical data included [sál'ü] 'saliva' for /sálio/, [téθk'üs] 'such' for /tétios/ and [xurγ'ǘ] 'village' (gen.) for /xoríu/ (but [xurγ'ó] (nom.) for /xorío/), as well as [panayö́ts] and [yümízu]. Thus it is at least the case that [ö́] occurs for [ó] after a sequence of vowel+yod and that stressed and unstressed [ü] arises for [u] not only after [y], but any palatal consonant. If we assume that true dialect will have [ö] for [eo] and [ü] for [eu], it is possible to state the fronting rule thus:

> **Fronting:** A vowel is front in the environment after front nonconsonantal segment, and if high, after a palatal consonant as well.[1]

Because [u] goes to [ü] after palatals whether it is of primary origin (as in χωριοῦ) or derives by raising from /o/ (as in σάλιο) we have a new point of ordering: the rule of raising must precede fronting. Consider the derivations of σάλιο, χωριοῦ, χωριό and Παναγιώτης in the dialects of Tyrnavos or Velvendos:

(25)	sálio	xoríu	xorío	panaγiótis
Glide formation	sályo	xoryú	xoryó	panaγyótis
Palatalization	sál'yo			panaγ'yótis
Postpalatal yod deletion	sál'o			panaγ'ótis
Consonantality		xorγ'ú	xorγ'ó	panayótis
High vowel loss				panayóts
Raising	sál'u	xurγ'ú	**xurγ'ó**	
Fronting	**sál'ü**	**xurγ'ǘ**		panayö́ts
Yod deletion (Tyrnavos)				**panaö́ts**

A sequence /eo/ as in /koréos/ 'bug' will develop to [ö] exactly as /ea/ goes to [ä] (i.e. /eo/ > [eö] > [ö]). It is not clear how /eu/ would develop in Tzartzanos' dialect; what, for example, would the accusative plural of [korö́s] be? One would expect it to be [korǘs]. In this case, the

[1] As roundness is a distinctive feature of /o/ and /u/ in dialects with [ö] and [ü], the rule will front the back vowels without affecting their roundness.

contraction rule, in addition to deleting vowels according to the usual hierarchy of dominance, will delete [e] adjacent to [ä], [ö] or [ü]. All that is involved here is the replacement of 'front' and 'back' by 'spread' and 'round' in part (*b*) of the original formulation. Thus, [e], being spread, drops before the round [ö], as it does before [ü] for the same reason. [e] will drop before [ä] by virtue of part (*c*), which reads 'a vowel is deleted in the environment adjacent to a lower vowel'.

The 'umlauted' [ä] and [ü] are also found in certain loans from Turkish ([baldürs] 'vagabond') and various onomatopoeic words ([ksü] used in chasing poultry). It is interesting that Tzartzanos cites [bäbä] as the conventional imitation of sheep's bleating, for this would correspond almost exactly to the βῆ βῆ of ancient Greek. [ä] is also frequent in various demonstrative expressions ([ä́tus] 'there they are').

It is not clear whether the dialects of Thessaly, Macedonia and Thrace constitute an exception to the general rule that unstressed [e] always undergoes height dissimilation and glide formation before [a] or [o]. There do not appear to be examples of /eá/, ancient φωλεά and γενεά having in modern dialects the underlying forms /foléa/ and /γenéa/ (see below). Tzartzanos (1909: 16) gives [ksärmin'ázo] 'have puerperal fever', which he says comes from /ksearmeniázō/, and his examples such as [säk'í] 'thither' may have underlying /ea/. For /eó/ Boundonas (1892: 32) has [θyö́s] 'god' from /θeós/, which suggests that at any rate /e/ before /ó/ behaves differently from /i/ before /ó/. Ancient ἑορτή 'holiday', however, is pronounced by informants [yürtí], which implies that if /eortí/ is the correct underlying form height dissimilation and glide formation do apply to unstressed /e/.

In central and western Crete /éa/ goes to [é] and it is tempting to connect this development with the phenomenon of fronting in the dialects of Thessaly, Macedonia and Thrace. That is, we might suppose that in western Crete /karéa/ 'walnut tree' went to [karéä], then [karä́], as did its northern cognate, and then, by a specifically Cretan development this [ä] was raised to [é]. In Ikaria, as we noted above, Chatzidakis actually found the [éä] pronunciation. In the eastern parts of Crete /éa/ is represented by [á] after /r/, but in other environments undergoes the normal height dissimilation, glide formation and consonantality processes, as is the case throughout the island with vowel sequences containing unstressed /e/, or /é/ and a vowel other than /a/. Let us consider the items ἀπιδιά 'pear tree', παιδιά 'children', χωριά 'villages', μεριά 'part', νιός 'young man', in western Crete:

(26)	apiδéa	peδía	xoría	meréa	néos
Fronting	apiδéä			meréä	
Contraction	**apiδé**			**meré**	
Height dissimilation					níos
Glide formation		peδyá	xoryá		nyós
Palatalization					n'yós
Postpalatal yod deletion					**n'ós**
Consonantality		**peδγ'á**	xorγ'á		
Softening			**xoržá**		

In eastern Crete we have [apiδγ'á], [peδγ'á], [xorž'á], [merá], [n'ós]. Because Cretan, as opposed to the north-eastern dialects, has a rule of height dissimilation, it is simpler to place the fronting rule first in the relevant rule sequence, for there is then no need to place any restrictions on the scope of the former. It applies generally, converting, e.g., /leontári/ 'lion' to [l'odári] and /θeós/ 'god' to [θx'ós]. Western Cretan [folé] 'nest', [žené] 'generation' go back to ancient φωλεά and γενεά and might be thought to constitute an exception to the rule that only /éa/ sequences convert to [é]. However, these items must have undergone a stress shift at some time, as is shown by the Old Athenian [foléa], [yenéa], so that their modern underlying forms are /foléa/, /γenéa/, yielding in the north east [fulä́], [yinä́], and most other places outside Crete [fol'á], [yen'á]. The feminine form of certain adjectives of the -ύς type, which show -εῖα in ancient Greek, also requires the assumption of underlying /éa/ in modern dialects. Thus Cretan [varé] 'heavy', [vaθé] 'deep', Old Athenian [varéa], [vaθéa], north-eastern [varä́], [vaθä́] imply /varéa/, /vaθéa/, and there is no reason not to accept these for common [varγ'á], [vaθx'á]. In Crete (but not the north east) the vowel of the feminine form is generalized throughout the singular, giving masculine [varés], neuter [varé]. The nouns in /éas/ go to [és] in Crete and [ä́s] in the north east according to the normal rules. Thus /fonéas/ 'murderer', /voréas/ 'north wind' become [fonés], [vorés] ([vorás] in eastern Crete). βασιλεύς 'king', gives Cretan [vasilés], thus suggesting /vasiléas/. However, the pronunciation [vasilés] is very widespread in the dialects other than Cretan and we ought rather to postulate two underlying forms, /vasiléas/ and /vasilés/. Either would yield [vasilés] in Cretan, but only the latter would do so elsewhere.[1]

[1] [vasilés] is found in most areas and may perhaps represent a popular approximation to learned [vasiléfs]; it is not clear how the presumably rare plural [vasiléyδes] can have provided a source of analogy (see Pernot 1913: 264). Various scholars have

Because the Cretan fronting is confined to /éa/, alternation is found in the nominal system. A typical paradigm would be that of μηλιά 'apple tree':

Nom.	milé	milés
Acc.	milé	milés
Gen.	milés	mil'ón

In Thessaly we have [milá̈] for nominative and accusative singular, [milés] in the plural. The genitive, as generally in the north, is replaced by a prepositional phrase (ἀπ' τὴ μηλιά [abdmilá̈]).

2.10 /γ/ epenthesis

We saw that glide formation tends to be impeded in certain dialects when the sequence /i/+vowel is preceded by a consonant+/r/ (τρία 'three', κρύο 'cold'). Such items therefore represent one source of continuing hiatus in modern Greek. Another source lies in the paradigms of vowel-final verb stems, where paradigmatic pressure has prevented the elimination of hiatus by glide formation or contraction; ἀκούω 'I hear', for instance, and κλαίω 'I cry' have not normally gone to [akwó], [kl'ó], and where such forms are found they are probably recent and subsequent to the loss of intervocalic /γ/ (see 3.1). A final source of persisting hiatus lies in the words which are taken into demotic from the learned or liturgical language (e.g. θεός 'God', ἁμαρτία 'sin', ἄδεια 'permission'). We find that where hiatus manages to resist glide formation or contraction it is often eliminated by the insertion of [γ] or [y] according as the following vowel is back or front. If we follow this rule by palatalization and consonantality we can state it simply as follows:

/γ/ **epenthesis:** Insert /γ/ in the environment between vowels.

Consider the Peloponnesian forms corresponding to standard ἀγαπάει 'he loves', ἀκούω 'I hear', ζούσανε 'they used to live':

(27)	aγapái	akúo	zíane
/γ/ epenthesis	aγapáγi	**akúγo**	**zíγane**
Palatalization	aγapáγ'i		
Consonantality	**ayapáyi**		

sought a source for Cretan [é] in the plurals ἀπιδές etc., but if ἀπιδές led to singular ἀπιδέ we might ask with Chatzidakis (1905: 345) why φωνές did not give φωνέ. Kapsomenos (1939) argues for a late Doric contraction of -εα to [ē].

There are two questions which merit brief discussion: (*a*) the areal distribution of /γ/ epenthesis and (*b*) its ordering within the rule sequence. As we shall see, these questions are intimately related.

The distribution of /γ/ epenthesis is on the face of it easy to state. We find epenthetic [γ] or [y] throughout the mainland, Crete, the Ionian Isles and Old Athenian dialects other than Maniot. The phenomenon does not occur in the south east. Now it is precisely this last group of dialects which has the rule deleting voiced fricatives intervocalically; thus while most dialects ***insert*** /γ/ between vowels, south-eastern ones ***delete*** it in that position. This may be illustrated by comparing the reflexes of ancient ἀκούω 'I hear', λόγος 'speech' in the Peloponnese and Cyprus:

Ancient	Peloponnese	Cyprus
ἀκούω	akúγo	akúo
λόγος	lóγos	lóos

Now it would have been a quite remarkable coincidence if the rules of /γ/ epenthesis and of voiced fricative deletion both selected the same isogloss; one would rather expect there to have been some degree of overlap. If in the area of overlap voiced fricative deletion occurred first, words such as /póδi/ 'foot', /kluví/ 'cage' would have gone to [pói], [kluí], giving us the situation found in most south-eastern dialects today, and then the subsequent /γ/ epenthesis rule would have converted these to *[póyi], *[kluyí]. Such cases are unknown. The opposite ordering would simply have inserted a /γ/ intervocalically only to remove it in conjunction with original /γ/ later. That is, we can explain the [akúo], [lóos] of south-eastern dialects equally well on the assumption that they underwent epenthesis followed by voiced fricative deletion as that they underwent only deletion. If we accept the former hypothesis, the relation between the two main groups of dialects can be shown as follows:

(28)	akúo	lóγos	póδi
/γ/ *epenthesis* (all dialects)	akúγo		
Voiced fricative deletion (S.E.)	**akúo**	**lóos**	**pói**

In addition to explaining what would otherwise be a freak of distribution this assumption is supported by two further considerations. (*a*) The insertion of /γ/ in the verbal ending -εύω occurs in the south east as well as Crete and Old Athenian. It did not drop by voiced fricative deletion because by the time the latter occurred the original [eúγo] (or [éwγo]) had gone to [évγo], thus destroying the intervocalic environment. (*b*) Unless we postulate an earlier stage of /γ/ epenthesis it is difficult to account for the long resistance of verb forms such as [kléo] 'I cry' (from /kléo/) to height dissimilation and glide formation. By assuming that /kléo/ went to [kléγo] very soon after /paléos/ went to [palyós] it is somewhat easier to account for modern [kléo]; we are still faced with the divergent development of /éo/ in the two cases, but the difficulty is shared by Peloponnesian [pal'ós], [kléγo]. The derivations of παλιός and κλαίω in the Peloponnese and south east would be as follows:

(29)	paléos	kléo
Height dissimilation	palíos	
Glide formation	palyós	
Palatalization	pal'yós	
Postpalatal yod deletion	**pal'ós**	
/γ/ epenthesis		kléγo
Voiced fricative deletion (S.E.)		**kléo**

An argument similar to the above can be made for those northern and other dialects which delete [y] < /γ/ before front vowels (see 3.3). Thus, while /lóγos/ 'speech' retains its /γ/, /kataγís/ 'on the ground' becomes [kataís]. Now in such dialects it is sometimes said that /γ/ epenthesis occurs before back vowels alone, giving, e.g., [θakaγó] 'I'll get burnt' for /θa+kaó/, but [θakaí] 'he'll get burnt' for /θa+kaí/. It is clearly more plausible, however, to assume that unrestricted /γ/ epenthesis occurred before yod deletion:

(30)	kataγís	θakaó	θakaí
/γ/ epenthesis		**θakaγó**	θakaγí
Palatalization	kataγ'ís		θakaγ'í
Consonantality	katayís		θakayí
Intervocalic yod deletion	**kataís**		**θakaí**

Further evidence for the relatively early position of /γ/ epenthesis in northern dialects is provided by the imperfect of oxytone verbs such as μπορῶ 'I am able'. Corresponding to Peloponnesian [bóriγa], [bóriyes], [bóriye], we there find [bórγa], [bórγ'is], [bórγ'i]. Now these forms derive historically from /boria/, /bories/, /borie/ (see 2.4), and the northern reflexes can be most easily explained as follows:

(31)	bória	bóries	bórie
/γ/ epenthesis	bóriγa	bóriγes	bóriγe
Palatalization		bóriγ′es	bóriγ′e
High vowel loss	**bórγa**	bórγ′es	bórγ′e
Raising		**bórγ′is**	**bórγ′i**

The dialect of Cargese as reported by Blanken (1951: 78) poses a rather interesting problem. There intervocalic [y], whether of epenthetic origin or corresponding to primary /γ/, fails to undergo softening, while all other cases of [y] go to [ž] as in Crete and Mani. Thus /γéros/ 'old man', /iatrós/ 'doctor', /karávia/ 'boats' are [žéros], [žatrós], [karávža], but /píγe/ 'he went', /aéras/ 'wind' are [píye], [ayéras]. Blanken concludes that the intervocalic [y] is of recent epenthetic origin even when it occurs at the position of historical /γ/, as in [píye]. If we assume for this dialect the common rule deleting intervocalic [y] before front vowels, κατώγι 'lower floor', κατώγια (pl.), γέρος 'old man' would have some such derivation as the following:

(32)	katóγi	katóγia	γéros
Glide formation		katóγya	
Palatalization	katóγ′i	katóγ′ya	γ′éros
Postpalatal yod deletion		katóγ′a	
Consonantality	katóyi	katóya	yéros
Intervocalic yod deletion	katói		
Softening		**katóža**	**žéros**
Yod epenthesis	**katóyi**		

The last four lines represent the dialectal possibilities actually found. All dialects possess the consonantality rule, and its output [katóyi], [katóya], [yéros] is found in certain Peloponnesian dialects. Most of these, and most northern dialects, delete intervocalic [y] before front vowels, giving [katói], [katóya], [yéros]. Cretan applies softening to yield [katói], [katóža], [žéros], and finally the dialect of Cargese epenthesizes a yod to yield [katóyi], [katóža], [žéros].

In various dialects [y] and not the expected [γ] occurs between [i] and a back vowel. Thus we find [kríyo] 'cold' for /krío/ in the dialect of Vourbiani in Epirus (Anagnostopoulos 1930), and [áδiya] 'permission' for /áδia/. However, more commonly than [kríyo] we find [kriyó], and similarly [γriyá] 'old woman' for /γréa/. Now if we accept the normal account, which treats these last forms as special cases of consonantal epenthesis, it is difficult to explain the stress shift. I would prefer in such cases to regard the underlying /i/ as the source of [y] and take the phonetic [i] to be of epenthetic origin:

(33)	krío	γréa
Height dissimilation		γría
Glide formation	kryó	γryá
[i] *epenthesis*	**kriyó**	**γriyá**

Whether in a given instance we are faced with glide formation and [i] epenthesis will depend on the general pattern of the particular dialect. In Vourbiani, for instance, the occurrence of [kríyo] confirms the existence of an epenthesis rule inserting [γ] before back vowels except when [i] precedes, otherwise [y] (cf. also in the same dialect [θeγós] 'god' < /θeós/). The [θiyós] of Astipalea is, on the other hand, not to be described as the outcome of /γ/ epenthesis (Karanastasis 1958) but rather as in derivation (33). For although no stress shift occurs in this particular item, it occurs in [ovriyós] 'Jew', and the sequence height dissimilation – glide formation – [i] epenthesis is certainly required there:

(34)	θeós	ovréos
Height dissimilation	θiós	ovríos
Glide formation	θyós	ovryós
[i] *epenthesis*	**θiyós**	**ovriyós**

It remains to mention that [y] epenthesis may occur between an [i] form of the definite article (ἡ, οἱ) and a following noun. Thus we find in various northern dialects [iyóra] 'the time', [iyelén'] 'Helen', [iyál'] 'the others' for ἡ ὥρα, ἡ Ἑλένη, οἱ ἄλλοι. In Crete and Mani this [y] goes, together with the [y] arising from /γ/ or /i/, to [ž] ([ižóra], etc.). That the appropriate conditions involved other forms of the article in the past is suggested by the restructuring of αἷμα 'blood' in many dialects as [yéma]. Presumably in some dialects [y] was epenthesized between the neuter article τό and a noun with initial front vowel. The [yóma] found in some dialects implies [y] epenthesis followed by rounding (as frequently between [y] and [m], see 2.3). The [óma] of Karpathos, however, suggests rather contraction of τὸ αἷμα to [tóma] followed by reinterpretation of this as /to + óma/.

The position of /γ/ epenthesis in the rule sequence is displayed in Figure 2.

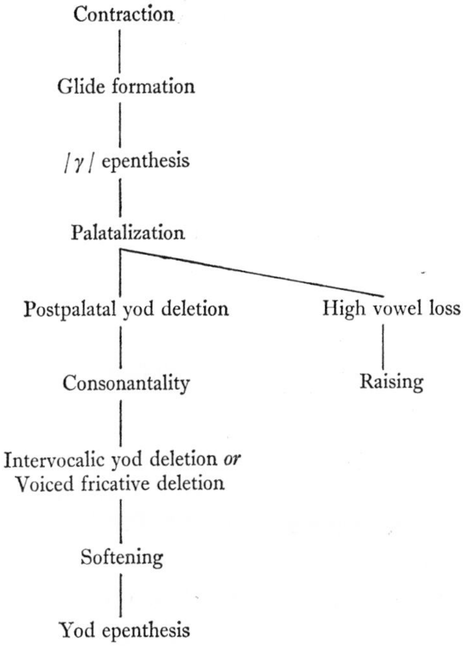

Figure 2. The position of /γ/ epenthesis in the normal rule sequence

2.11 Epenthesis in -εύω verbs

In south-eastern dialects, in Cretan and in Old Athenian (with the exception of Aegina but including Mani) verbs in ancient -εύω appear with [évγo], matching [évo] in other dialects. The south-eastern dialects, which apply manner dissimilation to sequences of voiced fricatives, convert this further to [évgo], and in Cypriot this may go by 'devoicing' (4.5) to [éfko]. Thus for δουλεύω 'I work' we find [δulévo] in Peloponnesian–Ionian, [δlévu] in the north, [δulévγo] in Crete, Mani, Megara and Kimi, as well as most south-eastern dialects, and [δuléfko] in parts of Cyprus. Furthermore certain other verbs with stems in β develop a /γ/ (e.g. κλέβω 'I steal', σκάβω 'I dig', ράβω 'I sew'). Finally the word Παρασκευή 'Friday' appears with an ending matching that of the -εύω verbs (e.g. Cretan [parasčevγ'í], Cypriot [paraššefk'í], and certain south-eastern dialects have [vγaŋg'él'o] for εὐαγγέλιο 'bible'.

The phenomenon has attracted considerable attention, although no completely convincing explanation has been offered. There is one account, however, that of Krumbacher (1886), which in addition to its intrinsic plausibility can be related to the phonological principles described in this book without the need to make any special assumptions. If we start with a stage at which ancient αυ and ευ had still a diphthongal pronunciation the derivation of the various forms of δουλεύω (and of δούλεψα, for which see below) can be represented as follows:

(35)	δuleúo	δúleusa
Glide formation	δuléwo	δúlewsa
/γ/ epenthesis II	δuléwγo	
Consonantality	**δulévγo**	δúlefsa
Manner dissimilation	**δulévgo**	**δúlepsa**
Devoicing	**δuléfko**	

While that form of epenthesis which inserts /γ/ between vowel applies to all dialects, what we are here labelling '/γ/ epenthesis II', and which inserts /γ/ in addition between the glide [w] and a vowel, is found only in certain dialects. Where it does not occur (in Peloponnesian–Ionian and the north), an extension of the consonantality rule has converted [w] to its consonantal counterpart [v] in all positions (and not just post-consonantally as with [y]).

By treating the epenthesis of /γ/ in -εύω verbs as an extension of the normal epenthesis rule we are implying that in south-eastern dialects /γ/ was epenthesized between vowels at one stage, only to be removed later by voiced fricative deletion (see 2.10). If this is correct, the course of events which led to south-eastern [klaévgo] 'I prune', [kléo] 'I cry' can be represented thus:

(36)	klaδeúo	kléo
Glide formation	klaδéwo	
/γ/ epenthesis II	klaδéwγo	kléγo
Consonantality	klaδévγo	
Voiced fricative deletion	klaévγo	**kléo**
Manner dissimilation	**klaévgo**	

One advantage of postulating a uniform underlying /δuleúo/ is that the derivation of the sigmatic forms of the verb will be identical in all dialects. The rules used in derivation (35) above to derive the aorist form [δúlepsa] from /δúleusa/ are found in all dialects. Manner dissimilation always converts [fs] to [ps], although it acts on voiced clusters such as [vγ] only in the south-east. Thus while every dialect has [ps] in its reflex of /δúleusa/, the present and imperfect will have [v] (where epenthesis acts only intervocalically), [vγ] (where it acts after [w]), [vg] (where voiced clusters undergo manner dissimilation) or (with devoicing) [fk].

One other proposal worth mentioning, for its ingenuity if nothing else, is due to Kretschmer (1905: 193–204). According to his account /δuleúo/ went to [δuleúwo] by a natural rule which can be paralleled in ancient dialects (and is analogous to the modern insertion of [y] in some dialects between /i/ and /a/). Then the [ww] resulting from glide formation became [gw] by a rule found in S. Italy ([δulégwo] occurs in Otranto). This is the weakest link, but from then on it is plain sailing. The conversion of [gw] to [gv] can be achieved by the normal consonantality rule and of this to [vγ] by the same rules of fricativity assimilation and metathesis as led from ancient ἐκβάλλω to [vγálo].[1]

[1] Other proposals have usually involved rather implausible analogical extensions. Chatzidakis (1892: 123) suggested that the [y] arising by glide formation in sequences such as βασιλεύει ὁ ἥλιος 'the sun sets' [vasilévyoíl'os] was blended with the [i] which remained in preconsonantal position (γυρεύει καλά 'he looks carefully' [yirévikalá]) to give [vasilévyi], and this was then taken to represent /vasilévγi/. The single verb ȝεύγω 'I yoke' has also been claimed to provide the operative analogical proportion (ézepsa : zévγo :: δúlepsa : *x*). Neither approach can account for Παρασκευγή.

3 *Secondary Hiatus*

3.0 Having examined the various ways in which underlying vowel sequences are eliminated at the phonetic level in modern Greek, we now turn to the development of those vowel sequences which arise through the loss of an intervening consonant. The first section deals with the loss of /v, δ, γ/ in the south east, and reference is then made in 3.2 to the possibly related phenomenon whereby one of these sounds is replaced by another. In 3.3 we consider that loss of [y] between any vowel and [i] or [e] which is particularly common in the north. The loss of intervocalic /r/ is discussed in 3.4 and the next section deals with the dissimilatory loss of intervocalic consonants; the extent to which the loss of /s/ may be regarded as a species of dissimilation is discussed in the final section. Throughout the chapter considerable attention is paid to the relative position of these deletion processes in the rule sequences of the different dialects. We shall usually find that consonant loss may be followed by height dissimilation and perhaps contraction, but not glide formation.

3.1 Voiced fricative deletion

In the Dodecanese and Cyprus, as well as in Chios, there is a regular loss of /v, δ, γ/ in intervocalic position. Furthermore, because sequences of definite article + noun, and particle or pronoun + verb, form closely-knit grammatical structures which tend to behave phonologically as single words, we also find that the initial voiced fricative of a noun or verb may drop when a vowel-final article, particle or pronoun precedes. The following examples are typical for the south east:

/v/	κάβουρας	'crab'	[káuras]
	φόβος	'fear'	[fóos]
	φλέβα	'vein'	[fléa]
	λιβάδι	'meadow'	[liái]
	βουβός	'dumb'	[vuós]

	ὁ βασιλιάς	'the king'	[oasil'ás]
/δ/	λάδι	'oil'	[lái]
	πηγάδι	'well'	[piái]
	πόδι	'foot'	[pói]
	κρομμύδι	'onion'	[krommíi]
	τὰ δόντια	'the teeth'	[taón'g'a]
	νὰ δώκῃ	'let him give'	[naók'i]
/γ/	ἀνοίγω	'I open'	[anníο]
	λίγο	'little'	[llío]
	ρόγα	'grape'	[róa]
	λυγαριά	'willow'	[liarg'á]
	ἐπῆγα	'I went'	[epía]
	ὁ γάμος	'the wedding'	[oámos]

Not all these pronunciations are found in every island. In some cases the item itself may be replaced by a synonym (e.g. [lákkos] in Cyprus for 'well', [eyáik'e] < ἐδιάβηκε in Karpathos for 'he went'), and, more importantly, standard pronunciations with intact fricatives are common, especially in the larger and more accessible communities. Only in small isolated islands such as Kastellorizo (between Rhodes and Cyprus) and in the remote villages of the larger islands (e.g. in Elimbos on Karpathos, certain villages in western Cyprus and southern Rhodes) have I found the rule of voiced fricative deletion applied with any degree of consistency, and even then the phenomenon is largely restricted to the older generation, especially the womenfolk.

It is obvious that the most striking effect of voiced fricative deletion will be the creation of vowel sequences. Indeed at least three-term clusters are possible, as in the [piái] cited above and in the pronunciation [traúi] for τραγούδι 'song'. The main question for consideration therefore is the fate of this secondary hiatus in respect to the rules which we have found to affect primary hiatus, in particular the rules of (*a*) glide formation, (*b*) height dissimilation and (*c*) contraction.

(*a*) *Glide formation and voiced fricative deletion.* We have seen that glide formation has the effect of converting a high vowel ([i] or [u]) to its corresponding glide ([y] or [w]) in the environment before and after a vowel. In the south-eastern dialects (other than that of Elimbos) the rule applies in its fullest form. That is, it applies to unstressed [i] before a vowel, to stressed [í] before a vowel, and to both of these after a vowel;

similarly for [u], although the evidence is minimal. With regard to secondary sequences arising from voiced fricative deletion it appears in general that glide formation does not in fact act on them. That is, it seems to be the case that historically glide formation no longer represented an active trend when voiced fricative deletion set in. The evidence for this statement lies in the study of items such as are presented in the following paragraph.

Unstressed [i] and [u] retain full vocalicity before another vowel. Compare, for instance, βουβός [vuós] 'dumb' and [piái] cited above. Other typical examples would be [tianízo] 'I fry' from τηγανίζω, [siá] 'slowly' from σιγά, and the various forms of πηδᾶ 'he jumps' (e.g. [appiá] in Cyprus, [piá] Elimbos). However, there are found occasional items in which glide formation does attack the output of voiced fricative deletion. Thus the Cypriot verb 'give' has an underlying stem /δiδa/ and in most parts of the island the intervocalic [δ] drops without occasioning further change. Thus we normally hear [δió, δiás, δiá, δiúme, δiáte, δiúsin] in the present active paradigm. In certain subdialects, though, one finds [θk'ó, θk'ás, θk'á], and so on, which implies the action of glide formation followed by the various rules which affect post-consonantal yod in Cypriot (see 6.4). Stressed high vowels enjoy, as one would expect, a similar immunity to the effects of glide formation; thus /epíγe/ 'he went' goes to [epíe], never *[epyé], /llíγo/ 'little' to [llío], /íδa/ 'I saw' to [ía] and /kalívi/ 'cottage' to [kalíi]. For /ú/ we may cite [vúi] 'ox', used in Cyprus and elsewhere for common βόδι, and reflecting an underlying /vúδi/, or [kopellúa], the Cypriot for 'girl' (underlying /kopellúδa/). For stressed [í] and [ú] after vowel, we may note /allaγí/, 'change, dress', which always goes to [allaí], never *[alláy], and /maγírevse/ 'he cooked', which yields [maírepse]. The only area where stressed high vowels in secondary sequences are known to be converted to glides appears to be south-western Rhodes, for which see below on height dissimilation. Finally unstressed [i] and [u] may come into position after a vowel as a result of voiced fricative deletion. Here the position is a little less straightforward. One sometimes has the impression that a word such as /póδi/ 'foot', /kávuras/ 'crab', is being pronounced [póy], [káwras], and, as in northern Greece, where [γ] drops before front vowels, /léγi/ 'he says' appears as [léy]. But the extent to which this impression is attributable to the non-distinctive lengthening of the stressed vowel is unclear. In any case, except in the case of the southern Rhodian dialects referred to below, this phenomenon has no further phonological implications (i.e. the resultant [y], [w] are not acted on by subsequent rules) and, as opposed to cases with prevocalic unstressed high vowels, no contrast between [i] and [y] is possible in a word such as [léy].

The principle which emerges from all this is that glide formation acts before the rule deleting intervocalic voiced fricatives. This can be illustrated within the single item πηγάδια 'wells' as pronounced in northern Rhodes:

(1)	piγáδia
Glide formation	piγáδya
Voiced fricative deletion	piáδya
Consonantality	piáδγ'a
Manner dissimilation	**piáδg'a**

(*b*) *Height dissimilation and voiced fricative deletion.*[1] The rule of height dissimilation, as we saw in 2.6, has the effect of raising /e/ to [i] when adjacent to /a/ or /o/ and of raising /o/ to [u] when adjacent to /a/. Does this rule affect the clusters such as [ea] which arise from the action of voiced fricative deletion? The answer appears to be that it in fact does so in certain dialects, especially those of Kos, Kalimnos, Karpathos and southern Rhodes. Consider, for instance, the derivational history we must postulate for the words ρόγα 'grape', φλέβα 'vein', in the dialect of Kalimnos compared to that implied for μηλιά 'apple tree':

(2)	róγa	fléva	miléa
Height dissimilation			milía
Glide formation			milyá
Voiced fricative deletion	róa	fléa	
Height dissimilation	**rúa**	**flía**	

[milyá] will go by the rules of palatalization and postpalatal yod deletion to [mil'á]. It will be observed that in order to account for the output [flía], [milyá], we must make assumptions regarding ordering constraints which appear on the face of it contradictory. To account for [milyá] we

[1] Most of the data presented in this section are drawn from Karanastasis (1963), Andriotis (1939) and Tsopanakis (1940). It is likely that standardizing influences are increasingly blocking the application of height dissimilation to secondary sequences. Andriotis cites from various sources [foíra] 'threat', [rúa] 'grape', [aúrasa] 'I bought' for φοβέρα, ρόγα, άγόρασα in Karpathos, but I found only [foéra], [róa], [aórasa] in Elimbos in 1963.

must apply first height dissimilation and then glide formation, but in the case of [flía] it is crucial that glide formation should precede height dissimilation, as otherwise [flía] would go incorrectly to *[flyá]. However, this air of paradox is dissolved when we remember that sound changes may represent trends active for considerable lengths of time and may therefore overlap according to various patterns. In this case we may suppose that height dissimilation operated continuously over a fairly long stretch of time, and that during its initial stages glide formation was also active, so that [milía], the output of the former, was immediately attacked by the latter. Then glide formation ceased to operate and voiced fricative deletion set in. [fléa], the output of this new process, was instantaneously affected by the still active process of height dissimilation, giving [flía], but not by glide formation, which was no longer alive.

Miscellaneous examples showing the effect of height dissimilation on the output of voiced fricative deletion in Kalimnos are as follows:

ἀπόγαλα	'starch'	[apúala]
πόδας	'foot'	[púas]
φοβᾶσαι	'you are afraid'	[fuáse]
ἔλεγα	'I was saying'	[ília] (< /íleγa/)
λέγω	'I say'	[lío]
ἀσφόδελος	'asphodel'	[aspóilos]
μεγάλος	'big'	[miálos]

It was mentioned above that glide formation acts exceptionally on the secondary vowel sequences resulting from voiced fricative deletion in south-western Rhodes. It is also true of these dialects that height dissimilation acts on the output of voiced fricative deletion, so that the relations between our rules can be easily expressed by stating that they apply in the order voiced fricative deletion – height dissimilation – glide formation. A few examples from Tsopanakis (1940) should make this clear; they are πηγαίνω 'I go', ρόγα 'grape', κοπελλούδα 'girl', γρήγορα 'fast':

(3)				
	paγénno	róγa	kopellúδa	γlíγora
Voiced fricative deletion	paénno	róa	kopellúa	γlíora
Height dissimilation	paínno	rúa		
Glide formation	**páynno**	**rwá**	**kopellwá**	**γlyóra**

Essentially what has happened in south-western Rhodes is the breakdown of all ordering constraints between our three rules; they each apply whenever their input conditions arise. Still a third ordering possibility would be for voiced fricative deletion to be followed by glide formation but not height dissimilation. This would yield [kopellwá], [γlyóra], but [paénno], [róa]. Such a situation is not apparently reported for any dialect.

In dealing with sequences of consonant and yod we shall frequently refer to a rule ('consonantality') which converts [y] to [γ'] after a voiced consonant, and to [x'] after a voiceless one. The dialects of south-western Rhodes suggest that the rule may be formulated more generally to apply to [w] as well as [y] and to include position before as well as after a consonant.[1] That is, just as [y] goes to its voiced fricative counterpart [γ'] before and after a voiced consonant and to its voiceless fricative counterpart [x'] before and after a voiceless one, [w] goes to [v] or [f] under parallel circumstances. Consider the derivations for μάγουλο 'cheek', σούδα 'sewer', ἀλογᾶς 'horse-dealer' in parts of south-western Rhodes:

(4)	máγulo	súδa	aloγás
Voiced fricative deletion	máulo	súa	aloás
Height dissimilation			aluás
Glide formation	máwlo	swá	alwás
Consonantality	**mávlo**	**sfá**	**alvás**

Dialects which possess pronunciations such as these are clearly more 'advanced' than those with [máulo], [súa], [aloás], current in most of Rhodes. Yet it is interesting to note that the difference between 'extreme' and 'conservative' dialects often lies entirely in the way in which rules are ordered. A typical Rhodian dialect with [kariδγ'á] for καρυδιά 'walnut tree' but [aloás] for 'horse-dealer' has exactly the same rules as are used in deriving [mávlo], [sfá], [alvás]. Only the sequencing differs:

(5)	kariδéa	aloγás
Height dissimilation	kariδía	
Glide formation	kariδyá	
Consonantality	**kariδγ'á**	
Voiced fricative deletion		**aloás**

1 This is also true of Zakinthian. There νὰ ἰδῶ 'let me see', βόϊδι 'ox', βοηθάω 'I help' go to [naγ'δó], [vóγ'δi], [vox'θáo], and then by palatality assimilation to [naγδó], [vóγδi], [voxθáo].

Were the rule of height dissimilation to act indiscriminately on the output of voiced fricative deletion quite extensive morphophonemic alternation would result; for it would frequently be the case that some, but not all, the allomorphs of a given morpheme would satisfy the conditions for height dissimilation. In the singular [róa] 'grape', for instance, which results by voiced fricative deletion from /róγa/, the [ó] of the stem meets these conditions, while in the plural [róes] it is the [e] of the ending which meets them, so that one would expect to find a singular [rúa] but plural [róis]. While it is not clear in this particular instance what happens, in certain other cases alternations are either explicitly mentioned in the literature or derivable from published data. Thus /póδas/ 'foot' is [púas] in Kalimnos, while /póδi/, for which informants claim a marginal coexistence in the same sense, is [pói]. Similarly /fováse/ 'you are afraid' is there [fuáse] while /fóvos/ 'fear' is [fóos]. Perhaps the most regular pattern of alternation is found in south-western Rhodes. There, just as /paγénno/ goes to [páynno], the plural ending /áδes/ of nouns in -άς and -άδα goes to [áys]. Thus for /evδomáδes/ 'weeks', /foráδes/ 'mares', /papáδes/ 'priests' we get [evdomáys], [foráys], [papáys], while the plural morpheme /es/ remains [es] when an intervocalic voiced fricative does not precede ([pórtes] 'doors', [náftes] 'sailors'). Likewise, while the masculine ending /os/ is directly realized as [os] in most words ([fílos] 'friend', [tópos] 'place') the deletion of a voiced fricative may be followed by height dissimilation and glide formation. Thus /káδos/ 'bucket' is reported to yield [káws] and /tráγos/ 'goat', [tráws]. The situation is complicated, however, by analogical influences. In Kalimnos, for example, while /foverízo/ 'I threaten' goes via [foerízo] to [foirízo], /papáδes/ 'priests' becomes [papáes], and so for other plurals in /es/. Again, while the unimpeded action of voiced fricative deletion and glide formation in south-west Rhodes would produce as the present paradigm of 'I say' (λέγω, λέγεις, λέγει), [lyó, léys, léy], this is not reported, although we find [lyó, lyís, lyí], the whole paradigm having been remodelled on the basis of the first person singular.

To summarize the above discussion we may repeat that voiced fricative deletion may theoretically be followed by height dissimilation, by glide formation, by both or by neither. When glide formation follows, the resulting [w] or [y] may be acted on by consonantality. Abbreviating these rules 'VFD, HD, GF, C' we may list the possibilities actually found together with their effect on /róγa/ and /súδa/ as follows:[1]

[1] I cannot find an actual citation of [rvá], but [arvát^{s}ina] occurs for ροδάκινα 'peaches'.

	róγa	súδa
VFD	róa	súa (Cyprus, Chios)
VFD – HD	rúa	súa (Kos, Kalimnos)
VFD – HD – GF	rwá	swá (S.W. Rhodes)
VFD – HD – GF – C	rvá	sfá (S.W. Rhodes)

(*c*) *Contraction and voiced fricative deletion.* In our discussion of secondary hiatus thus far we have mentioned that sequences of different vowels might be subject to height dissimilation and glide formation but have ignored the possibility of contraction. Thus, while primary /oe/ and /oi/ contract under certain circumstances to [o], we have assumed that a word such as καλόγερος 'monk' will go to [kalóiros] or perhaps [kalóyros], but not *[kalóros]. It is in fact the case that contraction does not in general affect sequences of different vowels arising from voiced fricative deletion. Counter-examples are at best sporadic; the word ἀδελφός 'brother', for instance, occurs in Cypriot as [arfós], implying that the sequence [ae] which arose as a result of voiced fricative deletion underwent contraction according to the normal rule (see 2.8). But this appears to represent an exception: /aδérfia/ 'brothers and sisters' is in Cypriot [aérk'a] and the plural of [arfí] 'sister' is [arfáes] from /aδelfáδes/, not *[arfás]. Another case is [kráttos] 'bed' from /krévattos/, reported for Kos. The only instance where contraction succeeds voiced fricative deletion with any regularity involves the paradigms of the 'semi-contracted' verbs. Thus λέγεις 'you say' is often [lés] and τρώγουνε 'they eat', [tróne]. In Cretan subdialects with intervocalic loss of /v/, a verb such as χορεύω 'I dance' conjugates [xoréo, -és, -éi, -éme, -éte, -éne],[1] again implying contraction subsequent on voiced fricative deletion. But as was noted in 2.8, these verbs cannot be studied in purely phonological terms.

When we turn to repeated occurrences of the same vowel, however, the situation is different. When a sequence of two identical vowels occurs and the first is stressed, there is at least a strong tendency in many dialects for the second one to drop by contraction. Consider, for instance, the following miscellaneous examples in which voiced fricative deletion has been followed by contraction:

ἑβδομάδα 'week' [vdomá] (Elimbos), [ftomá] (Rhodes, Cyprus)
βιδολόγος 'screw-driver' [violós] (Elimbos, Cyprus)

[1] See Pangalos (1955: 193).

παιχνίδι 'game' [pexní(n)] (Rhodes, Cyprus)
μολύβι 'pencil' [molí] (Elimbos)
γάδαρος 'donkey' [γáros] (commonly in S.E.)

However, even when the appropriate conditions are met and the dialect in question regularly has [á] for the ending -άδα and [í] for -ίδι exceptions are common. /fóvos/ 'fear' seems to contrast everywhere in the south east as [fóos] versus [fós] 'light' from /fós/, although a contracted accusative is possible in the expression ἀπὸ τὸν φόβον του 'in his fear', at least in Cyprus, where we hear [putoffóndu]. It would be unwise to assume that the widespread fluctuation found is due entirely to the influence of standardizing pronunciations. For instance, φορά 'time, occasion' (for speakers who use the word rather than βολά for this sense) will always have the form [forá], while φοράδα 'mare' might fluctuate between [forá] and [foráa]. The second [a] of this last pronunciation might be due not so much to standard [foráδa] as to the fact that its plural [foráes] implies underlying /foráδes/ (or /foráves/, /foráγes/), and this in turn a singular /foráδa/. [forés] 'times', on the contrary, implies /forés/, singular /forá/. In other cases evidence occurs elsewhere than in the contracted form not only for the underlying vowel structure but for the precise voiced fricative. Thus the item [psomn'á] 'loaves' implies underlying /psomía/, singular /psomí/, but [psallíδg'a] 'pairs of scissors' implies /psallíδia/, singular /psallíδi/. Thus 'loaf' will be pronounced [psomí] but 'pair of scissors' either [psallíi], with voiced fricative deletion or, optionally, [psallí], with contraction as well.

Sequences of identical vowels which have one of the other two possible stress patterns (vv́ or vv) do not normally contract. Thus we find [aapó] rather than *[apó] for ἀγαπῶ 'I love', [saáto] rather than *[sáto] for /savàto/ 'Saturday', [rooloó] rather than *[roló] for ρογολογῶ 'I pick grapes'. Exceptions occur: while [áloo] is usual for ἄλογο horse', [álo] ([áo] in Naxos) is not unknown.[1]

The spellings [áa], [aá], [aa] etc., used in the present discussion, must not be taken to imply that two separate syllabic pulses are discernible. The reason for using 'geminate' spellings rather than, say, 'ā' is purely practical: the final uncontracted vowel sequence of a word such as [krommíi] 'onion' (from /krommíδi/) is phonetically distinct from that of [klií] 'key' (from /kliδí/). Although what we have in both cases can be described as a long vowel, in the first case there is diminuendo stress and

[1] See the Ἱστορικὸν Λεξικόν *sub voce* ἄλογο. /savàto/ appears to underlie all dialectal forms of Σάββατο and Athenian [sávato] probably lacks a vernacular source.

(when the word is uttered in isolation or bears sentence stress) a fall in pitch, while in the second case the stress is crescendo and the pitch rises. The spellings [íi], [ií] indicate this difference quite naturally.[1]

Outside the south east no dialect appears to show a regular loss of intervocalic voiced fricatives, although the phenomenon occurs sporadically in Crete and the Cyclades, and in Thrace.[2] Thus in Naxos, where Cretan-type dialects are spoken, we find [oámos] for ὁ γάμος 'the wedding' and [traúi] for τραγούδι 'song'; indeed this loss of /γ/, combined with the loss of /l/ characteristic of Naxian dialects, sometimes yields quite unusual vowel sequences (e.g. /eγélasene/ 'he laughed', [eéasene]). It appears that in Naxos, as in the south east, glide formation does not affect the output of voiced fricative deletion; this is neatly illustrated by the proverbial expression cited by Emellos (1964), ἐμεγάλωσενε μὰ δὲν ἐμυάλωσενε 'he's grown but has not acquired sense', [emeáosene ma δén emyáosene]. The adjective μεγάλος 'big' and its derivatives frequently appear with [i] even in dialects which do not in general follow voiced fricative deletion by height dissimilation. We may note in this connexion the Cretan word [aylé] 'cow', which apparently derives from ancient ἀγελαία rather than from medieval ἀγελάς, as does standard [ayeláδa]. We must suppose that the /γ/ dropped from /aγeléa/ by the form of voiced fricative deletion which operates in Crete to remove /γ/, especially before front vowels, but only rarely /v/ or /δ/, and that height dissimilation and glide formation then took effect.

Although voiced fricative deletion is regular only in the south east, the item 'Devil' occurs in expletives without /v/ from Zakinthos ([δγ'áolos]) to Cyprus ([θk'áolos]) and from Macedonia ([δγ'áulus]) to Crete ([δγ'áolos]).

We turn finally to a brief examination of voiced fricative deletion as a source of morphophonemic alternation. Because our rule takes effect when a voiced fricative is flanked by vowels, we shall get alternation when a particular underlying morpheme begins or ends with a voiced fricative and in some, but not all, of the environments in which the morpheme occurs, the appropriate condition of intervocalic position is met.

1 See Seiler (1958) and Newton (1968) for some discussion of these points.

2 For Thrace I rely on Kyriakidis (1923). /γ/ is occasionally lost in other northern dialects before back vowels. Tzartzanos (1909) cites [saón'] for σαγόνι 'jaw', [tráws] for τράγος 'goat' in Tyrnavos, and Skiros has [laós], [traúδi] for λαγός 'hare' τραγούδι 'song', according to Phavis (1909).

The first set of cases concerns morphemes with final voiced fricative. Consider the declension of λάδι 'oil' (root morpheme /laδ/) in a typical south-eastern dialect:

	Singular	Plural
Nominative	lái	láδg′a
Accusative	lái	láδg′a
Genitive	laδg′ú	laδg′ón

Here the rule of glide formation has acted on the genitive singular /láδiū/ and plural forms /láδia/ and /láδiōn/ before voiced fricative deletion could operate. Compare the derivations of the nominative–accusative singular and plural:

(6)	láδi	láδia
Glide formation		láδya
Voiced fricative deletion	**lái**	
Consonantality		láδγ′a
Manner dissimilation		**láδg′a**

Once /láδia/ has gone to [láδya] it is immune to the action of voiced fricative deletion. A similar situation arises with /v/ in neuter forms. /kluví/ 'cage', for instance, will in south-eastern dialects have a singular [kluí] but plural [kluvγ′á] (or some development of this such as [kluvg′á], [klufk′á], [kluvzá]). In the case of /γ/ the situation is parallel, although not so obvious. Consider the singular and plural forms of ρολόγι 'clock':

(7)	rolóγi	rolóγia
Glide formation		rolóγya
Voiced fricative deletion	**rolói**	
Palatalization		rolóγ′ya
Postpalatal yod deletion		rolóγ′a
Consonantality		**rolóya**

It would be technically possible to derive the forms [rolói], [rolóya] from /rolói/, /rolóia/, but the sequence /oi/ is otherwise absent from underlying forms and the derived form [roloás] would imply /roloás/, with an equally unusual diphthong. Another important consideration is that the postulation of underlying /γ/ enables us to relate dialectal to standardizing pronunciations; thus standard [roloγás] differs from [roloás] only in having failed to undergo voiced fricative deletion.

There appears to be only one south-eastern dialect where alternation of the [lái]:[láδγ'a] type fails to occur, that of the isolated village of Elimbos in Karpathos. There [lái] is pluralized to [láya], [karái] 'slice from end of round loaf' to [karáya]. The last item corresponds to [karái] (plural [karávγ'a]) 'ship' elsewhere, which requires an underlying /v/.[1] Now if we assume underlying voiced fricatives in [lái] and [karái], we may relate the dialect of Elimbos to that of the other villages by postulating a transposition of voiced fricative deletion and glide formation:

(8)	*Elimbos*			*Elsewhere*	
	láδi	láδia		láδi	láδia
VFD	**lái**	láia	GF		**láδya**
GF		**láya**	VFD	**lái**	

Because glide formation does not affect stressed [í] in Elimbos, items such as παιδιά 'children' from /peδía/ and κλουβιά 'cages' from /kluvía/ throw no light on the situation, for only voiced fricative deletion affects them, giving [peía], [kluía]. A further complication is that the dialect of Elimbos appears to convert [δy] to [y]. Thus /δiavázo/ 'I read' appears there as [yaánd͡zo] and /δiávolos/ 'Devil' as [yáolos].[2] It is thus not impossible to apply glide formation first to /láδia/ and then convert [δy] to [y] by this special rule; however there is no evidence that [vy] goes to [y], and there are other difficulties.

Alternation between morpheme-final voiced fricatives and zero is also possible in verb paradigms. Thus /travó/ 'I pull' will yield [traó], while /etrávie/ 'he was pulling', [etrávg'e]. Compare also cases such as /appíδin/ 'pear', usually [appíi(n)] or [appí(n)], versus /appiδéa/ 'pear tree', in most dialects [appiδg'á].

Finally, alternation is possible morpheme-initially. The commonest case involves nouns in prevocalic /v, δ, γ/. The consonant may drop in some dialects when a vowel-final form of the definite article precedes. Thus in Karpathos, the forms ὁ δάσκαλος 'the teacher' (nom. sing.) and τὸν δάσκαλο (acc. sing.) are derived as follows:

(9)	oδáskalos	tonδáskalo
Nasal assimilation		**toδδáskalo**
Voiced fricative deletion	**oáskalos**	

[1] [karávi], plural [karávγ'a], also occurs in Elimbos in the meaning 'ship' (καράβι) as a synonym for [pambóri], a corruption of [vapóri]. A similar doublet is [molívi] 'lead' but [molí] 'pencil'.

[2] We cannot easily derive [yáolos], [yaánd͡zo] from sequences such as /o+δiávolos/ by applying voiced fricative deletion and glide formation in that order, for the accusative /ton+diávolo/ would then presumably develop to [toδδiávolo] > [toδδiáolo] > [toδδyáolo], while what we find is [toyyáolo]. For the [nd͡z] of [yaánd͡zo] see 4.1.

These rules are unordered; if we applied voiced fricative deletion first there would be no change of output. The full paradigm of this item in Karpathos is as follows:

	Singular	*Plural*
Nominative	o áskalos	i askáli
Accusative	toδ δáskalo	tuz δaskálus
Genitive	tu askálu	toδ δaskálon

Were a dialect with voiced fricative deletion also to possess the rule of degemination, the position of this latter rule in the sequence would be crucial, for we would have as accusative [toáskalo] or [toδáskalo] according as the order was degemination, then voiced fricative deletion, or the converse; however only 'geminating' dialects have voiced fricative deletion. A similar example for /v/ would be [oasil'ás] 'the king' (ὁ βασιλιάς) versus [tovvasil'á], [tuzvasil'áes], and for /γ/, [oámos] 'the wedding' (ὁ γάμος) versus [toγγámo], [tuzγámus]. Verb stems can also be affected by alternation of this type. Thus the aorist stem /δok/ of the verb meaning 'give' will in Cyprus and Rhodes, say, have allomorphs with and without [δ] according as a consonant or vowel precedes. Thus /an + δóki/ 'if he gives' will appear as [aδδók'i], /ás + δóki/ 'let him give' as [azδók'i], while /na + δóki/ 'let him give' and /éδoken/ 'he gave' will be [naók'i] and [éok'en]. Normally such items show the voiced fricative in utterance-initial position (e.g. [δómmu] 'give it me!'), but the negative particle δέν usually drops its /δ/ in the south east when initial (e.g. [embirázi] 'it doesn't matter!').

3.2 Voiced fricative interchange

The dialects which have a rule of voiced fricative deletion also display a tendency to interchange voiced fricatives in intervocalic position, in particular to replace them by [v] or [γ] ([y] before front vowels). Thus [γóndi] occurs for /δónti/ 'tooth' in Cyprus and Chios, while [vóndi] is found in Rhodes and some villages in Cyprus. Similarly /δulía/ 'work' appears as [vul'á] in Karpathos, [γul'á] in parts of Rhodes and Cyprus. The phenomenon seems to involve a sporadic and irregular restructuring of underlying forms, although both Pernot (1907: 532) and Dawkins (1904) have attempted to establish appropriate principles. Pernot suggests that in Chios a rule deleting intervocalic /γ/ came into operation early on and was succeeded by one of [v] epenthesis. Thus we find developments such as /trayúδi/ 'song' > [traúδi] > [travúδi], /alóyata/ 'horses' > [alóata] > [alóvata], /eyó/ 'I' > [eó] > [evó]. Unfortunately counter-examples are about as frequent in his data as positive instances; thus /fléva/ 'vein' > [fléya], /perivóli/ 'garden' > [periyóli]. Dawkins' proposal for Karpathos is based on a putative tendency for intervocalic fricatives to be replaced by [v] before back vowels and [y] before front, and this hypothesis does stand up fairly well for his data: /δáktilas/ 'finger' > [váxtilas], /yála/ 'milk' > [vála], /víxas/ 'cough' > [yíxas], /δimítris/ 'Dimitris' > [yimítris]. Outside Karpathos, however, there is little support for this account. What is reasonably clear is that the dialects characterized by voiced fricative deletion and those interchanging voiced fricatives are coextensive, so that Pernot is probably correct in his general thesis that the phenomenon reflects deletion and subsequent replacement rather than a single replacive change.

3.3 Intervocalic yod deletion

While voiced fricative deletion affects /v/, /δ/ and /γ/ no matter what vowel follows, the rule we shall call 'intervocalic yod deletion' removes [y], whether from /i/ or /γ/, when it is preceded by any vowel and followed by a front vowel. It is found in perhaps all northern dialects, and is at least widespread in the Ionian Isles. Typical northern examples are the following:

λαγένι	'jug'	[laén']
παγίδα	'trap'	[paíδa]
καλόγερος	'monk'	[kalóyrus]
ἔλεγε	'he was saying'	[éliy]
καταγῆς	'on the ground'	[kataís]

For Corfu we may cite from Salvanos (1918) [kalóeros], [floéra] 'flute' (φλογέρα), [kataís], and for Zakinthos from Minotou (1932), [epíe] 'he went' (ἐπῆγε), [máisa] 'witch' (μάγισσα), [éfae] 'he ate' (ἔφαγε). In the Peloponnese, although pronunciations such as [léyi] 'he says' (λέγει), [payéno] 'I go' (παγαίνω, standard πηγαίνω) represent the norm, the rule is reported for certain villages in Laconia by Koukoules (1908), who gives [paniíri] 'fair' for πανηγύρι, [laína] 'jug' for λαγῆνα. In Cretan and various Cycladic dialects intervocalic yod deletion is also usual, but the picture is complicated here by the sporadic activity of voiced fricative deletion, especially involving /γ/ before back vowels. The widespread loss of intervocalic /γ/ in certain semicontracted verbs before back vowels is usually attributed to generalization from forms in which a front vowel follows: northern [éfaa] 'I ate' develops by this account from ἔφαγα under the influence of ἔφαγε 'he ate', and [léw] 'I speak', [élia] 'I was speaking' betray the influence of models such as λέγει 'he says', ἔλεγε 'he was saying'.

The relation of the present rule of intervocalic yod deletion to glide formation appears to be similar to that found to connect the latter rule with voiced fricative deletion. That is, the output of yod deletion does not undergo the general rule of glide formation, although an unstressed [i] or [u] in the position after a vowel usually goes to [y], [w]. In the north this seems to be the case even when the preceding vowel is unstressed. If we call this limited type of glide formation 'weak glide formation', the following derivations may be proposed for the usual northern pronunciations of πήγαινε 'go!', πηγή 'source', ποιοί 'who?', ἔλεγε 'he was saying':

(10)	píγene	piγí	píi	éleγe
Glide formation			pyí	
Palatalization	píγ'ene	piγ'í		éleγ'e
Consonantality	píyene	piyí	**px'í**	éleye
Raising	píyini			éliyi
Intervocalic yod deletion	píini	**pií**		élii
Weak glide formation	**píyni**			**éliy**

It may be observed that 'weak glide formation' acts on the second member of a sequence of two identical high vowels, while the normal rule of glide formation acts on the first. Thus, in the present instance, normal glide formation, if it acted on the output of intervocalic yod deletion, would convert [píini], [élii] to *[pyíni], *[élyi].

The derivation of the above items in themselves does not require the operation of palatalization and consonantality, as it would be quite feasible to frame our rule so that it would delete [γ] rather than [y] before front vowels, enabling us to go directly from /píγene/ to [píene].] However, we shall find later (see 7.2) that palatalization at least must precede high vowel loss, and high vowel loss is crucially ordered before yod deletion, as may be seen by observing the derivational histories required for πανηγύρι 'fair' and θὰ κυνηγήσω 'I shall hunt':

(11)	paniγíri	θakiniγíso
Palatalization	paniγ′íri	θak′iniγ′íso
Consonantality	paniyíri	θak′iniyíso
High vowel loss	**panyír**	θak′inyíso
Raising		**θak′inyísu**

If the [y] of, say, [paniyírí] were lost by intervocalic yod deletion before high vowel loss took place we would get [paniíri], and there would be no means of converting the first [i] to [y], normal glide formation, as we have just seen, not affecting the sequences resulting from yod deletion. In other words, high vowel loss may have the effect of saving a yod from deletion by bringing it into position adjacent to a consonant. That this ordering of high vowel loss before intervocalic yod deletion is general in the north is supported by the fact that in Skiros, where /γ/ is lost intervocalically before back as well as front vowels, /éfiγa/ 'I left' goes to [éfγa], while /fíγame/ 'we left' yields [fíame]. As Phavis (1909) observes, these forms can most easily be accounted for by supposing that the first was protected from deletion of its voiced fricative by the prior occurrence of high vowel loss:

(12)	éfiγa	fíγame
High vowel loss	**éfγa**	
Intervocalic /γ/ deletion		**fíame**

In the [píyni] and [éliy] of derivation (10) the source of the [y] was shown to be underlying /e/, while in [panyír] it is plausible to derive the [y] from /γ/. When we have an underlying sequence consisting of a vowel +/γ/+unstressed /i/, the form considered in isolation can be derived in two ways. Consider one possible derivation of λέγει 'he says' and κυνήγησα 'I hunted':

(13)	léγi	kiníγisa
Palatalization	léγ′i	k′iníγ′isa
Consonantality	léyi	k′iníyisa
High vowel loss	**léy**	**k′iníysa**

This derivation has the advantage that it accounts for [k′iníysa] by the same rules as are required in any case for [k′inyísu] above; however, the account it gives of [léy], and other similar semi-contracted forms such as [páy] 'he goes' (πάγει), [tróy] 'he eats' (τρώγει), as well as of nouns such as [rolóy] 'clock' (ρολόγι), will differ according as the item occurs in a northern dialect, or some other dialect with intervocalic yod deletion. [léy], [rolóy], for instance, are widespread, and we might wish to account for them in terms of a general principle of weak glide formation converting postvocalic unstressed [i] to [y]. As intervocalic yod deletion must follow high vowel loss (see on derivation (11) above) we must suppose that the latter was impeded from acting on the sequence [yi]:

(14)	léγi	kiníγisa
Palatalization	léγ'í	k'iníγ'isa
Consonantality	léyi	k'iníyisa
High vowel loss	—	—
Intervocalic yod deletion	léi	k'iníisa
Weak glide formation	**léy**	**k'iníysa**

The source of the yod in [léy] is on this account not [γ], as is implied by derivation (13), but [i]. Because the present account applies generally to all dialects with [léy], [páy] and so on, it is to be preferred; it also seems to reflect the intuitions of Greek scholars who have dealt with the matter.

3·4 Intervocalic liquid deletion

In the Sphakia area of Crete /l/ has a retroflex pronunciation before back vowels and is reported to convert to [w] or drop intervocalically before back vowels in certain villages; thus we find [γáa] for γάλα 'milk', [ksía] for ξῦλα 'wood'.[1] As is the case with voiced fricative deletion, the rule may operate across word boundaries: [toáδi] 'the oil' (τὸ λάδι). A similar conversion to [w] or loss is reported for part of Naxos (see 6.4). /r/ drops in all positions in a dialect spoken in southern Santorini (ἔρχεται 'he is coming' > [éx'ete], μωρό 'child' > [moó]). In Crete, Naxos and Santorini these liquid deletions do not appear to involve further changes in the words in which they occur, and must accordingly represent late rules.

The most interesting, and best studied case of liquid deletion occurs in the northern island of Samothraki, where /r/ is lost in all positions except final, and there apparently occurs a loss of /l/ at least intervocalically and initially before back vowels. This latter phenomenon is

[1] For Crete see Pangalos (1955: 219) and Kondosopoulos (1959), and for Naxos, Emellos (1964). My data for Samothraki are drawn largely from Heisenberg (1921) and Andriotis (1939); I was able to check a few points during a brief stay in the main town of the island in 1963, but did not visit the smaller communities.

not, however, found in the island's main village, and is probably of recent date; that it must be placed late in the rule sequence is indicated by the fact that its output is not affected by height dissimilation, as is the output of the rule deleting /r/. Consider the derivations of κόλλα 'starch' and τώρα 'now':

(15)	kóla	tóra
/r/ deletion		tóa
Height dissimilation		**túa**
/l/ deletion	**kóa**	

The details of /r/ deletion in Samothraki are as follows:

(*a*) /r/ drops intervocalically:

τυρί	'cheese'	[tií]
ψαράδες	'fishermen'	[psaáδis]
ὥρα	'hour'	[úa]
φορά	'time'	[fuá]
κάβουρας	'crab'	[kávuas]
μέρα	'day'	[mía]

(*b*) /r/ between word-boundary or consonant and vowel drops with lengthening of the vowel:

ἄντρας	'man'	[ádās]
Σαμαθράκη	'Samothraki'	[samaθāk']
πράσινος	'green'	[pāšnus]
παντρειά	'marriage'	[padīyá]
ροῦχα	'clothes'	[ū́xa]
ρώτα	'ask!'	[ṓta]
ρωτῶ	'I ask'	[ūtó]

(*c*) /r/ between a vowel and consonant converts to [i]:

χαρτί	'paper'	[xaití]
καρδιά	'heart'	[kaiδγ'á]

(*d*) /r/ initially before a consonant converts to [ī]. This environment can only arise as a result of high vowel loss:

ρουφῶ	'I sip'	[īfó] (via [rfó])
ρουθούνια	'nostrils'	[īθún'a] (via [rθún'a])

(*e*) Word-finally /r/ remains:

παρακόρη	'maid'	[paakór]
σαμάρι	'pack-saddle'	[samár]

Perhaps the most puzzling feature of our data is the sheer multiplicity of reflexes (zero, [i], [ī], lengthening of following vowel, [r]). Leaving this question for the moment let us first examine certain points of ordering. The main rules whose position in the rule sequence relative to /r/ deletion is crucial are (*a*) glide formation, (*b*) height dissimilation, (*c*) contraction, (*d*) high vowel loss and raising, and (*e*) palatalization.

(*a*) *Glide formation and* /r/ *deletion.* The fact that τηρῶ 'I watch' and τυρί 'cheese' appear as [tió], [tií] shows that glide formation precedes /r/ deletion. That is, as in the case of voiced fricative deletion, when /r/ was lost historically, glide formation was no longer active.

(*b*) *Height dissimilation and* /r/*deletion.* Height dissimilation must follow the deletion rule, for μέρα 'day', ὥρα 'hour' go to [mía], [úa]. Notice however, that as glide formation is ordered before /r/ deletion, these new sequences of high vowel + vowel are not converted to [yV], [wV]. We again have the situation noted in connexion with derivation (2) above, in that height dissimilation is seen to have operated over a period of time sufficiently long to have overlapped at one end with glide formation and at the other with /r/ deletion. The derivations of μέρα 'day', καλαμιά 'reed-bed' and μιά 'one' are as follows for Samothraki:

(16)	méra	kalaméa	mía
Height dissimilation		kalamía	
Glide formation		kalamyá	myá
/r/ deletion	méa		
Height dissimilation	**mía**		
Consonantality		**kalamn'á**	**mn'á**

It will be remembered that the rule of height dissimilation raises /e/ to [i] adjacent to /a/ or /o/ and /o/ to [u] adjacent to /a/. This means that while, say, /méra/ goes to [mía], and /óra/ to [úa], their respective plurals /méres/ and /óres/ will retain their stressed mid vowels; thus the paradigm of ὥρα contains the forms /óra/ (nom., acc. sing.), /óras/ (gen. sing.) and /óres/ (nom., acc. pl.) and these develop as follows:

(17)	óra	óras	óres
Raising			óris
/r/ deletion	óa	óas	**óis**
Height dissimilation	**úa**	**úas**	

In this instance it would be possible to account for the [i] of [óis] by applying height dissimilation to [óes]. However, in the cases of [méis], the plural of [mía], this is not possible as the [mées] arising by /r/ deletion from /méres/ would be unaffected by the rule of height dissimilation as formulated. Furthermore, we shall see that there are independent grounds for placing the raising rule before /r/ deletion.

While alternation of this type is found, it is sometimes eliminated by analogical levelling. Thus /xóra/ 'county' and /psóra/ 'mange' have the plurals [xúis], [psúis] rather than expected *[xóis], *[psóis].

(*c*) *Contraction and /r/ deletion.* There is no evidence in my own data that the output of /r/ deletion can be subject to contraction. Thus /psaráδes/ 'fishermen' goes to [psaáδis], /tirí/ 'cheese' to [tií].[1]

(*d*) *High vowel loss and raising in relation to /r/ deletion.* Because the only condition under which /r/ is directly realized as [r] is in final position, and because /r/ can occur finally only as a result of high vowel loss, it is clear that this latter rule precedes deletion. Thus the normal situation may be illustrated by the derivation required to account for παρακόρη 'maid' and its plural παρακόρες:

(18)	parakóri	parakóres
High vowel loss	parakór	
Raising		parakóris
/r/ deletion	**paakór**	**paakóis**

In the above case, because the singular form, but not the plural, contains a final /ri/ sequence, alternation arises, and the same is true of neuters in /ri/ such as χέρι, 'hand', σαμάρι 'pack-saddle':

(19)	samári	samária
Glide formation		samárya
High vowel loss	**samár**	
/r/ deletion		**samáiya**

[1] Heisenberg (1921) claims that when /r/ deletion leads to a sequence of identical vowels, any stress carried by the second is transferred to the first, which suggests contraction. Thus /karávi/ 'ship' > [káav], /kurúna/ 'crow' > [kúun]. But cases with underlying high vowel sequences can be explained on the assumption of loss followed by the normal rule for /r/: /kurúna/ > [krúna] > [kűna]. Furthermore, his [miíδa] 'share' from /meríδa/ implies that his stress shift precedes raising (as otherwise we would get *[míiδa]), while his [ksiénu] 'I dry' from /kseréno/ requires the converse order.

There do seem to be cases, however, in which the [r]-less form has been generalized. Thus θυμάρι 'thyme' and μαχαίρι 'knife' are [θmái], [max'éi]; this is equivalent from the synchronic viewpoint to a transposition of high vowel loss and /r/ deletion.

For raising, we may note that μέρος 'place', γέρος 'old man' go to [méus], [yéus]. If raising did not precede /r/ deletion, the output of the latter, [méos], could be expected to go by height dissimilation to *[míos]; the easiest way to block this incorrect result is to place raising before /r/ deletion.

(*e*) *Palatalization and* /r/ *deletion.* It is not possible to determine from published studies of the dialect of Samothraki whether [x], [k] and [γ] before [r] + front vowel are palatalized when the [r] drops. My own data contain [yiyá] for /γréa/ 'old woman', which implies that palatalization in fact follows. Velar palatalization in general is a rule which applies whenever its input conditions arise, and a pronunciation such as [γi] or [ki] would constitute a striking exception to this principle. However, until precise data are forthcoming the question must be left open.

We turn finally to the nature of the rule of /r/ deletion itself. Must we treat it as a cluster of unrelated parts, or is it possible to detect some pattern in the apparent confusion?

We note first of all that before another vowel /r/ drops if a vowel precedes, and if not, is reflected in the lengthening of the following vowel. Thus /karávi/ 'boat' goes to [kaávi], while /kráta/ 'hold!' yields [kā́ta]. It is possible, however, to relate these apparently disparate outcomes by supposing that in both cases /r/ was first replaced by a vocalic element of a quality identical to that of the following vowel. This would be phonetically plausible; compare the replacement of postvocalic /r/ in British English by a lengthening of the previous vowel (e.g. [art] > [āt]). This would give us the outputs [kaā́vi], [kā́ta]. In the case of the first item the long vowel was shortened by an equally natural process acting on long vowels adjacent to other vowels. The following derivations may therefore be proposed for τυρί 'cheese', μέρα 'day', ροῦχα 'clothes', ἄντρας 'man' (starting with intermediate [ádras]):

(20)	tirí	méra	rúxa	ádras
/r/ deletion	tiī́	méā	**ū́xa**	**ádās**
Vowel shortening	**tií**	méa		
Height dissimilation		**mía**		

More perplexing is the replacement of preconsonantal /r/ by [i] or [ī] The length difference can be disposed of first by noting that our rule of vowel shortening provides a ready explanation of the fact that [i], but not [ī], occurs between a vowel and consonant. That is, we can assume that preconsonantal /r/ is replaced by [ī] in both instances and that this [ī] is then subject to vowel shortening. The difficulty lies in accounting for the replacement of /r/ by [ī] rather than by some other vowel; in particular it is odd that while prevocalic /r/ is replaced according to the quality of the succeeding segment, postvocalic /r/ should behave in a manner apparently independent of its vocalic context. Furthermore, of all possible vowels, [i] is surely the one least likely to have been generated by [r], for the usual effect of [r] is to lower to [e] precisely that vowel (e.g. ancient σίδηρος > [síδeros]); and even if we accepted this possibility, why should the initial [r] of an item such as [rfó] lead to long [ī] rather than [i]? One obvious suggestion would be to derive the [ī] of [īfó], [xaītí], not directly from [r], but from [ri]. Thus [rifó], [xarití] would go to [īfó], [xaītí] by the same rule of /r/ deletion as we used above, and the [xaītí] would then be reduced to [xaití] by vowel shortening. What we still require, therefore, is a rule which would epenthesize [i] between [r] and a consonant. Now the required process of [i] epenthesis occurs precisely in the dialect of Samothraki and others in the north east to break up certain clusters. In Lesbos, for example, the verbal ending -ουν is replaced after consonant-final stems by [in], which implies derivations such as /éxun/ 'they have' > (high vowel loss) > [éxn] > (epenthesis) > [éxin] > [éx'in] (see 7.4). In Samothraki itself [i] is regularly inserted between the final [n] or [s] of certain pronouns, articles and particles and a following consonant-initial word. Thus we find [tunimkrón] for τὸν μικρόν 'the little boy', [δeniθélu] for δὲν θέλω 'I don't want'. What may be proposed, therefore, is that the rule of vowel epenthesis should be appropriately extended to insert an [i] between [r] and a following consonant in Samothraki. We can now derive ρουφῶ, 'I sip', χαρτί 'paper', χωριά 'villages' as follows:

(21)	rufó	xartí	xoría
Glide formation			xoryá
High vowel loss	rfó		
Raising			xuryá
Vowel epenthesis	rifó	xarití	xuriyá
/r/ deletion	**īfó**	xaītí	xuīyá
Vowel shortening		**xaití**	**xuiyá**

3.5 Dissimilatory consonant loss

Secondary hiatus can arise as a result of dissimilatory consonant loss, and such loss is particularly common in the south east. The general tendency is for an intervocalic consonant to drop when separated by a single following vowel from an occurrence of the same consonant or a cluster containing it.[1] Thus κάμωμα 'ripening' and its plural καμώματα 'goings on' occur as [káoma], [kaómata] in Chios and elsewhere. The item πενήντα 'fifty' is found as [peínda] in Cyprus and other islands ([peídda] in Simi). The adjective κανένας 'no' appears commonly (Chios, Karpathos, Naxos etc.) as [kaénas], while the form κανείς 'no one', where it exists in contrast to κανένας, always retains its nasal (cf. Cretan [čanís], Chian [kanís]). ἀποπάνω 'above' is [aopáno] in parts of Crete and ἐτοῦτος 'this' is found as [eútos] in Simi and Chios. There appears to be no evidence that dissimilatory loss can be followed by height dissimilation, glide formation or contraction, and this merely reflects the sporadic (and presumably late) action of the rule in question. With regard to the nature of the consonants typically subject to dissimilatory loss, most instances involve stops and nasals. This preponderance, though, largely reflects the fact that voiceless fricatives do not normally occur in successive syllables (this itself reflecting an ancient dissimilatory process which deaspirated the first of two aspirated stops, the source of modern [f, θ, x]). Liquids tend not so much to drop as to shift in articulation, /r/ to [l], and /l/ to [n]. Cases involving /l/ are quite rare, but ἀμπελόφυλλο 'vineleaf' is reported to occur as [ambenófillo] in Chios and Nisiros.[2] The replacement of /r/ by [l] when an /r/ occurs later in the word (not necessarily in the next syllable) is so regular in all dialects that it cannot be treated as sporadic in spite of the relatively restricted number of items. Examples are [γlíγora], exceedingly common for etymological and standard γρήγορα and [pelistéri] for περιστέρι 'dove'. Standard [fevráris] 'February' is commonly in the dialects [fleváris], implying metathesis as well as dissimilation. Other common cases are [paleθíri] for παραθύρι 'window', [kliθári] for κριθάρι 'barley'; [alétri] for ancient ἄροτρον 'plough' and [plóri] for πρῷρα 'prow' appear to be universal.

[1] Pernot (1907: 442 ff.) presents an impressive catalogue of instances. He claims that the second consonant drops when either it but not the first is intervocalic or the intervening vowel is stressed, although his data are not entirely unambiguous; he also asserts that the Chian [ái] for the diminutive suffix -άκι arises from sequences in which καί 'and' follows.

[2] See the Ἱστορικὸν Λεξικόν *sub voce*.

The most interesting questions are posed by the loss of intervocalic /s/; while many cases look like instances of straightforward dissimilation, the replacement in northern Greek of items such as πειράζεις 'you annoy' by [piráys] or [piráyz] represents a major crux, and we shall devote the next section to the issues involved. There is a certain amount of unavoidable technical and speculative detail which is not strictly relevant to the overall picture of Greek phonology and the section may be omitted without loss.

3.6 Intervocalic /s/ loss

Intervocalic /s/ is lost in modern Greek in circumstances which fall into two broad categories:

(*a*) In south-eastern dialects the /s/ which marks the punctual aspect of verbs is lost in intervocalic position in some or (rarely) all of the members of the paradigms in which it occurs. Thus in parts of Chios ἔχασες 'you lost' and θὰ χάσῃς 'you will lose' are [éxaes], [axáis]; in some of the island's villages this loss affects the whole paradigm ([axáo, axáis, axái etc.]). In Rhodes and parts of Cyprus this /s/ is not lost outright but replaced by [h] (a glottal fricative similar to English *h*). Thus we find forms such as Cypriot [ennaskotóho] for θὰ σκοτώσω 'I will kill', [epótiha] 'I watered' for ἐπότισα, [epk'áhan] 'they took' for ἔπιασαν. Outside the verb system intervocalic /s/ normally resists loss, although [kambóhes] is heard for κάμποσες 'several' (fem. pl.) in those Rhodian and Cypriot dialects which convert /s/ to [h] in verbs. In the case of this last item it is significant that the /s/ remains in the other members of the paradigm such as [kambósi] (nom. pl. masc.) and [kambósa] (nom. pl. neut.); this suggests that the phenomenon is dissimilatory, although [kambósus] (acc. pl. masc.) does not seem to occur without the intervocalic sibilant. Similarly the Chian dialects with /s/ deletion only in the second person singular, in which a second /s/ occurs, but not the other persons, in which this is not so, point in the same direction. It is therefore very tempting to accept the explanation put forward by Pernot (1905) that the above cases result from dissimilatory consonant loss, generalized in some dialects throughout certain verbal paradigms.

(*b*) In northern dialects it is usual for the first sibilant in the underlying sequences consisting of stressed vowel and /sis/, /zis/, /siz/ to drop.[1] There are six classes of forms containing these sequences:

[1] /ziz/ seems not to occur.

(i) Second singular present verb forms in -εις:
πειράʒεις 'you annoy' [piráys] (Thessaly [piráyz])
παίʒεις 'you play' [péys] (Thessaly [péyz])
(ii) Second singular aorist subjunctives in -σῃς
θὰ λούσῃς 'you will wash' [θalúys]
θὰ ρωτήσῃς 'you will ask' [θarutíys]
(iii) Certain nominative singular forms (usually names):
'Αθανάσης 'Athanasis' [aθanáys]
Λουίʒης 'Louis' [luíys] ([luíyz] Thessaly)
(iv) Genitive singulars of feminine nouns in -η:
τῆς βρύσης 'of the spring' [dzvríys]
τῆς κρίσης 'of the judgement' [tskríys]
(v) The aorist singular and third plural forms of certain verbs:
ἀποφάσισα 'I decided' [apufáysa]
ἀποφάσιʒα 'I was deciding [apufáyza]
φύσησα 'I blew' [fíysa]
(vi) Neuters in -ʒι + σου
τὸ καρπούʒι σου 'your melon' [tukarpúys]

The sibilant deletion is blocked when the underlying vowel is other than unstressed /i/. Thus ἐσεῖς is always [esís], and βρύσες 'springs' is always [vrísis]. This latter implies that the rule deleting /s/ must precede raising. Compare, for instance, βρύσης with βρύσες:

(22)	vrísis	vríses
Sibilant deletion	vríis	
Raising		**vrísis**
Weak glide formation	**vríys**	

The proposals which have been put forward to account for the above data have been essentially two. The first relates the present set of phenomena to the dissimilatory process assumed by Pernot to underlie cases such as [éxaes] referred to in (*a*) above. The second proposal has assumed various forms, but all embody reference to the action of northern high vowel loss on /i/ and subsequent reintroduction of [i] or [y]. Its adherents criticize the applicability of the dissimilation hypothesis on two main grounds. It is pointed out that dissimilation would affect equally sequences such as /ses/, whereas, as we have seen, only underlying sequences with /i/ are affected. Secondly, in Thessaly /zis/ goes to

[yz] rather than to [ys], which one would expect on the assumption of simple dissimilation.[1]

The argument that dissimilation would necessarily affect vowels other than /i/ is weak. In terms of articulation the sibilants have the same high front articulation characteristic only of [i] among the Greek vowels and a dissimilatory rule applying to segments separated by another sharing some of their own features would be by no means implausible. That secondary [i] fails to trigger sibilant loss is no real difficulty either, as we can merely assume that dissimilation had ceased to operate when raising took place.

The voicing in [piráyz] constitutes the real problem. The dissimilatory hypothesis can be made to work only if we supplement it by an assumption of prior voicing metathesis:

(23)	pirázis
Voice metathesis	pirásiz
Dissimilatory loss	piráiz
Weak glide formation	**piráyz**

Unfortunately there seems to be no real evidence for the occurrence of a process metathesizing voice state in modern Greek. The [δexatéra] found in Old Athenian for θυγατέρα 'daughter' is quite isolated, and is sometimes claimed to be based on popular etymology with δέχομαι 'I receive'.

The alternative proposal in one of its various forms assumes that high vowel loss acts on, e.g., /pirázis/ to yield [pirázs], that the final cluster is reduced to [z] (by, say, voice assimilation and degemination) and that the resultant [piráz], now homophonous with the third singular from /pirázi/, has its identity restored by a borrowing of the [i] vowel which still survives in the stressed [ís] of μπορεῖς 'you can', θαρρεῖς 'you believe' and ȝῇς 'you live'. But this appeal to analogy brings its own difficulties. Why, for instance, should the ending [áz], for the vowel of which the considerable number of verbs in the ἀγαπάω conjugation might be held to provide a parallel, be felt to be more aberrant than [áyz]? Again, in most northern dialects the sibilants are palatalized before primary /i/, yielding the normal third singular form [piráž], so that homonymic clash between the second and third persons would not in fact occur. In any case this explanation cannot even attempt to deal

[1] See especially Boundonas (1892: 20 ff.), Kretschmer (1905: 80 ff.), Tzartzanos (1913), Anagnostopoulos (1915).

with more than the first two of the six classes of case listed above. No appeal to analogy can explain, for instance, why [aθanás] should be replaced by [aθanáys].

If the hypothesis of high vowel loss and assimilation followed by the development of a new [i] or [y] is correct at all, then we must surely accept the view that this segment has a phonological source. One suggestion, due to Boundonas, is that a [y] developed before the palatalized [s′] of items such as [θaplís′s] from θὰ πουλήσῃς 'you will sell', and the [s′] subsequently dropped.[1] It is not however clear why this development should occur before [s′s] and not before the [s′] of the third person form [θaplís′] 'he will sell', nor is there any good evidence to suppose that such a prothetic [y] occurs anywhere in modern Greek (see 2.5).

The clue to the problem lies perhaps in the observation that in Cretan, Maniot and some south-eastern dialects the [y] arising from /i/ in post-consonantal position goes by consonantality and softening to [š] or [ž], and that assimilatory processes often have dissimilatory analogues; thus voice assimilation may be matched under certain circumstances by a rule of voice dissimilation. In this case one might suggest that the [šs] arising from [sis] by palatalization and high vowel loss went to [x′s] by a process of 'softness dissimilation' which removes the stridency from a palatal continuant ([š] or [ž]) in the environment before a strident segment. That such a process actually occurs is shown by the dissimilatory conversion of /s/ to [h] in Rhodes and Cyprus (although in this case more is involved than loss of stridency); a parallel closer both phonetically and in terms of dialectal affiliation is the conversion of /s/ to [x] before a /s/ in the following syllable which is found in the Thracian town Soufli. There ὁ γαμπρός της 'her son-in-law' goes to [oγabróxts] and ἀρρώστησα 'I took ill' to [aróxtsa]. The final step in our proposed derivation will lead from [x′] or [γ′] before sibilant to [y], i.e. will have an effect opposite to that of consonantality, which converts [y] after a consonant to [x′] or [γ′]. That there is independent evidence for this is perhaps suggested by the fact that ἔχυσα 'I poured' often goes to [éysa] in northern dialects, although only one scholar (Anagnostopoulos 1915) appears to have suggested a direct conversion here of [x′] to [y]; the common view is that the original /x/ undergoes dissimilatory loss, so that the sequence is /éxisa/ > [éisa] > [éysa] rather than /éxisa/ > [éx′isa] > [éx′sa] > [éysa]. That [x′] can be lost by the sort of process which deletes the first of two sibilants in a word is shown by the Cretan

[1] See Boundonas (1892: 21).

[éys] for ἔχεις 'you have'; however, in the case of northern [éysa] we may attribute the loss of [x′] to the same process as eliminates [š]. If we label the rule converting [s] to [x′] and [z] to [γ′] 'softness dissimilation' and that replacing [x′] and [γ′] by [y] 'consonantality dissimilation', the derivation for ἔχυσα 'I poured' and ἔσεισα 'I shook' in a northern dialect would run somewhat as follows:

(24)	éxisa	ésisa
Palatalization	éx′isa	éšisa
High vowel loss	éx′sa	éšsa
Softness dissimilation		éx′sa
Consonantality dissimilation	**éysa**	**éysa**

Thessalian dialects which convert sequences of /zis/ to [yz] will also require the assumption of a rule of voice assimilation which will convert intermediate [žs] to [žz]; the normal direction of voice assimilation is regressive (e.g. [vt] > [ft]), but progressive assimilation is implied by the conversion of, say, [fy] to [fx′], [vy] to [vγ′] by consonantality, and the northern [éfx′i] for ἔφυγε 'he left' provides another example, as does the common [tombzéfti] for τὸν ψεύτη 'the liar'. We conclude this section with a derivation for παίζεις 'you play', θὰ λούσῃς 'you will wash', and τῆς βρύσης 'of the spring' in a northern dialect of the Thessalian type; those which have [péys] for the first item will apply voice assimilation to [péžs] in the usual regressive direction:

(25)	pézis	θalúsis	tisvrísis
Palatalization	péžis	θalúšis	tisvríšis
High vowel loss	péžs	θalúšs	tsvríšs
Voice assimilation	péžz		dzvríšs
Softness dissimilation	péγ′z	θalúx′s	dzvríx′s
Consonantality dissimilation	**péyz**	**θalúys**	**dzvríys**

4 *Consonant Clusters*

4.0 In this chapter we shall be concerned with the action on consonant clusters of certain phonological processes which have the general effect of reducing the combinatorial possibilities realized in underlying structures. For instance, to simplify somewhat, modern dialects permit only one type of obstruent sequence – that which consists of fricative and stop, usually in that order. We can account for this by positing a rule of 'manner dissimilation' which will specify a dyadic obstruent cluster as having a continuant first member and non-continuant second, unless the second member is sibilant, in which case the first must be non-continuant. Our rule will have two main functions: it will explain the relation between certain learned forms and their vernacular cognates, and it will clarify certain alternations. For instance, learned forms may have fricative+fricative and stop+stop sequences, while any vernacular cognate will be derived from them by manner dissimilation: thus λεπτά /leptá/ 'minutes' may resist manner dissimilation, in which case we have the more learned pronunciation [leptá], or it may undergo it, giving colloquial [leftá]; learned [fθinós] 'cheap' from /fθinós/ has a spoken equivalent [ftinós]; [efxaristó] 'thank you' is common, but does compete with a pronunciation [efkaristó] dialectally. Often systematically related doublets result: /elefθería/ 'freedom' is nowadays normally [elefθería], but in the expression καλή ἐλευθερία (a wish addressed to pregnant women) we always find [kalílefterγ'á]. Examples could be multiplied; more important for our purpose is the role played by manner dissimilation in accounting for alternation. κουράστηκα 'I'm tired' has the underlying form /kuraz+θi+k+a/, as may be seen by comparing [kurázo] 'I tire (someone)' and, e.g., φοβήθηκα [fovíθika] 'I was afraid'; but the sequence /zθ/ violates (*a*) the prohibition against obstruent clusters other than those consisting of fricative and stop and (*b*) a restriction against contiguous voiced and voiceless obstruents. It is accordingly acted on by manner dissimilation and voice assimilation to yield [st]. /pemp+θi+k+a/ 'I was sent' from πέμπω undergoes several of the rules to be discussed to yield [péftika]. Indeed this is a good example of the way in which in a language such as Greek, with systematic diglossy, an explanation of morphophonemic alternation will often throw light on the relation between learned and colloquial pronunciations of one and the same underlying form: Πέμπτη 'Thursday' or 'fifth' (as in πέμπτη τάξη 'fifth class') is pronounced by urban speakers [pém(p)ti] but dialectally in the first sense as [péfti].

The study of consonant clusters will be broken down as follows:

(*a*) Geminate clusters (long consonants) (4.1) and their reduction by 'degemination' in mainland and Cretan dialects.

(*b*) Nasal-initial clusters (4.2) and the action on them of postnasal voicing (converting, e.g., /páNta/ 'always' to [páNda]) and of nasal assimilation (leading from [páNda] to [pánda] in some dialects and to [pádda] in others).

(*c*) Word-final consonants (4.3), and in particular the loss of final /n/ in most, but not all dialects.

(*d*) Other dyadic clusters as they are affected by voice assimilation (4.4), manner dissimilation (4.5), and 'delateralization' (4.6).

(*e*) Triadic clusters, especially in relation to the rule of cluster simplification, which deletes the middle consonant of a sequence of three (4.7).

(*f*) Learned and foreign clusters, which often violate the above rules (4.8).

Some of these rules apply to the secondary consonant clusters arising from the action of the consonantality rule on postconsonantal [y] (see 6). The clusters arising as a result of high vowel loss in the north may also serve as input to them (see 7.4).

4.1 Geminate clusters

Ancient Greek, besides contrasting long and short vowels, also displayed an opposition of length in its consonantal system. Modern Greek has in all dialects lost the original long versus short opposition in the vowels, at least as far as the overt phonetic form of words is concerned, and the consonantal opposition has usually been neutralized, so that minimal pairs of the ἄλη : ἄλλη type ('wandering' : 'other') are no longer possible. However, in south-eastern dialects, in the variety of Old Athenian spoken in the Kimi area of Euboea, and in certain Cycladic dialects (at least those of Seriphos, Siphnos and Kimolos), the ancient contrast between long ('geminate') and short ('simple') consonants has not only survived, but has been extended.[1] The following examples are drawn from Cypriot, but 'geminating' dialects differ only very slightly in the distribution of long consonants within their respective lexicons.

/pp/	ἄππαρος	(< ἱππάριον)	'horse'	[áp̄ʰaros]
	πέφτω	(< πίπτω)	'I fall'	[pʰéfto]
/tt/	μύτη	(< μύτη)	'nose'	[mút̄ʰi]
	τέλι	(< Tk. *tel*)	'wire'	[tʰéli]
/kk/	λάκκος	(< λάκκος)	'well'	[lák̄ʰos]
	κέλης	(< Tk. *kel*)	'bald'	[kʰélis]
	κουκκί	(< κοκκίον)	'bean'	[kuč̄ín]
/ff/	νύφη	(< νύμφη)	'bride'	[níf̄i]
/θθ/	πεθερός	(< πενθερός)	'father-in-law'	[peθ̄erós]
/xx/	βήχω	(< βήσσω)	'I cough'	[víx̄o]
	συγχωρῶ	(< συγχωρῶ)	'I forgive'	[six̄oró]
/ss/	θάλασσα	(< θάλασσα)	'sea'	[θálas̄a]
/sk/	σκύλλος	(< σκύλλος)	'dog'	[š̄íl̄os]
/mm/	γράμμα	(< γράμμα)	'letter'	[γrám̄an]
	μάτι	(< ὀμμάτιον)	'eye'	[m̄átin]
/nn/	πέννα	(< Lat. *penna*)	'pen'	[pén̄a]
	ναί	(< ναί)	'yes'	[n̄é]
/ll/	φύλλα	(< φύλλα)	'leaves'	[fíl̄a]
	λίγο	(< ὀλίγον)	'a little'	[l̄íon]
/rr/	χαράμι	(< Tk. *haram*)	(a curse)	[xar̄ámi]

It will be observed that these long consonants are of miscellaneous origin. Some reflect ancient geminates; these are still pronounced long with the exception of ρρ (ἄρρωστος [árostos] 'ill') and the κκ of ἐκκλησία (Cypriot [eklišá] 'church'). A large number result from the action of nasal assimilation on sequences of nasal + fricative. Thus we have [níf̄i] for underlying /níNfi/ and [six̄oró] for /sinxoró/. This indeed is the only source of the long voiced fricatives [v̄, δ̄, γ̄], which can arise at word boundaries when a final /n/ is assimilated to an initial simple /v, δ, γ/. Thus δὲν βάλλει 'does not put' (standard βάζει or βάνει) goes to [ev̄ál̄i], and τὸν γάμον 'the marriage' (acc.), ἂν δώκῃ (standard δώσῃ) 'if he gives' to [toγ̄ámon], [aδ̄ók'i] (see end of 3.1). Many instances again result from borrowing, in which case a foreign geminate remains (Italian *cappello* > [kap̄ʰél̄o] 'hat') and, especially in the case

[1] The dialects of S. Italy also retain geminate consonants, and in Cappadocia it appears that at least the diminutive suffix -όκκος and [ll] in loans from Turkish show contrastive length.

of Turkish borrowings, a voiceless simple stop becomes long in Greek, while a voiced one becomes a simple voiceless stop (cf. [tʰéli] from Turkish *tel*, [maytanós] from *maydanoz* 'parsley'). Still another source lies in ancient words which have undergone 'spontaneous gemination'; thus ναί appears as [n̄é], μύτη as [mút̄ʰi], κῦμα 'wave' as [čím̄a], οὐδέποτε 'never' as [pot̄ʰé]. When such spontaneous gemination occurs it affects only one consonant within the word. If there is a pretonic intervocalic consonant it will affect that (/poté/ > [pot̄ʰé]), if not, any post-tonic intervocalic consonant (/míti/ > [mít̄ʰi]); if not even that occurs, an initial pretonic consonant will undergo gemination (/péfto/ > [pʰéfto]).[1]

As may be seen from the data, and from the above remarks on borrowings and spontaneous gemination, long consonants may occur initially before vowels in modern Greek, as well as in the intervocalic position permitted them by the ancient language. The continuant long consonants differ from their simple counterparts in length alone in both positions: compare for instance [m̄átin] 'eye' versus (in western Cyprus) [mátin] 'coat' (< ἱμάτιον), [éf̄oros] 'fertile' (< εὔφορος) but [éforos] 'superintendent' (< ἔφορος), [fíl̄a] 'leaves' (< φύλλα) but [fíla] 'kiss!' (< φίλα).

The phonetic clues differentiating long and short stops, however, are not identical for initial and intervocalic position. Intervocalically (whether word-medially or initially after a vowel) not only is the period between closure and release longer in the case of geminates but there is an audible puff of aspiration and the whole articulation is tenser. In utterance-initial position tenseness and aspiration become the sole auditory indication of length. Thus [péfti] 'Thursday' differs from [pʰéfti] 'he falls' only in having a lax, unaspirated [p]. It is sometimes claimed that certain Dodecanesian dialects have [p^f], t$^\theta$], [k^x] for the (p̄ʰ], [t̄ʰ], [k̄ʰ] used in Chios, Rhodes and Cyprus for /pp/, /tt/, /kk/, but I have never heard these pronunciations and it is not clear to what extent the spellings π$^\phi$, τ$^\theta$, κ$^\chi$ found in various publications indicate genuine affricates as opposed to aspirated stops.

Phonetically speaking 'geminates' are clearly long rather than doubled consonants. Phonologically the arguments cut both ways. On the one hand, any rule which applies to simple consonants will usually have the same effect on geminates, so that it will be easier to consider a geminate stop as differentiated from a simple one by the possession of

1 See Seiler (1958), Newton (1968) for a more detailed discussion.

a feature of length. For instance, palatalization acts on both simple and geminate /x/; if we wish to regard [x̄] as /xx/, though, then we shall have to make special provision for the fact that both segments are affected. On the other hand our morphophonemics will be complicated unless we accept the possibility of geminate sequences. Thus if δὲν νομίζω 'I don't think' has the underlying form /δén+nomizō/ it is easier to suppose that πανví 'sail' is /panní/ rather than /pañí/. We shall follow the common practice of treating underlying long consonants as double. For convenience geminate spellings may be used in phonetic representations as well.

The only consonant which does not appear to participate in the system of length contrast in any position is /z/. In most geminating dialects it is pronounced long intervocalically and utterance-initially before vowel, short otherwise. This means, among other things, that while other continuants in word-initial position provide a source of phonetic length contrast according as a nasal does or does not precede, this is not possible in the case of /z/. Thus ἡ σόμπα 'the stove' gives [isópa] in, say, Cyprus, while its accusative τὴν σόμπα appears as [tissópan]; compare with this the reflexes of ἡ ζώνη 'the belt' (nom.) and its accusative: [iz̄óni], [tiz̄ónin] from /i+zóni/, /tin+zónin/.

In various south-eastern dialects /z/ is pronounced [dz] or [ndz]. These pronunciations are usually treated as of ancient origin, but the possibility of a modern source cannot be dismissed outright. A lengthened [z̄] may have gone to [dz] by the same process as converts [s̄] to [ts] in Karpathos; in dialects in which voiced stops cannot occur postvocalically, only after a nasal, a nasal was prefixed; where nasal assimilation type II operates (converting, e.g. /nt/ to [dd]), the [dz] remains, or there was a reconversion to this from [ndz]. The available data on the distribution of [dz] and [ndz] are at least compatible with this hypothesis; the dialects of Karpathos, Chios and Kastellorizo do not permit postvocalic voiced stops and show [ndz]; Simi and Santorini, which do permit them, have [dz]. That Santorini, a dialect which has undergone degemination, has [dz] implies that the development of the [d] predates historically the reduction of geminates.

Most dialects do not distinguish primary geminate clusters from their simple counterparts. Thus, while in geminating dialects /fílla/ 'leaves' contrasts with /fíla/ 'kiss!' as [fílla] versus [fíla], mainland speakers have [fíla] for both. The 'degemination' rule which we require in order to account for this operates both within and between words so that τὸ φῶς σου /to+fós+su/ 'your light' becomes [tofósu] and in at least casual speech τοῦ στέλνω 'I send to him' and τοὺς στέλνω 'I send them' both appear as [tustélno]. Where the action of degemination would destroy a crucial contrast it is inhibited in certain circumstances, in particular τόν 'him' (in dialects which have this rather than τόνε) and τό 'it' would both go to [to] before [n] by degemination. Thus τὸν νομίζω 'I consider him' and τὸ νομίζω would converge to [tonomízo] if degemination applied, but in practice the first is pronounced [tonnomízo]. When τόν precedes a continuant other than [n] it is rather nasal assimilation which is inhibited in dialects with degemination; thus τὸν φέρνω 'I bring him' is pronounced [tonférno] and not *[toférno] which would be generated by the unimpeded action of nasal assimilation and degemination. See further on τόν and similar items in 4.3.

In northern and central Cyprus, northern Rhodes, Simi, Kalimnos and parts of Chios [θθ] goes to [tt]. Apart from the item ἀνάθεμα /anáθθema/ 'curse', which may represent a case of spontaneous gemination, [θθ] arises as a result of the action of nasal assimilation on /nθ/.[1] Thus in the dialects mentioned πενθερά 'mother-in-law', ἂν θέλεις 'if you want' and ἀνάθεμα develop as follows:

(1)	penθerá	anθélis	anáθθema
Nasal assimilation	peθθerá	aθθélis	
[θθ] > [tt]	**petterá**	**attélis**	**anáttema**

Thus the sequences /nθ/, /θθ/ and /tt/ merge phonetically in [tt] (pronounced [t̄ʰ]).

4.2 Nasal-initial clusters

Nasals may be followed in underlying structures, at least across word boundaries, by any consonant. Word-medially, if the following consonant is a stop it is subject in all dialects to the rule of postnasal voicing:

> **Postnasal voicing:** A stop is voiced in the environment after a nasal consonant and before vowel or sonant.

Thus /áNtras/ 'man', /éNporos/ 'merchant', /sinkenís/ 'relative' have voiced stops everywhere, the commonest pronunciations being either

[1] The rule for spontaneous gemination as formulated above would yield *[annáθema], but several informants have asserted that this item represents 'katharevusa' ἀνάνθεμα; this suggests the attribution of the form rather to popular etymology.

[ándras], [émboros], [sin′g′enís] or [ádras], [éboros], [sig′enís].[1] The blocking of this rule in foreign words and the integration of loans with original voiced stops are discussed in 4.8, but as far as inherited items are concerned we may say that modern Greek [b, d, g] always reflect underlying /p, t, k/ preceded by a nasal (but see p. 109); similarly [g′, ǰ, dᶻ̌] can arise only from underlying sequences of nasal + /k/ before front vowel or yod. Thus standard [an′g′ía], Cretan [aǰá], Cypriot [anǰá], Lesbian [adᶻ̌á], Peloponnesian [ag′á] all derive from /aNkía/ 'pots' (ἀγγεῖα).

The nasal itself is subject in all dialects to a rule assimilating it to a following consonant. This rule occurs in two main forms:

> **Nasal assimilation I:** A nasal is assimilated completely to a following continuant and in point of articulation to a following stop, except that /mn/ remains [mn].
>
> **Nasal assimilation II:** A nasal is assimilated completely to a following consonant, except that /mn/ remains [mn].

Nasal assimilation is followed in the rule sequence by degemination in such dialects as have this rule. This induces a four-fold classification of dialects as follows:

Group A. Nasal assimilation I occurs but not degemination. The items κουμπί 'button', πέντε 'five', νύμφη 'bride', πεθερός 'father-in-law' would in a dialect of this group develop as follows:

(2)	kuNpí	péNte	níNfi	peNθerós
Postnasal voicing	kuNbí	péNde		
Nasal assimilation I	**kumbí**	**pénde**	**níffi**	**peθθerós**

Dialects of this type are found in the variety of Old Athenian spoken in Kimi, and throughout the south east. The only known exceptions within this area appear to be the dialects of Simi and Kalimnos, which possess nasal assimilation II. In parts of Cyprus and elsewhere, as we noted in 4.1, the [θθ] arising from /nθ/ goes to [tt], so that in such dialects the last item will be pronounced [pet̄ʰerós].

Group B. Nasal assimilation I occurs, and is followed by degemination. The above items now become [kumbí], [pénde], [nífi], [peθerós]. This output is characteristic of most of northern Greece and much of the Peloponnese.

[1] Where there is no clear ground for identifying the point of articulation of underlying nasals, 'N', the general symbol for 'nasal segment', is used.

Group C. Nasal assimilation II occurs, but not degemination. This combination yields the reflexes [kubbí], [pédde], [níffi], [peθθerós], and is found at least in the Dodecanesian islands of Simi and Kalimnos.

Group D. Nasal assimilation II occurs, and is followed by degemination. The output of this combination will be as follows:

(3)	kuNpí	péNte	níNfi	peNθerós
Postnasal voicing	kuNbí	péNde		
Nasal assimilation II	kubbí	pédde	níffi	peθθerós
Degemination	**kubí**	**péde**	**nífi**	**peθerós**

This group comprises all Cretan, Thracian and eastern Macedonian dialects, as well as those spoken in the islands which belong to the northern complex (at least Thasos, Samothraki, Lesbos, Skiros, Samos). The Old Athenian dialects of Mani (with Cargese) and Megara also belong here, as does present-day Aeginetan (as well as the obsolete variety of Old Athenian previously spoken on the island). Of the Ionian dialects, Kephalonia, Ithaki and Zakinthos have [b, d, g] for /mp, nt, nk/, and there appear to be speakers in at least the southern part of Corfu with this pronunciation. It is also found in the north of Euboea, which has a northern dialect, and appears to have been characteristic of the older generation in Tyrnavos (N. Thessaly) (Tzartzanos 1909), although my own data from various parts of Thessaly consistently show the nasal element. In the Peloponnese there do seem to be speakers, particularly among the younger generation, whose speech would place them here rather than in group B; indeed in Athens itself the nasal is rarely perceptible at least as far as fairly rapid speech is concerned.

It may be added that it is often quite difficult to determine whether a given idiolect is to be treated as belonging to a group B or a group D pronunciation. While some dialects such as Cretan, Thracian and Lesbian show no trace of a nasal in, say, [péde], [kubí], and others such as Rhodian and Cypriot have a clearly enunciated nasal, many speakers in the Peloponnese and northern Greece have a very slight nasal onset ([pé^{n}de], [ku^{m}bí]) and indeed often seem to show fluctuation in the clarity with which the nasal element is articulated. While the phonetic facts are perhaps best described in terms of a continuous scale from [nd] to [d], our phonological statement requires a clear-cut decision which will entail some degree of arbitrariness. That is, a dialect with a very lightly articulated nasal must either be claimed to have nasal assimilation I, in which case a late phonetic rule will specify that nasals before voiced stops have a very reduced articulation, or be assigned nasal assimilation II, a late rule then prenasalizing voiced stops; this latter seems the less satisfactory choice, except perhaps for speakers who fluctuate between light and zero nasalization.

A further dimension of complexity is introduced when we consider nasal-initial clusters at word boundaries. All dialects appear to delete any nasal utterance-initially before a stop. Thus we find that all dialects have a simple [b] before the vowel of μπορῶ 'I am able'. Consider, for instance, this item compared with ἔμπορος 'merchant' when uttered in isolation in a dialect of types A or B:

(4)	Nporó	éNporos
Postnasal voicing	Nboró	éNboros
Initial nasal deletion	**boró**	
Nasal assimilation I		**émboros**

In a dialect of type D, which will reduce any [bb] to [b] by degemination, there is, strictly speaking, no need for a special rule of nasal deletion; in group C dialects, which do not have degemination, though, the rule is required, and must be ordered as in the above derivation. Thus in Simi we have /Nporó/ > (postnasal voicing) > [Nboró] > (initial nasal deletion) > [boró]; if nasal assimilation preceded initial nasal deletion the latter (as formulated above) would be blocked.

While the situation encountered after an actual pause is fairly straightforward, we cannot say the same of utterance-medial intervocalic nasal + stop clusters where a word boundary either precedes or follows the nasal. The problem is to determine under what circumstances and in what respect a given dialect treats these sequences differently from word-medial intervocalic nasal + stop sequences. The proper study of this question would take us beyond the scope of this book, but a few comments are in order.

First of all, we may observe that in several of the rather limited sets of words which retain a final nasal at all in modern dialects this does not participate in the normal assimilatory processes affecting nasals within words nor does it voice with any degree of regularity a following stop (see 4.3); rather in such cases the initial consonantal element of the second word behaves as it would after pause, and the nasal of the first is assimilated, if at all, only in respect of point of articulation. Thus ἂν πᾶς 'if you go', ἂν μπορεῖς 'if you can' will usually appear as [anpás] (or [ampás]), [amborís]; thus dialects which reduce medial /mp/ to [b] will yet have [mb] and [mp] across boundaries, although there is occasional evidence in the literature that some dialects do not make a systematic distinction between nasal followed by nasal+stop or stop alone in the following word on the one hand and medial nasal+stop on the other.

There are certain types of close syntactic structures in which clusters straddling word boundaries are often treated as if they were word-medial. These include in particular the nasal-final forms of the article before a following noun and the verbal particles θά(ν) or νά before a verb. Thus the cluster of τὸν τόπο 'the place' (acc. sing.) will usually be treated as is that of κοντά 'near'; that is, dialects of group A or B will have [tondópo], [kondá], those of group C [toddópo], [koddá] while Cretan and other dialects in group D will show [todópo], [kodá]. In cases where the boundary falls between the vowel and nasal we find in general the same situation. A minimum pair for testing this is in many dialects θὰ μπῶ 'I shall go in' and θαμπό 'dull'. Cretan-type dialects, which replace /mp/ by [b] medially, will not make a difference in any case. It is those which have [mb] medially and [b] after pause which might have different outputs for these items. At least Cypriot among the south-eastern dialects never makes a distinction in such instances: [θambó] occurs for both items there (and perhaps everywhere else in group A dialects). In Simi we again have no distinction ([θabbó]). Group B speakers, who have [θambó] for θαμπό but apply degemination, would represent the pronunciation described in the typical handbooks of standard demotic, and might be expected to have a [θabó]:[θambó] contrast on the basis of the conventional formulation to the effect that μπ is pronounced [mb] word-medially and [b] word-initially. Unfortunately I have not been able to find a speaker who appears to do this at all regularly. In the Peloponnese and Athens, where the 'standard' pronunciation would be expected, if anywhere, both items are pronounced [θa^{m}bó] or [θabó]. My impression is that only in Athenian *Bühnesprache* would one find a consistent distinction.

To summarize the discussion, we may first formulate the rule of initial nasal deletion as follows:

Initial nasal deletion: A nasal is deleted between # (word boundary) and stop.

Using this formulation we may suggest that speakers may differ in whether they have # or + (a morpheme boundary) in certain types of construction. A speaker who pronounces θὰ τὸ ντύσω 'I shall dress it' [θatodíso] but κοντά [kondá] can be said to assign the underlying structure /θa + to # ntisō/ to the first phrase, while one who has [nd] in both instances will have /θa + to + ntisō/. For speakers with [d] in each case the considerations under discussion would not suffice to impose a decision.

For a speaker representing the maximally distinctive treatment of nasal + stop sequences, we could derive ἂν πῇς 'if you say', ἂν μπῇς 'if you enter', νὰ μπῇς 'enter!' as follows:

(5)	an # pís	an # mpís	na # mpís
Postnasal voicing		an # mbís	na # mbís
Initial nasal deletion		an # bís	**na # bís**
Weak nasal assimilation	**am # pís**	**am # bís**	

The 'weak nasal assimilation' referred to above will affect point of articulation alone and will operate across word boundaries when the rule cycle governing word phonology has been completed.

It remains to mention the rather puzzling treatment of nasal + stop sequences in Karpathos. Within words we normally find the postnasal voicing and nasal assimilation I typical of most south-eastern dialects. Thus, ἄντρας > [ándras], πέντε > [pénde], κουμπί > [kumbí]. When a word boundary intervenes (including the one between article and noun) we find what appears to be a failure of postnasal voicing followed by nasal assimilation II. Thus τὴν πόρτα 'the door' (acc.) goes to [tip-pórta], τὴν κόρη 'the girl' to [tikkóri]. Because nasal assimilation takes the other form medially in Karpathos, it is tempting to suppose that what we have is rather a failure of the stop to voice through analogical pressure of positions other than the postnasal one, followed by some process of gemination; then the nasal drops as commonly in the south east before a geminate stop. This method of preserving the voicelessness of a stop may be illustrated by the replacement of Italian *pantaloni* by [patteláni] in Cyprus and elsewhere. The phenomenon is also found in the verbal endings -ουνται, -ουντο (e.g. [érkutte] 'they come', [írkutto] 'they were coming'). The preservation of the [t] in this case may be motivated by the third singular counterparts of these endings.[1]

Nasal assimilation is one of the most persistent of phonological rules and applies in most dialects whenever its input conditions arise. For instance, δόντια 'teeth' is in some Chian dialects [δóδγ'a] and it will

[1] See Dawkins (1904).

be suggested later (see 6.5) that this implies the derivational sequence /δóntia/ > [δóntya] > [δóndya] > [δóndγ'a] > [δónδγ'a] > (nasal assimilation) > [δóδδγ'a] > [δóδγ'a]. This means that it is still required after 'fricativity assimilation' has converted [dγ'] to [δγ']. It must also follow the rule deleting the middle of three consonants ('cluster simplification'), for the other, commoner form of this item in the south east is [δón'g'a], which requires the action of nasal assimilation after [nδg'] has been simplified to [ng']. However, when a nasal-initial cluster arises in a northern dialect through the loss of an intervening high vowel, nasal assimilation does not always affect it. For instance, /γínika/ 'I became' often goes to [yín'ka], showing that neither postnasal voicing nor nasal assimilation occur after the [i] drops. We may note also that when the aorist plural imperative morpheme -ετε is reduced to -τε and the verb stem ends in a nasal, postnasal voicing may again fail to act. Thus κάνετε 'do!' may be pronounced [kánte], although [kánde] and [kánete] appear to be commoner outside urban dialects.[1] There is no clear evidence on whether nasal assimilation affects [m] before this reduced -ετε, for dialects which have [m] in the aorist stem of κάνω and other verbs do not use the syncopated ending (cf. south-eastern [kámete]).

4.3 Word-final consonants

As was noted in 1.6, one of the characteristic features of the south-eastern dialect complex is the retention of an ancient final nasal in various groups of words. For instance, 'he said' appears as [ípen] before a pause, and when in close grammatical association with a following word as [ípem], [ípes], and so on, according to the rules governing nasal-initial clusters within words. Thus we find [ípemmu] 'he said to me', [ípessu] 'he said to you' and [ípendu] 'he said to him' from underlying /ípen/ followed by /mu/, /su/, /tu/ respectively. In other dialects, however, word-final nasals are found only in certain items such as the article and the negative particles δέν and μήν. It is worth while to distinguish three basic cases.

(1) A final nasal occurs subject to the rules of assimilation in all dialects. This is true of the accusative singular forms of the articles τόν, τήν, ἕναν, the feminine accusative singular pronoun τήν 'her', the negative particles δέν, μήν, and the conjunction σάν 'when'. For these forms we must assume an underlying /n/. δὲν θέλω 'I don't want', δὲν

[1] [mínde], [míde] appear to be particularly common in Roumeli and N. Euboea.

παίρνω 'I don't take' and δὲν ἔχω 'I don't have' will then derive as follows in a dialect which has nasal assimilation of type II and degemination (e.g. Cretan and various Peloponnesian dialects, as well as many standard idiolects):

(6)	δenθélo	δénpérno	**δénéxo**
Postnasal voicing		δénbérno	
Nasal assimilation II	δéθθélo	δébbérno	
Degemination	**δéθélo**	**δébérno**	

A dialect without degemination and with nasal assimilation of type I would have [δéθθélo], [δémbérno], [δénéxo].

In addition to the items cited above, the masculine singular accusative forms of certain 'pronominal adjectives' (e.g. τόσον 'so much', ἄλλον 'other') as well as of the demonstratives (αὐτόν, ἐκεῖνον, τοῦτον) frequently retain their ancient nasal subject to assimilation, as does to a lesser extent the masculine singular accusative form of adjectives. In general, where variation does occur the nasal is more likely to be retained in the local dialect than in the standard. In Athenian, for instance, while τὸν κακὸν ἄνθρωπο 'the bad man' (acc.) may be pronounced [toŋgakónánθropo], the nasal is rare in positions other than before vowel. In Cretan, on the contrary, this particular form of the adjective bears an underlying nasal no matter what follows. Thus, while τὸν κακὸν τόπο 'the bad place' (acc.) appears as [toŋgakótópo] in Athens, Cretan has [togakódópo].

(2) A final nasal occurs subject to the rules of assimilation in some dialects but does not occur in others. Roughly speaking, the south-eastern dialects alone have a final underlying nasal in (*a*) the nominative–accusative of neuter nouns and adjectives: thus, τὸ καλὸ παιδί 'the good child' and τὸ μικρὸ ὄνομα 'the first name' appear as [tokalómbeδín], [tomikrónónoman] or something similar. (*b*) The accusative singular forms of nouns, adjectives and pronouns usually retain their original nasal: τὸν φίλον του 'his friend' (acc.) > [toffílondu]. (*c*) Many dialects outside the Peloponnese have /θan/ as the particle of futurity matching standard /θa/.

In describing dialects outside the south-eastern ones it is important to distinguish carefully these two groups of words. Those belonging to the first group may not show a nasal phonetically, but this must be attributed to the action of the phonological rules operating in the dialect, while in the second group there may be no point in talking about an underlying nasal at all. To make this clear, let us consider the expression τὸν φόρο 'the tax' (acc.) in Athenian and a south-eastern dialect: [tofóro] and [toffóron] respectively. Athenian differs superficially in not having final nasals in either article or noun, but there is an important distinction. The article has an underlying nasal in Athenian, as is shown by the fact that in positions other than before continuant consonants we find overt realizations of it. Thus, τὸν τόπο 'the place' (acc.) > [tondópo], τὸν ἄνθρωπο 'the man' > [tonánθropo]. The noun, on the other hand, never behaves as if it had an underlying nasal, and if we wished to assert that 'final nasals drop' in Athenian, we would either be commenting on a purely historical fact or summarizing in a somewhat misleading way the relation between Athenian and dialects which retain final nasal. However, there do appear to be dialects for which we must assume a rule dropping nasals in utterance-final position. Thus in Karpathos τὸ παιδὶ ἦρθε 'the child came' is pronounced [topeínírte], but when the same words occur in marked order we get [írtendopeí]. In such dialects we have a clear case for setting up a rule of 'final nasal deletion', applicable before pause. Dialects which lost most ancient final nasals also tend to delete such ones as remain (or have developed since) in utterance-final position: thus, /mín/ 'don't' is regularly pronounced [mí] in isolation in, e.g., Athenian.

(3) A final nasal occurs in all dialects but does not necessarily undergo assimilation before continuant consonants. Perhaps the commonest of such cases involves the accusative pronoun τόν 'him'. δὲν τὸν θέλω 'I don't want him' is pronounced [δéndonθélo] rather than *[δéndoθélo] in dialects with degemination and the reason is not far to seek. The latter pronunciation could arise equally well from δὲν τὸ θέλω 'I don't want it' (referring to a neuter noun). That the explanation does in fact lie in the need to distinguish τόν from τό is confirmed by noticing that τήν 'her' belongs to group (1) (δὲν τὴν θέλω [δéndiθélo] is unambiguous); furthermore, dialects which lack degemination do seem to apply assimilation to τόν: [δéndoθθélo] 'I don't want him', but [δéndoθélo] 'I don't want it'. A similar non-assimilated nasal is regular in all genitive plural forms (e.g. τῶν φίλων μου 'of my friends' [tonfílonmu]) and in the conjunctions ἄν 'if' and πρίν 'before'.

The final nasal of certain verb forms can be properly discussed only within the context of a description of dialectal verb morphology. It may be mentioned, though, that south-eastern dialects tend to show a final nasal in the first plural active endings of verbs, as well as in the third singular active past endings, and the phenomenon is sometimes reported for the north: εἴδαμε 'we saw' [íδamen], ἔφυγε 'he left' [éfien]. Final /n/ is also found in many dialects in the first and second plural forms of the imperfect passive (e.g. northern [kaθómastan] 'we were sitting'). However, in most mainland dialects and in Cretan, an originally final /n/, especially in the third plural endings, is followed by an /e/ or /a/ of analogical origin. Thus ἔλεγαν 'they were saying', ἔχουν 'they have' are usually [léγane], [éxune]. This, in conjunction with the common replacement of τόν 'him', τήν 'her' by [tone], [tine] and, utterance-finally, of the masculine singular accusative demonstrative forms αὐτόν, ἐκεῖνον, τοῦτον by [aftóne], [ek'ínone], [tútone], has the effect of eliminating occurrences of final nasal except in the articles, in δέν, μήν, σάν, θάν, and in the genitive plural of adjectives and nouns. Even this last instance is avoided in Zakinthos, where instead of, e.g., [tongalómbeδyón] for τῶν καλῶν παιδιῶν 'of the good children' we find [tongalónepeδyóne], τῶν καλῶνε παιδιῶνε.

While many dialects display a strong tendency to delete final /n/, /s/ is in general preserved in final position. In Chian it assimilates completely to a following continuant, so that we find, for instance, that ἔχεις δουλειά 'you have work' may be pronounced [éx'iδδul'á]. In all other dialects it converts to [z] before a voiced consonant or glide. In the variety of Old Athenian spoken in Corsica it appears from the account of Blanken (1951) that /s/ drops prepausally, so that ὀκτὼ μέρες 'eight days' goes to [oxtómére], τῆς μάνας 'of the mother' to [tizmána]. In Crete dissimilatory loss of final /s/ occurs before the first plural possessive μας: ὁ ἀδελφός μας [oaδerfómas]; in Chios this happens before any word with initial [ts], [ks], [ps]: τοὺς ψεῦτες 'the liars' [tupséftes].

If we leave out of account a few exclamations we can say that no other consonants apart from /s/ and /n/ both occur in final position in underlying forms and are directly represented phonetically, although we may wish to claim that at least /t/ can occur finally in underlying forms. Thus various neuters in -α which have -άτου in the genitive singular and -ατα in the nominative–accusative plural may be held to have an underlying /t/ which is deleted prepausally: [ónoma] 'name', plural [onómata] may be assigned to /ónomat/. However, no dialectal variation turns on this alternation between [t] and zero. More important is the fact that in northern dialects consonants and indeed consonant clusters may occur word-finally as a result of high vowel loss. Thus μάτι 'eye', πόδι 'foot', βαπόρι 'boat' are in most northern dialects [mát], [póδ], [vapór].

Indeed a fuller range of contrasts is possible in final consonants in northern dialects than southern ones allow non-finally, for the palatal variants of the velars and at least /n, l, s, z/ can there contrast finally with their nonpalatal counterparts: φίλοι 'friends' > [fíl′], but φίλου 'friend' (gen.) > [fíl]. This rich set of contrasts is limited only slightly in the dialect of Saranda Ekklisies (E. Thrace), which devoices final stops.[1] The derivations of φεγγάρι 'moon' and φέγγει 'shines' in this dialect would run as follows:

(7)	feNkári	féNki
Postnasal voicing	feNgári	féNgi
Nasal assimilation II	feggári	féggi
Degemination	fegári	fégi
Palatalization		fég′i
High vowel loss	**fegár**	fég′
Final devoicing		**fék′**

4·4 Voice assimilation

The following rule applies to primary consonant clusters in all dialects:

> **Voice assimilation:** An obstruent agrees in voice state with an immediately following obstruent and in addition a sibilant is voiced before a following sonant (liquid, nasal or glide).

The consonant combinations not included in this formulation are (*a*) nasal-initial sequences, (*b*) liquid-initial sequences, (*c*) stop + sonant sequences and (*d*) sequences of non-sibilant fricative + sonant:

(*a*) Nasal-initial sequences are governed by the rules of nasal assimilation and postnasal voicing discussed in 4.2.

(*b*) Liquid-initial sequences undergo delateralization, which converts any /l/ to [r] (see 4.6). This [r] may be devoiced before a stop whether this is of primary origin ([pór̥ta] 'door') or secondary ([ír̥te] 'he came' < /írθe/, [xor̥kó] 'village' < /xorío/).

(*c*) Stop + sonant sequences. Stop + liquid sequences in underlying structure are represented directly as [pr, tr, kr, kl, pl] in all dialects. Thus /plekō/ 'I knit' > [pléko], /kríma/ 'pity' > [kríma], /trís/ 'three' > [trís], /klistós/ 'closed' > [klistós]. Stop + nasal sequences are rare and may undergo shifts of manner and point of articulation or be

[1] See Psaltis (1905: 46).

broken up by epenthesis, but there appears to be no clear case of voice assimilation acting directly on them. Thus πνίγω 'I drown' > [piníγo] in Laconia (Peloponnese) and elsewhere; ἀτμός 'steam' is usually [axnós] or, with voice assimilation in Cyprus, [aγnós]. /kn/ may perhaps remain everywhere; πυκνός 'thick', if it occurs at all, seems always to have [kn], and the sequence is found in apparently dialectal items such as Cypriot [knizzín] 'bunch of grapes'.

(*d*) Non-sibilant fricatives + sonant undergo voice assimilation in certain dialects. In the Kimi dialect of Old Athenian /xn/ converts to [γn]: /páxni/ 'frost' > [páγni], /δíxno/ 'I show' > [δíγno]. This phenomenon is found also quite widely in the Peloponnese (cf. [ríγno] 'I throw' for standard [ríxno]), and in addition /fn/ is sometimes reported to go to [vn] (e.g. in the Triphylia region we get [áksavnos] 'sudden' for standard [éksafnos]).[1] Only in Cyprus, however, does there appear to be a general rule voicing fricatives before sonants. Thus /δáfni/ 'laurel' > [δávni], /éθnos/ 'nation' > [éδnos], /xrónos/ 'year' > [γrónos], /fléva/ 'vein' > [vléa], /ánθropos/ 'man' > [áδropos] (or [áγropos]).

We shall now illustrate the effects of the normal voice assimilation rule on (*a*) non-sibilant fricatives, (*b*) sibilants and (*c*) stops.

(*a*) The non-sibilant fricatives [f, θ, x] occur before voiceless obstruents and their voiced counterparts [v, δ, γ] before voiced ones. Sometimes there is no evidence that any change in voice state has been produced by the voice assimilation rule, in which case it merely represents a statement of what sequences are phonetically possible (it is a 'morpheme structure rule'). For instance [avγó] 'egg' cannot be shown to have an underlying cluster other than /vγ/ and [péfko] 'pine' must go back, failing evidence to the contrary, to /péfko/. In other cases the rule has resulted in a shift of voice state. Thus [rávo] 'I sew' must come from /rávo/, so that [érapsa] (aorist) can be assumed to derive from /éravsa/ by voice assimilation and manner dissimilation: /éravsa/ > [érafsa] > [érapsa]. Similarly [ráftis] 'tailor' presumably represents the realization of /rávtis/ and [náftis] 'sailor' of /návtis/ (cf. [navaγó] 'I get shipwrecked'). Other examples are [δúlepsa] 'I worked' from /δulevsa/ (cf. [δulévo] 'I work') and [élikse] 'it ceased' from /éliγse/ (cf. [líγi] < /líγi/ 'it ceases').

[1] For Triphylia see Λεξικογραφικὸν Δελτίον (1963: 80) and for Kimi, Phavis (1911). The pronunciations [ríγno] 'I throw', [δíγno] 'I show', and so for other verbs in -χνω, are widespread in the Peloponnese.

(*b*) Morpheme-final /z/ is found in verb stems, in which case it converts to [s] before the aorist passive formative /θi/: /kurázθika/ 'I am tired' > [kurásθika] > [kurástika] (cf. [kurázo] < /kurázo/ 'I tire'). But the commoner situation arises when a morpheme final /s/ goes to [z]. /prosméno/ 'I await' > [prozméno] (cf. [prosefx'í] 'prayer' implying /prosefxí/). The action of voice assimilation on /s/ is particularly common at word boundary in certain close constructions: /tus+máγus/ 'the magicians' (acc.) > [tuzmáγus], /tis+rómis/ 'of Rome' > [tizrómis], /tus+léo/ 'I tell them' > [tuzléo]. Again, in many cases no actual change is involved: [spíti] 'house' < /spíti/, [kózmos] 'world' < /kózmos/, [zlávos] 'Slav' < /zlávos/. It may be added that sibilant+liquid clusters occur only in borrowings and as commonly in such cases may be subject to fluctuation. [slávos] is not unknown, for instance, and 'slide' may be pronounced [sláyd] rather than, as commonly, [zláyt].

(*c*) Assimilatory voicing of a stop is possible when the ancient preposition ἐκ precedes a voiced fricative in certain compounds, usually relatively learned. Thus /ekδótis/ 'publisher' may be pronounced [egδótis], /ekδíkisi/ 'revenge' [egδík'isi]. But the sequence [gδ] is not truly dialectal and violates the rule of manner dissimilation; the inherited forms with original κδ have [γδ] in modern Greek: ἐκδέρω gives modern [γδérno] 'I scratch'. Indeed this process may affect even learned words. In Kephalonia, for instance, we find [eγδík'isi]. An example with /kv/ is /ekviázo/ 'I blackmail', which may be realized as [egviázo], but again the sequence [gv] is not truly demotic (ancient ἐκβάλλω is represented by the metathesized [vγállo] 'I take out' in modern dialects, and this in turn may go to [vgállo] or [fkállo], see 4.5).

We have been assuming throughout that voice assimilation is always regressive, going from second to first element, so that, say, /évkolos/ 'easy' becomes [éfkolos], never *[évgolos]. However, there is evidence that under certain circumstances [γ'] may convert to [x'] after voiceless stops or fricatives. Thus the normal result of the consonantality rule is to convert a sequence such as [ty] to [tx'], which may be held to collapse two changes, [ty] > [tγ'] (by strict consonantality) and [tγ'] > [tx']; one reason for treating consonantality in two stages is indeed that in some dialects [ty] may go via [tγ'] to [dγ'] (and this to [δγ']), in which case the difference turns on the direction of voice assimilation (see 6·3). Furthermore ἔφυγε 'he left' is frequently [éfx'i] in northern dialects and this is most easily explained by deriving /éfiγe/ > [éfiγ'e] > [éfγ'e] > [éfx'e] > [éfx'i]. Again, the normal order may assert itself;

while ἄκουγε 'he was listening' usually goes to [ákγ'i] in the north, [ágγ'i] is found in Skopelos, and even [évγ'i] is reported for a village in Thessaly.[1]

With regard to the position of voice assimilation in the rule sequence, we may note that it appears to act in all dialects whenever its input conditions arise; the only exception is provided by certain northern dialects which fail in some cases to apply voice assimilation to the output of high vowel loss so that, e.g., κουδούνι 'bell' is pronounced [kδún'] rather than [gδún'] (see 7·4).

4·5 Manner dissimilation

Except in learned or foreign items, underlying dyadic obstruent clusters consist of a continuous (fricative) and non-continuous (stop) member, although [sf], [zv] occur in most dialects and [vγ, vδ, γδ, zγ] are allowed outside the south east. In many dialects the only non-sibilant obstruents permitted after [r] (whether from /r/ or /l/) are [t, k, p, f, v]. The phonological rule which accounts for this severe restriction on consonantal clustering patterns ('manner dissimilation') exists in three main forms. In its commonest (but phonologically least general) form it operates on voiceless obstruent clusters as follows:

> **Manner dissimilation I:** Voiceless heterogeneous dyadic obstruent clusters other than those with /s/ or /f/ as second member consist of fricative + stop. If the second member is /s/, the first is a stop.

While the rule of manner dissimilation is of striking simplicity and generality even when limited to voiceless obstruents, its historical origins are relatively complex, and some of the processes which have led to the modern rule have had little to do with dissimilation in respect of continuity. It may be worth while to consider briefly the underlying obstruent cluster classes of modern Greek in relation to their origins.

(*a*) *Stop + stop.* Ancient Greek had /pt/ and /kt/ and these are now converted to [ft], [xt]. Thus ancient πτερόν 'feather', ἑπτά 'seven', κτίζω 'I build', ὀκτώ 'eight' are now [fteró], [eftá], [xtízo], [oxtó]. Whether we assign underlying /pt/, /kt/ to such items will often depend on whether we wish to relate dialectal to 'learned' pronunciations. While [eftá], for example, does not participate within any dialect in

[1] See Kretschmer (1905: 179), Boundonas (1892: 18).

morphophonemic alternations which would justify us in deriving [ft] from anything but /ft/, the postulation of underlying /eptá/ makes it possible to account for the fact that many speakers have rather [eptá]. In other cases doublets may be related by simply showing that manner dissimilation may be blocked for specific meanings. If [γraftó] 'fate' is interpreted /γraptó/, for instance, we can give a straightforward account of its phonological relation to [γraptó] 'written examination'. In other cases the semantic links may be quite tenuous; [leftá] 'money' has little apparent connexion with [leptá] 'thin', and what about 'minutes', pronounced either [leptá] or [leftá]? However the synchronic reality is interpreted, ancient λεπτά provides the common source for all three.

(*b*) *Stop+fricative.* Ancient Greek had /ps/ and /ks/ and these carry over unchanged into the modern dialects. Thus ξένος > [ksénos] 'foreigner', ὑψηλός > [psilós] 'tall'. Modern [tˢ], perhaps so to be regarded rather than as a cluster (see 5.1), derives largely from borrowing (e.g. [tˢánda] < Tk. [čánta]) but Greek /t/ or /k/ may provide a source ([tˢíxla] 'thrush' < κίχλη) and in [kátˢe] 'sit' the fricative and stop of [káθise] have undergone manner dissimilation after an irregular vowel loss. In the case of items such as [ksénos] and [psilós] there is no reason to assign the initial clusters to anything but /ks/, /ps/.

Underlying /pθ/ and /kθ/ occur in modern Greek when a verb stem in final /p/ or /k/ is followed by the aorist passive formative /θi/. Manner dissimilation converts them to [ft] and [xt]. Thus /pempō/ 'I send' has as its typical aorist passive from /e+pemp+θi+k+a/ [epéftika] (see derivation (13)), and /plekō/ 'I knit' has the third person singular aorist passive [epléxtik'e] from /e+plek+θi+k+e/. In this case the conversion of /pθ/ to [ft] and /kθ/ to [xt] reflects the collapsing of two distinct historical changes. First πθ, κθ had gone to φθ, χθ by the ancient period; the conversion of these latter to [ft], [xt] is modern.

(*c*) *Fricative+stop.* Ancient /sp/, /st/, /sk/ are taken over as [sp], [st], [sk] (although the latter may undergo various modern processes including palatalization and softening). Modern [ft], [fp], [fk] may take their fricative element from the second element of the ancient diphthongs αυ, ευ. Thus ancient αὐτός went from [awtós] to modern [aftós] 'he' and εὔπορος, εὔκολος yield modern [éfporos] 'prosperous', [éfkolos] 'easy'. Manner dissimilation applies vacuously to these cases.

(*d*) *Fricative+fricative.* Underlying modern fricative+fricative sequences, which will be acted on by manner dissimilation except in the case of /sf/, have miscellaneous ancient sources. Ancient φθ, χθ, σφ, σθ, σχ occurred within morphemes as well as across boundaries and are represented by modern [ft, xt, sf, st, sk]. For intramorphemic position we have φθάνω > [ftáno] 'I arrive', ἐχθρός > [oxtrós] 'enemy', ἀσφαλίζω > [sfaló] 'I close', ἀσθενής > [astenís] 'ill', ἄσχημος > [ásk'imos] 'ugly'. In these cases the motive for assigning underlying /fθ/, /xθ/, /sθ/, /sx/ rather than /ft/ etc. would be based on the correlation of katharevusa and vernacular forms. The pronunciations [fθáno], [exθrós], for instance, are common in standardizing idiolects. It is interesting to note, however, that these correspondences between fricative+fricative in katharevusa and fricative+stop in demotic do not necessarily reflect directly a historical occlusivization of the second term, for it is not certain that a cluster such as ancient σχ ever went through a [sx] stage; rather what occurred was a deaspiration of [sk^h], and [sx] represents a modern reading pronunciation.

Underlying /fs/ and /xs/ can occur across morpheme boundary and go to [ps], [ks]. Thus /γrafō/ 'I write', aorist /e+γraf+s+a/ yield [γráfo], [éγrapsa] and [vréxo] 'I wet' and its aorist [évreksa] imply the underlying /vrex/. Here again, the synchronically valid observation that fricatives go to stops before /s/ may reflect the ancient deaspiration of φ and χ before a sibilant (cf. ancient γράφω, ἔγραψα). In other cases, though, the synchronic and diachronic statements may be parallel. The verbs in -εύω, for instance, have modern aorist stems in [eps] for ancient [ews] and this appears to reflect a shift [w] > [f] > [p] before [s].

Finally modern /f/ or /v/ before /x/ or /θ/ may reflect ancient [w] (see above). Thus /efxí/ 'blessing', /evxaristó/ 'I thank', /efθís/ 'immediately' come from εὐχή, εὐχαριστῶ, εὐθύς and receive in a typical dialect the pronunciations [efk'í], [efkaristó], [eftís].

While voiceless obstruent clusters are affected in all dialects by manner dissimilation, there is a slightly more general form which in addition converts /rθ/ and /rx/ to [rt] and [rk] (more general, that is, if we regard /r/ as continuous). In this form ('manner dissimilation II') the rule operates in Mani, Ikaria and Samos; in the northern islands of Lesbos, Samothraki and Imbros, as well as in Kephalonia, /rθ/ goes to [rt], but not apparently /rx/ to [rk].

The most general form of manner dissimilation in addition to performing the work of the first and second types, operates on any voiced counterparts of the clusters mentioned. This means that it encompasses manner dissimilation I and also occlusivizes the second member of /rθ, rx, rγ, rδ, vδ, vγ, γδ/ (and /zγ/ when it occurs). We can state it thus:

> **Manner dissimilation III:** A heterogeneous dyadic cluster consisting of oral consonant + non-sibilant, non-labial obstruent is continuous + non-continuous; one consisting of obstruent + sibilant is non-continuous + continuous.

If we did not apply the rule before nasal assimilation had removed sequences such as [nθ] we would be able to omit even reference to nasality. In any case the net effect of nasal assimilation and manner dissimilation is to ensure that the only clusters other than those with a continuous and non-continuous member have either [f], [v] or sonant as second term, or consist of [rs].

Manner dissimilation III is characteristic of south-eastern dialects and is found in at least Chios, Rhodes, Cyprus, Kos and Karpathos.

Manner dissimilation, of whatever type, is normally ordered before the consonantality rule which converts [y] to [x′] or [γ′] after consonants. Thus in most dialects ἀλήθεια 'truth' goes from [alíθya] to [alíθx′a], but this is not further converted by manner dissimilation to [alíθk′a] as, say, εὐχή 'blessing' goes from [efx′í] to [efk′í]. However, in south-eastern dialects the order is reversed and we get [alíθk′a]. See on this 6.2, and on the relation of manner dissimilation to high vowel loss 7.4.

The following examples are intended to illustrate the effects of voice assimilation and manner dissimilation in the dialects of the Peloponnese, Zakinthos and western Cyprus, where manner dissimilation operates in forms I, II and III respectively:

			I	II	III
/kt/	ὀκτώ	'eight'	oxtó	oxtó	oxtó
/fx/	εὐχή	'blessing'	efk′í	efk′í	efčí
/vx/	εὐχαριστῶ	'thank you'	efkaristó	efkaristó	efkaristó
/xθ/	χθές	'yesterday'	xtés	xtés	extés
/fs/	ἔγραψα	'I wrote'	éγrapsa	éγrapsa	éγrapsa
/vs/	κλάδεψα	'I pruned'	kláδepsa	ekláδepsa	ekláepsa
/xs/	ἔβρεξε	'it rained'	évrekse	évrekse	évreksen
/zθ/	σχίστηκε	'it was torn'	sk′ístik′e	esk′ístik′e	eššístin
/kθ/	πλέχτηκε	'it was knitted'	pléxtik′e	epléxtik′e	epléxtin
/rθ/	ἦρθε	'he came'	írθe	írte	írten
/rx/	ἀρχή	'beginning'	arx′í	arx′í	arčí

			I	II	III
/rδ/	σκόρδος	'garlic'	skórδos	skórδos	skórdos
/rγ/	ἀργά	'late'	arγá	arγá	argá
/vδ/	ραβδί	'stick'	ravδí	ravδí	ravdín
/vγ/	αὐγό	'egg'	avγó	avγó	avgón
/γδ/	γδέρνω	'I scratch'	γδérno	γδérno	γdérno

The application of manner dissimilation III to /rδ, rγ, vδ, vγ, γδ/ yields [rd, rg, vd, vg, γd], as is illustrated by the last five items in the above list. However, in parts of Chios, Rhodes, Cyprus and Kos what we find is [rt, rk, ft, fk, xt]. Thus in central Cyprus these same items appear as [skórtos], [arká], [raftín], [afkón], [xtérno]. It is therefore apparent that in these dialects we have a rule which devoices stops in the position after fricative and [r]; as we shall observe later (see 6.4) this rule also acts on the output of the consonantality and manner dissimilation rules in the case of clusters such as /vy, δy, ry/. Consider the forms which αὐγό 'egg', κλουβιά 'cages' will take in a dialect of this type:

(8)	avγón	kluvía
Glide formation		kluvyá
Consonantality		kluvγ'á
Manner dissimilation	avgón	kluvg'á
Devoicing	avkón	kluvk'á
Voice assimilation	**afkón**	**klufk'á**

The devoicing rule may be expressed simply as follows:

Devoicing: A stop is voiceless except between nasal and vowel or sonant.

Phrased thus, the devoicing rule, rather than being viewed as specific to certain south-eastern dialects, may be seen to be characteristic of all dialects; in dialects with [avgó] for /avγó/, [ravdí] for /ravδí/, it fails to operate after manner dissimilation. In Central Cypriot it does follow it. Furthermore, it will be noted that its conditioning environment complements exactly that for postnasal voicing, and it is possible to treat it as merely an aspect of postnasal voicing, which may accordingly be revised as follows:

Postnasal voicing: A stop is voiced in the environment between a nasal consonant and a vowel or sonant, otherwise voiceless.

We may therefore represent the difference between a dialect with [avgó] and one with [afkó] in terms of the relative ordering of postnasal voicing and manner dissimilation. Cypriot πέντε 'five', αὐγό would then be accounted for thus (using 'T' for a dental stop unspecified for voice):

(9)	péNTe	avγón
Manner dissimilation		avgón
Postnasal voicing	péNde	avkón
Nasal assimilation	**pénde**	
Voice assimilation		**afkón**

A dialect with [avgó] would derive these items by placing postnasal voicing before manner dissimilation:

(10)	péNTe	avγó
Postnasal voicing	péNde	
Manner dissimilation		**avgó**
Nasal assimilation	**pénde**	

By taking advantage of the fact that voice assimilation acts whenever its input conditions arise, we do not need to make our devoicing rule act on a preceding fricative, although it appears probable that the actual historical change acted on the cluster as such (e.g. [vg] > [fk]). The devoicing rule appears at first sight phonetically unmotivated, but it may be noted that its effect is to bring the new clusters created by manner dissimilation III into line with existing patterns of combination. The voiced stops of [skórdos] and [argá] are aberrant in dialects which have these pronunciations in that they entail contrast at the phonetic level between voiced and voiceless stops, for until manner dissimilation takes effect only voiceless stops occur after [r] (e.g. [pórta] 'door', [arkúδa] 'bear'). The clusters [vd], [vg] and [γd] are also exceptional in that voiced stops occur otherwise within words only after nasals. In other words, the effect of manner dissimilation is to create phonemic contrast where none existed by destroying the complementarity of voiced and voiceless stops.

We may conclude by noting that the joint effect of manner dissimilation III and devoicing is to restrict severely the range of possible obstruent structures. Thus the dyadic clusters with labial and dental points of articulation allowed by our choice of underlying segments are /pt, pθ, pδ, ft, fθ, fδ, vt, vθ, vδ/ and all but /pδ/ and /fδ/ are actually found. Yet phonetically the only output allowed by our rules is [ft]:

/eptá/	'seven'	[eftá]
/na+pemp+θi+ī/	'let him be sent'	[napeftí]
/aftín/	'ear'	[aftín]
/na+γraf+θi+ī/	'let it be written'	[naγraftí]
/ráv+ti+s/	'tailor'	[ráftis]
/na+rav+θi+ī/	'let it be sewn'	[naraftí]
/ravδ+í+n/	'stick'	[raftín]

4.6 Delateralization

In all core dialects /l/ goes to [r] before another consonant in primary clusters.[1] Thus /aδelfós/ 'brother' > [aδerfós], /ílθa/ 'I came' > [írθa], /fθalmós/ 'evil eye' (ancient ὀφθαλμός) > [ftarmós] ([eftarmós] Chios). In these particular cases there is in fact no justification within the vernacular dialects themselves for setting up underlying forms with /l/ at all, for the two liquids do not enter into any alternation. In other cases, however, alternation can be found which does justify a 'delateralization' rule: /psállo/ 'I chant' (the underlying form found in south-eastern dialects, rather than /psálno/) forms an agentive noun /psáltis/ 'cantor' which goes to [psártis]. /vállo/ 'I put', found in the same group of dialects for /váno/ or /vázo/, has in its paradigm forms such as /válθkike/ (aor. pass. third sing.) and /valménos/ (perf. pass. part.), which undergo the present rule to yield [várθik'e] (or [vártik'e]), [varménos]. In Cyprus /vále+to/ 'put it!' is syncopated to [válto] and this goes to [várto].

Foreign and learned items, as one might expect, often form exceptions to the general rule. /vólta/ 'stroll', /balkóni/ 'balcony', both of Italian origin, are often pronounced [vólta], [balkóni], but forms with [r] are certainly not unknown (e.g. [vórta] is cited as current in Kimolos and Naxos and [parkóni] is usual in Cyprus). Even pronunciations such as [δérta], [árfa] for the letters delta, alpha are sometimes found. Although most monographs list the specific items which undergo delateralization in the dialect described, there is no evidence known to me that any core dialect lacks the rule (although Pontic and Cappadocian might); what we do find is that standard pronunciations have been reintroduced at different rates. In some idiolects of standard Greek, for instance, [aδerfós] might be used only in the familiar vocative expression [aδerfé]; [írθa], on the other hand, is normal. /elpíδa/ 'hope' and /elpízo/ 'I hope'

[1] For numerous examples see Pernot (1907: 300 ff.).

usually have [l] but the dialectal forms with initial [o] also have [r]: [orpíδa], [orpízo] (as in [δéssórpiza] 'I didn't expect it of you'). It is because of this variation that we justify the postulation of underlying forms with /l/ in all such cases.

Delateralization must be ordered before high vowel loss, for secondary lateral + consonant clusters in northern dialects are unaffected: /θélis/ 'you want' > [θél'is] > [θél's] (never *[θérs]); /élusa/ 'I washed' > [élsa]. In parts of Rhodes /ly/ goes to [lǰ] (e.g. /eléa/ 'olive' > [elǰá]), so that at least there we must place delateralization before the consonantality rule which leads from [elyá] to [elγ'á]. An indication of the early position of delateralization is also provided by Zakinthian [aδrefós], which implies the sequence /aδelfós/ > (delateralization) > [aδerfós] > (metathesis) > [aδrefós].

It was mentioned in a previous chapter (see 3.5) that in all dialects a process is found which is directly opposed to delateralization: /r/ converts to [l] by 'dissimilatory lateralization' when a second /r/ occurs in the word. Thus περιστέρι 'dove', γρήγορα 'quickly' usually go to [pelistéri], [γlíγora]. The question therefore arises as to what happens when these rules pull in different directions. The items ἁλμυρός 'salty' and καρτερῶ 'I wait' would go to [almirós], [kalteró] if dissimilatory lateralization took precedence but in fact we find [armirós], [karteró]. Similarly the Spanish and Italian loans *alburo* and *saltare* are not prevented by the existence of dissimilation from appearing in Greek as [árburo] 'mast', [sarpári] 'it sets sail'. One way of putting this would be to say that both rules applied, and in the following order:

(11)	almirós	karteró
Dissimilatory lateralization		kalteró
Delateralization	**armirós**	**karteró**

4.7 Triadic clusters

The rules of voice assimilation, manner dissimilation, postnasal voicing, nasal assimilation and degemination apply between consonant pairs whether these occur in a dyadic cluster or as part of a longer one. Thus the existence of these rules alone eliminates vast numbers of theoretically possible clusters from the phonetic output of modern Greek dialects. Furthermore, within morphemes only stops are permitted as the middle terms of three-term clusters (ἄρθρο 'article' and πορθμός 'strait' hardly classifying as dialectal). Now the rules of manner dissimilation and nasal assimilation allow a stop to be followed by a sonant or sibilant and to be preceded by a sonant or fricative, but only a few of the possibilities allowed by this restriction are realized. Within inherited words we find the following morpheme-internal clusters:

(1) /s/+stop+sonant. The sequences found are illustrated by σκληρός [sklirós] 'cruel', σκνίπα [sknípa] 'midge', ἄσπρος [áspros] 'white', σπλάχνα [spláxna] 'bowels', ἀστραπή [astrapí] 'lightening', σκρόφα [skrófa] 'sow'.

(2) Nasal+stop+liquid. We find nasals before all six stop+liquid clusters: ἀμπλέω [ambléo] 'I swim' (Cypriot), ἐμπρός 'forward' [embrós], ἄντρας [ándras] 'man', 'Αγγλία [aŋglía] 'England', φαγγρί [faŋgrí] 'sea-bream', ἐξαντλῶ [eksandló] 'I exhaust' (if indeed dialectal).

(3) /xtr/ occurs in various items such as [oxtrós] 'enemy' < ἐχθρός.

Across morpheme boundaries triadic clusters other than those which occur intramorphemically are possible, in which case they are acted on by the usual rules for dyadic sequences, as well as by three rules specific to triadic clusters. These are the rules of 'nasal deletion in clusters', 'geminate reduction in clusters' and 'cluster simplification'.

(1) *Nasal deletion in clusters.* We saw in our discussion of postnasal voicing (see 4.2) that a stop is voiced between a nasal and vowel or sonant. The rule does not therefore cover cases in which a nasal precedes a cluster of stop+obstruent. As the only obstruent permissible after a stop in terms of the rule of manner dissimilation is /s/, and as /Nts/ does not appear word-medially in inherited items, the question concerns the development of /Nps/ and /Nks/. These clusters arise when a morpheme-final /Np/ or /Nt/ precedes an initial /s/. Thus /peNp+ō/ 'I send' has the aorist /e+peNp+s+a/ and /sfiNk+ō/ 'I squeeze' forms the aorist /e+sfiNk+s+a/. We may also notice certain deverbal nouns such as /láNp+si/ 'flash' (cf. λάμπω 'shine') and /sfíNk+si+mo/ 'squeezing'. In such cases the nasal is found to drop, so that in all dialects we have [ps], [ks], typical pronunciations being [épepsa], [ésfiksa], [lápsi], [sfíksimo]. In dialects which permit double consonants it may be noted that nasals are deleted before geminate stops whenever such sequences arise at word boundaries; thus /ton+tteNpélin/ 'the lazy one' (acc.) goes to [tottembélin] in Cypriot. This suggests that the required prohibition is against nasals in the environment before voiceless stop:

Nasal deletion in clusters: Delete a nasal in the environment before voiceless stop.

If we accept the suggestion made at the end of 4.5 that the rule of postnasal voicing determines the voice state of stops, then again using a capital for an underlying stop unspecified for voice state, we may derive πέμπω 'I send', ἔπεψα 'I sent' as follows:

(12)	PéNPo	éPeNPsa
Postnasal voicing	péNbo	épeNpsa
Nasal assimilation	**pémbo**	épempsa
Nasal deletion in clusters		**épepsa**

When a cluster of [m] + [s] arises in a northern dialect as a result of high vowel loss, a buffer [p] is often inserted, so that, e.g., /pukámiso/ 'shirt' goes via [pkámsu] to [pkámpsu]. As this [mps] is no longer subject to nasal deletion in clusters, this latter rule must be crucially ordered before the rule of consonantal epenthesis in such a dialect.

It may be added that across word boundaries the rule of nasal deletion in clusters does not apply in all dialects. When a nasal-final morpheme occurs in close construction before one with initial /ps/, /ks/ or /ts/ one of three possibilities may be realized:

(i) Nasal deletion in clusters applies. This is characteristic of the dialects of Chios, Rhodes and Cyprus at least in the south east and is in all likelihood general there; it also appears to be normal in northern dialects including those of Lesbos and Samos. Thus for τὸν ψεύτη 'the liar', τὸν ξένο 'the foreigner', τὴν τσιμπᾶ 'he pinches her' we find in Cyprus [topséfti], [tokséno], [titsimbá].

(ii) Both stop and sibilant undergo postnasal voicing. This is characteristic of Peloponnesian–Ionian, Old Athenian and Cretan. Thus in some Peloponnesian dialects we shall get [tombzéfti], [toŋgzéno], [tind^{z}imbáyi]. Where nasal assimilation II operates, as in many Peloponnesian dialects, in Cretan and in Old Athenian, we find [tobzéfti], [togzéno], [tid^{z}ibáyi].

(iii) Neither nasal deletion nor postnasal voicing occurs. Pronunciations such as [tompséfti], [toŋkséno], [tint^{s}imbáyi] may be possible in all dialects, especially in slow, deliberate speech, and are usual in constructions less intimate than those of article + noun (e.g. ἂν ξέρω 'if I know' [aŋkséro]).

In the case of pronunciations of the second type, it is clear that nasal + stop + /s/ clusters develop differently word-medially and at word boundary. Medially /mps/ and /nks/ will go to [ps], [ks] and when split between words to [(m)bz], [(ŋ)gz].

It may be added that the affricates [t̂ˢ] or [č] which arises from the action of softening on palatalized /k/ in many dialects always behave like stops in postnasal environments, not like clusters. Thus while in, say, Cypriot, /δén + tsimpá/ appears as [étsimbá], /δén + kentá/ 'it does not prick' is [enǰendá]. Similarly in Chios we find that /ton + tsíro/ 'the dried mackerel' goes to [totsíro], while /ton + keró/ 'the time' is [tond͡ᶻeró] (on [ts] versus [t̂ˢ] see 5.1).

(2) *Geminate reduction in clusters.* In most dialects outside the south east a rule of degemination acts to remove the distinction between long and short consonants. Furthermore dialects of the south-eastern type which permit initial and intervocalic geminates do not allow them to cluster with other consonants. Thus ἄνθρωπος 'man' develops in the dialects of Rhodes and Cyprus to [áθθropos] by nasal assimilation and then by 'geminate reduction in clusters' to [áθropos], whence it may go by various local processes to [áδropos], [áxropos] or [áγropos]. Consider also in these dialects the derivational history implied by νὰ σφιγχθῇ 'let it be squeezed' and νὰ πεμφθῇ 'let him be sent'. We may set up as the stems of these verbs /sfiNK/ and /PeNP/ on the basis of the present forms such as [sfíŋgo] and [pémbo]. Starting from a convenient point, and using capitals for stops of unspecified voice state, we may proceed as follows:

(13)	nasfiNKθí	naPeNPθí
Manner dissimilation	nasfiNXtí	naPeNFtí
Postnasal voicing		napeNFtí
Nasal assimilation	nasfiXXtí	napeFFtí
Geminate reduction	nasfiXtí	napeFtí
Voice assimilation	**nasfixtí**	**napeftí**

The rule of geminate reduction in clusters is also required in order to account for various correlations between dialectal forms and their learned cognates. The item συγγνώμη in the sense 'I'm sorry!', for instance, may be pronounced [siŋγnómi] and is normally so pronounced in the meaning 'pardon'; [siγnómi], the usual pronunciation for the first sense, requires an assumption of the derivation [nγn] > [γγn] > [γn] and in dialects which lack the normal degemination rule this can be achieved only by the present rule. We may note also the normal dialectal form of Πέμπτη 'Thursday', which develops /PéNPTi/ > [PéNFTi] > [péNFti] > [péFFti] > [péFti] > [péfti], according to the same rule sequence as we posited for [napeftí].

There is evidence that in some of the less well-known south-eastern dialects geminates do not reduce adjacent to a consonant. Thus ἄνθρωπος is reported to be pronounced [áθθropos] in various islands and where [θθ] goes to [tt] we get [áttropos] (see on derivation (1) above).[1]

Dialects which have geminate reduction in clusters do not always apply it across word boundaries. Thus τὸν δρόμο 'the road' (acc.) may appear as [toδδrómon] or [toδrómon] in Cyprus.

(3) *Cluster simplification.* The most general of the rules which apply to triadic clusters is one which deletes the middle term of such a sequence:

> **Cluster simplification:** Delete the middle term of a sequence of three consonants unless it is either (*a*) a sibilant or (*b*) a stop followed by sibilant or liquid or (*c*) any consonant followed by a palatal fricative.

This formulation is to be regarded as at most tentative; not only does the set of phonetic triadic clusters actually found permit of more than one extrapolation, but it is quite possible that the rule operates in different versions in different dialects. The rule as phrased suggests that a sufficient condition for deletion is that the second and third terms do not form permissible dyadic clusters; thus stop + stop sequences are excluded, as are those with stop and non-sibilant fricative. In northern dialects, for instance, which provide most of the evidence for the rule, κουράστηκα 'I was tired' goes by high vowel loss to [kurástka] and this by cluster simplification to [kuráska]. The plural form κλέφτηδες 'thieves' reduces via [kléftδis] to [kléfδis] and this may undergo voice assimilation to [klévδis]. The rule also disallows the sequence stop + nasal, though, in spite of the fact that this cluster-type is found within morphemes in a few words such as καπνός 'smoke', πνοή 'breath'. However, it may be the case that cluster simplification acts more readily on such stop + nasal sequences as do not occur in primary clusters; thus /aftunú/ 'of him' usually goes to [afnú] in the north while /sxiní/ 'rope' often develops /sxiní/ > [sx'iní] > [sk'iní] > [šk'iní] > [šk'ní] (although [šní] is also found). This may be connected with the fact that [kn] but not [tn] is found as reflex of underlying clusters. A similar suggestion may be made in respect to stop + liquid clusters. δικράνι 'fork' develops in the north /δikráni/ > [δikrán'i] > [δkrán'] > [θkrán'], and the [k]

[1] The Ἱστορικὸν Λεξικόν gives ἄθ-θρωπος for Karpathos, Kos, Kastellorizo and Nisiros, ἄτθρωπος for Kalimnos and Kos.

may be held to remain because the second and third terms of [θkr] (but not, it may be noted, the first and second) cluster freely elsewhere. The item δάχτυλο 'finger', however, often goes to [δáxlu], perhaps because [tl] is absent from dialectal forms (but not certain learned items such as ἐξαντλῶ 'I exhaust'). Cluster simplification as it is found to operate in the north is further discussed in 7.4.

In southern dialects the action of cluster simplification is virtually confined to certain /CCy/ clusters in which the yod is converted to [x′] or [γ′] and then [k′], [g′]. Thus in south-eastern dialects δόντια 'teeth' may go to [δónδγ′a] and this by manner dissimilation to [δónδg′a], which now meets the input conditions for simplification, and goes to [δóng′a]. Similarly ἀδέλφια 'brothers and sisters' goes often to [aérfx′a], then to [aérfk′a] > [aérk′a] (see 6.5).

Evidence for the action of cluster simplification on primary sequences is negligible. The verb ζεύγω 'I yoke', has an aorist ἔζεψα, and if we assume as the underlying stem of this verb /zevγ/, this can be derived as follows:

(14)	ézevγsa
Cluster simplification	ézevsa
Voice assimilation	ézefsa
Manner dissimilation	**ézepsa**

However, this alternation is isolated, and there is perhaps no evidence that the comparable cluster [fks] reduces to [fs]. On the contrary, dialectal [aksáno] 'I increase' is related to 'learned' [afksáno] by deletion of the initial segment of its cluster. It is true that in many dialects [évγo] occurs in verbs which have [évo] elsewhere and that these accordingly show regular alternation between [vγ] and [ps], but here it is possible to treat the present stem as having underlying /eu/ rather than /evγ/ (see 2.11), so that the need for cluster simplification does not arise.

The rule also plays a marginal role in accounting for pronunciations such as [pémti] for Πέμπτη 'Thursday' (in careful pronunciation [pémpti] and dialectally [péfti]); compare also Cypriot [kumg′á] 'buttons', which derives by simplification and postnasal voicing from [kumpk′á] (underlying form /kumpía/).

Our rule leaves a sibilant unaffected and the evidence for this restriction lies in northern forms such as [msták′] for /mustáki/ 'moustache', [piršnós] for /persinós/ 'last year's', [kšlén′us] 'wooden' for /ksilénios/. There is, however, slight evidence that simplification may have affected sibilants historically (cf. modern [pséftis] 'liar' < ψεύστης), and /s/ is lost regularly in at least Peloponnesian dialects when [pst] and [kst] arise as a result of the syncopation of aorist plural imperative forms in -ετε. While many dialects have κοιτάξ(ε)τε 'look', γράψ(ε)τε 'write', Peloponnesian and many Athenian speakers have [k'itáxte], [γráfte]:

(15)	kitáksete	γrápsete
Imperative syncopation	kitákste	γrápste
Palatalization	k'itákste	
Cluster simplification	k'itákte	γrápte
Manner dissimilation	**k'itáxte**	**γráfte**

In this last derivation we may note that cluster simplification precedes manner dissimilation in so far as the former creates a potential input for the latter, and the same ordering was required in derivation (14) above for [ézepsa]. In the case of south-eastern [δón'g'a] for δόντια 'teeth', however, the ordering appears to be reversed. To obtain the correct output from intermediate [δónδγ'a] we must first produce [δónδg'a] by manner dissimilation, for cluster simplification is not normally triggered when the last term is [x'] or [γ'] (e.g. many dialects have [karδγ'á] 'heart'). But even if we found that a certain dialect which converted [kst] to [xt] also converted [nδγ'] to [ng'] this would merely reflect the fact that historically the rules overlapped. If we assume a stage at which both rules are in operation any [kst] cluster will meet the input conditions of a cluster simplification rule formulated to include in its scope sibilants flanked by stops, but not those of manner dissimilation; the output [kt] will then be acted on by manner dissimilation. [nδγ'], on the other hand, will meet only the conditions for manner dissimilation, and the output of this, [nδg'], will then be subject to simplification.

4.8 Learned and foreign clusters

We have outlined in this chapter the development of underlying clusters in inherited words. Although this book is not much concerned with katharevusa or with foreign elements in Greek, a few words may be in order regarding dialectal differences in the treatment of learned and foreign clusters. The matter can best be approached by considering the various rules in the order in which they have been presented.

Dialects do not appear to distinguish inherited words from learned and foreign ones in their application of degemination. That is, south-eastern dialects pronounce [pénna] 'pen', [kólla] 'glue', [pullín] 'bird', [pítta] 'pie', [káppellos] 'hat' (or [kappéllon]) and similarly other words of Italian or Latin origin, retaining the original geminate, while the dialects which apply degemination to inherited words apply it to these as well: [péna], [kóla], [pulí], [píta], [kapélo]. Similarly for learned words drawn from the written language: speakers of geminating dialects will pronounce as long consonants which are written double. Thus ἐκκεντρικός 'eccentric', διάγραμμα 'diagram', συμμορία 'conspiracy' are pronounced [ek'k'endrikós], [δiáγramma], [simmoría] in the south east, but by other speakers with simple consonants, although the katharevusa of certain university professors is said occasionally to distinguish simple from double spellings. Because αυ and ευ are pronounced with [v] or [f] depending on whether the following segment is voiced or not, geminating dialects will contrast εὔφορος 'fertile' with ἔφορος 'supervisor' as [éfforos] versus [éforos], while elsewhere they are homophonous; similarly while Εὔβοια 'Euboea' normally rhymes with εὐσέβεια 'reverence' south-eastern speakers will have [évvia] but [efsévia].

Clusters of nasal + stop are, as we saw in 4.2, subject to the rules of postnasal voicing, nasal assimilation in one of its two forms, and, in most dialects outside the south east, degemination. Leaving aside the dialects of Simi and Kalimnos, in which nasal + stop clusters go intervocalically to [bb], [dd], [gg], we may say that /mp/, /nt/, /nk/ will be represented everywhere after a word boundary (#) as [b], [d], [g] and intervocalically as either [mb], [nd], [ŋg] (where nasal assimilation I operates) or as [b], [d], [g] (where the second type is in force). Thus, within words, while in all dialects voiced and voiceless stops will contrast initially, no dialect can have [mp], [nt] or [ŋk] and none can have both [mb], [nd], [ŋg] on the one hand and [b], [d], [g] on the other. Now in the languages from which modern Greek has borrowed most heavily, Italian and Turkish, a three-way contrast of this nature is possible; a speaker who reproduces the original clusters of Italian [lámpa], [ombrélla] and [kabína], while pronouncing inherited κουμπί [kumbí], will accordingly have a greater range of phonological oppositions in his speech than is required in an analysis limited to inherited items. From the point of view of his phonological rule system he will be excluding the item [lámpa] from the action of postnasal voicing and in the case of [kabína] the simplest and most natural interpretation would be to posit the occurrence of underlying voiced stops in the non-Greek portion of his lexicon, directly realized as [b, d, g].

Now while precisely this system of contrasts is ascribed to standard Athenian in most grammars of demotic, the situation even for native-born Athenians is far from clearcut, and the practice of an individual speaker will often depend on his knowledge of the donor language. One source of confusion is, of course, the inability of conventional Greek spelling to distinguish, say, [mb], [b] and [mp] – they are spelt alike as μπ. Mistakes are frequent; one recent writer castigates, for instance, pronunciations such as [yuŋgozlavía] (for [yugo]-) and [eksadrík] for [eksantrík] (Makrymichalos 1961) and proposals for spelling reform have been mooted.[1] In general one has the impression that the literature over-emphasizes the existence of contrasts even for standard speech. The last-mentioned author asserts, for example, that καμπάνα 'bell' differs from the similarly spelt borrowing meaning 'bathing cabin' as [kambána] versus [kabána], but not a single one of the dozens of Athenians I have questioned on the subject is aware of it; similarly λάμπα is regularly reported to be [lámpa], but only in the Ionian Isles have I found this. There do, however, appear to be various items frequently pronounced in Athens with non-Greek nasal + voiceless stop: [antíka], [sampán'a], [γánti] 'glove' may be so pronounced. With regard to foreign voiced stops Athenian speakers seem always to have [b], [d], [g] in fairly common items. [babás] 'dad' (< Tk. *baba*?) is always so pronounced, as is [adío] 'goodbye', [kabína] 'cabin', but it must be remembered that many Athenian speakers have nasal assimilation II in any case, and will have [b], [d], [g] for inherited /mp, nt, nk/.

In the dialects the treatment of foreign borrowings with sequences such as [b], [mp], [mb] seems to depend partly on the phonological rules operating for inherited words and partly on familiarity with the donor language. It is not possible on the data available to me to offer more than a brief characterization of a few typical situations.

The only important dialect area where a distinction is made with any degree of regularity between foreign nasal + voiced stop and nasal + voiceless stop in intervocalic position appears to be the Ionian Isles. There inherited /mp, nt, nk/ go to [b, d, g] intervocalically, as well as initially, but Italian loans may retain their original nasal + voiceless stop. Thus we may find [kantáδa] 'song', [kónte] 'count', [lámpa] 'lamp', [veraménte] 'truly', [ménta] 'mint', [γánti] 'glove' in violation of the

[1] One such proposal (Makrymichalos 1961) would spell voiced stops ββ, δδ, γγ, but, as is pointed out by Phoris (1961), this would entail alternate spellings for all stop-initial words (ἡ πόλις, τὴν ββόλι) and speakers show fluctuation in their application of postnasal voicing.

locally operative rules of postnasal voicing and nasal assimilation, but [kadáδa], [lába], [γádi] appear to be at least possible for some speakers. The original opposition between nasal + voiced stop and voiced stop is lost, however: [kumadáro] 'I command' and [agazáro] 'I engage' are so pronounced rather than with their original [nd], [ng].

In the Peloponnese many speakers use [mb], [nd], [ŋg] not only for foreign nasal + voiced or voiceless stop sequences, but for [b, d, g]. Thus for Turkish *soba*, Italian *roba* we find [sómba] 'stove', [rómba] 'dressing-gown', and those Peloponnesian speakers who have [b] for inherited /mp/ will have this for foreign [mp], [mb] and [b] alike.

While Peloponnesian speakers maintain the complementarity between voiced and voiceless stops by prefixing a nasal to foreign voiced stops, Cypriot speakers achieve the same result by devoicing them: [sópa], [rópa]. In Cypriot foreign voiceless stops are regularly identified with Greek geminates and voiced ones with Greek simple voiceless stops. Thus Turkish *kel*, *tel* become [k'k'élis] 'bald', [ttéli] 'wire', while 'gabardine' appears as [kapartína], 'cabin' as [kapína]; standard [babás] 'dad' and [papás] 'priest' are both [papás]. Elsewhere in the south east as well, it appears that voiced stops are allowed only after nasals, foreign intervocalic voiced stops being replaced by nasal + voiced stop, as in the Peloponnese, or by voiceless stop, as in Cyprus. Thus Rhodian has [parpéris] 'barber', [paklavás] 'baklava' (oriental sweetmeat) as in Cyprus, but [sómba], [kambína]. Still a third possible treatment of foreign voiced stops is to replace them by fricatives, perhaps particularly after [r]. Thus Rhodian has [kaparδína] 'gabardine', Karpathian [bárvas] 'uncle' (< Italian *barba*). It may also be noted that when the initial voiced stop of a foreign word is pronounced utterance-initially with [b, d, g], the south-eastern dialects introduce a nasal when the preceding word has a final vowel. Thus [bakkális] occurs in Rhodes for Turkish *bakal* 'grocer' but the articulated form is [ombakkális]. Similarly, in south-eastern dialects where 'tomato' is pronounced [domáta], as in Athens, rather than [tomáta], as in Cyprus, we find [indomáta] 'the tomato'.

Dialects such as Cretan, Lesbian and Thracian, which have post-vocalic [b, d, g] for inherited /mp, nt, nk/, take over foreign voiced stops in all positions without any need for adjustment. It is rather the assimilation of foreign nasal + stop sequences which poses a problem. In north-eastern Greece, Turkish nasal + voiceless stop sequences tend to be reproduced; thus I found [čánta] or [t̑ánta] 'bag' in Thrace, Thasos and Samothraki while elsewhere the rules for inherited /nt/ are followed; the pronunciation of nasals before both voiced and voiceless stops is said to be common in words of relatively recent origin in northern dialects of the Thracian type. Thus we find [kudá] 'near' for /kontá/, but [lámba], [γámba] 'leg' (< Italian *gamba*).[1] In Lesbos and Crete there appears to be a marked tendency nowadays to pronounce foreign [mp], [mb] and [b] alike as [b], and similarly for the other points of articulation, although publications on these dialects frequently refer to pronunciations such as [antíka], [pantalóni], [γánti].

In learned words of native origin we find the same underlying sequences as we do in vernacular forms, which means that /mp/, /nt/, /nk/ are possible initially and after vowels, while voiced stops are not found in any position. As postnasal voicing always affects learned and colloquial elements alike, a dialect with nasal assimilation I will represent the above sequences as [mb], [nd], [ŋg] in both cases, although a dialect with softening may have [nǰ] or [nd͡ᶻ] before front vowels and yod in colloquial, but not learned elements: ἔγκυος 'pregnant', being an elevated synonym for some such term as γκαστρωμένη, will be pronounced [én'g'ios], while ἀγγεῖα 'pots' is [anǰá] or [and͡ᶻá]. Apart from this no distinction can be made: /nt/ goes to [nd] in [endomoloyía] 'entomology' just as it does in [kondá] 'near'.

Dialects which have the second type of nasal assimilation, which assimilates nasals completely to following stops, may avoid this full assimilation in the case of learned items. Thus in Athens and Corfu, speakers with [ádras] 'man' for /ántras/, [péde] 'five' for /pénte/, [θabó] 'dull' for /θampó/ will yet have a clearly enunciated nasal in [éndomo], [éndimos], [embólemos] for /éntomo/ 'insect', /éntimos/ 'honourable', /enpólemos/ 'belligerent'. In Thrace also it is reported that while /mp, nt, nk/ normally go to [b, d, g], the nasal is articulated in numerals, Christian names and words subject to learned influence: [péndi] 'five', [saránda] 'forty' (but [pidára] 'coin of five lepta', [saradízo] 'be forty days, years old'), [andón's] 'Anthony'.

This avoidance of complete nasal assimilation in learned items is particularly noticeable in the case of nasal + fricative sequences. Thus /énxromos/ 'coloured' (of films), /énγrafa/ 'documents', /sinδromí/ 'subscription', /sinféron/ 'advantage' go to [éŋxromos], [éŋγrafa], [sinδromí], [siɱféron] (this last with labio-dental nasal) rather than *[éγγrafa] or *[éγrafa] etc.

[1] See Andriotis (1931: 172). At Saranda Ekklisies the participial ending -οντας was pronounced [ondas] through the influence of Constantinopolitan (Psaltis 1905: 47).

Just as Turkish [b] becomes [p] in the south east, and [p], [pp], we find in at least Cyprus that Turkish [ǰ] is equated with Greek [č] and Turkish [č] with [čč] (= [tš]). Thus we find [čámi] 'window pane', [ččái] 'tea'; elsewhere [tˢ], which occurs in a few words of native origin, is used for [č], and [dᶻ] for [ǰ]: [tˢái], [dᶻámi]. Turkish [nǰ] appears as [ndᶻ] in dialects which have [nd] for inherited /nt/, while those with [d] tend to pronounce [dᶻ]. Thus we find either [flindᶻáni] 'cup' or [flidᶻáni]. Similarly many speakers have [kazandᶻák′is] for the well-known Cretan author, while the Cretans themselves prefer [kazadᶻáčis]. In Chios both [ǰ] and [nǰ] become [zz].

One very common item which regularly resists nasal assimilation even in the speech of quite uneducated people is ἄνθρωπος 'man'. Although [áθropos] (Cypriot [áδropos]) occurs perhaps in all dialects it does not apparently oust 'learned' [ánθropos].

Manner dissimilation is characteristically blocked in learned items: ἔκπτωσις 'discount', σύμπτωσις 'coincidence', πτῆσις 'flight', εὐθύνη 'responsibility' are always [ékptosis], [símptosis], [ptísis], [efθíni]. In numerous cases a given morpheme will undergo manner dissimilation in a colloquial formation, but fail to do so in a more learned context. The word for 'seven' (underlying form /eptá/) will normally be heard as [eftá] while [eptaγonikós] 'heptagonal' will always have [pt]; similarly /pteró/ 'feather' is realized as [fteró], but /elikóptero/ 'helicopter' as [elikóptero].

Finally, learned items are not subject to cluster simplification. This is particularly noticeable in the large number of words compounded from εὐ-, προσ-, συν-, ἐκ-, ἐν-, and forms with fricative-initial clusters. Thus we find ἐκδρομή [egδromí] 'excursion', εὔθραυστος [éfθrafstos] 'fragile', ἔγχρωμος [éŋxromos] 'coloured'. The failure of nasal deletion in clusters may be observed in the items ἔμψυχος [émpsixos] 'animate' and κομψός [kompsós] 'smart'. It may be observed, however, that in [egδromí] voice assimilation has applied and that weak nasal assimilation (i.e. assimilation of point of articulation) is evident in the pronunciation [éŋxromos].

To summarize, we may say that the main phonological distinguishing features of learned words arise from their immunity to the normal rules of nasal assimilation, manner dissimilation, cluster simplification, and nasal deletion in clusters. Foreign items of relatively recent origin are more likely to betray themselves by their failure to undergo postnasal voicing, and in dialects with [mb] for inherited /mp/ in postvocalic position they may stand out in having [b, d, g] other than after nasals or initially. Very recent borrowings may display more extreme forms of aberrance; in [fílm] 'film', for instance, not only is there a violation of the restriction against the occurrence of any consonantal element at all in final position other than /n/ and /s/, but the cluster [lm] is impermissible even medially as it violates the rule of delateralization. However, the discussion has been limited to borrowings fully integrated into the grammatical system of Greek.

5 *Palatalization*

5.0 In this chapter we shall consider two closely related phenomena involving sequences of consonant and vowel, velar palatalization (5.1) and dental palatalization (5.2). The velar consonants /k, x, γ/ are fronted in all dialects to [k′, x′, γ′] when followed by a front vowel or yod, and in many insular dialects [k′] is then softened to [č], and [x′] may go to [š], so that καί 'and' and χέρι 'hand' are pronounced [če], [šéri], or, if 'depalatalization' follows, [t͡se], [séri]; there is even an important dialect, Cretan, which also softens [γ′], so that γέρος 'old man' becomes [žéros]. Dental palatalization affects /n, l, s, z/, and occasionally /t/, and is particularly important in the north, for while [n′, l′, š, ž] are elsewhere little more than positional variants, in northern dialects the loss of unstressed /i/ establishes phonemic contrasts of the type [róz] 'pink' versus [róž] 'corns' (ρόʒ, ρόʒοι). The final section deals mostly with the conversion of [sk′] to [šk′], [šš] or [ss] in various dialects, giving pronunciations such as [ššíllos] for σκύλος 'dog'.

5.1 Velar palatalization and softening

We may start by tabulating the reflexes of the items καιρός 'weather', χέρι 'hand' and γῆ 'land' in five typical dialects:

/kerós/	/xéri/	/γí/	
k′erós	x′éri	yí	(Peloponnese)
t͡serós	x′éri	yí	(Megara)
t͡serós	séri	yí	(N. Rhodes)
čerós	šéri	yí	(Cyprus)
čerós	šéri	ží	(Crete)

In order to account for these pronunciations of the velar obstruents, we require four separate but related rules; (*a*) velar palatalization (*b*) softening, (*c*) depalatalization and (*d*) consonantality.

(*a*) *Velar palatalization.* This has the effect of shifting forward the point of articulation of velar stops and fricatives before a front vowel or [y]:

Velar palatalization: A velar obstruent becomes palatal before a front non-consonantal segment.

The effect of this is to change /k/ to [k′], /x/ to [x′] and /γ/ to [γ′] before [i], [e] or [y]. Velar palatalization probably affects all core dialects, and while many speakers of a dialect such as Cypriot may resist the further conversion of [k′, x′] to [č, š] by 'softening', they will always have some fronting of the point of articulation. This has sometimes been denied. It is stated, for example by Pangalos,[1] against the authority of Chatzidakis (another Cretan) that in some Cretan dialects the word καιρός 'weather' is heard with the 'velar' pronunciation of καλός 'good', and a similar claim is sometimes made about the dialect of Elimbos in Karpathos. But my own observations at the last point indicate a normal fronted [k′] as in Athens and it is perhaps significant that 'velar' pronunciations are only reported for dialects where most speakers in the region have [č], suggesting that perhaps the idiosyncrasy lies in lack of stridency rather than of palatality. The pronunciation which /θ/ has before vowels, including front ones, in parts of Rhodes and Cyprus is sometimes transcribed as χ by Greek scholars but should, I believe, be [h] (with glottal rather than velar friction).[2]

Differences between dialects arise not in the application of palatalization itself, which is universal, but in the further development of the fronted variants which it creates. We shall call the conversion of [k′, x′, γ′] to [č, š, ž] 'softening' and assume that [t͡s, s, z] may then arise from these latter by a process of 'depalatalization' (not an ideal term, as it suggests a reversal of the palatalization trend, whereas it represents in a sense its end-point).

(*b*) *Softening*. It will be seen from the list of reflexes presented above for καιρός, χέρι, γῆ that the process of 'softening' may affect only [k′], converting it to [č] (this then going in Megara to [t͡s]), it may affect both [k′] and [x′] (as in Rhodes and Cyprus), or it may affect all three of [k′], [x′] and [γ′], converting them to [č], [š], [ž], as in Crete. There are no dialects in which [x′] is softened but not [k′], or which have [ž] for [γ′] without both [k′] and [x′] acquiring stridency.

The conversion of [γ′] to [y] in most dialects outside Crete is discussed

[1] See Pangalos (1955: 149).

[2] Pangalos (1955: 184) reports that /áxna/ 'breath' appears as [áxina] 'with velar [x]' in Crete; there is reason, though, to believe that he again means 'unsoftened'. For [x] instead of [h] see below in this section.

below and represents a facet of the process we call 'consonantality'. In the meantime we may note that [ž] arises in Cretan not only from underlying /γ/ as in γῆ but from an /i/ or /e/ which goes to [y] in prevocalic position by glide formation. Thus the Cretan forms of ἰατρός 'doctor', ἑορτή 'holiday', κλουβιά 'cages' and of γῆ could be derived as follows:

(1)	iatrós	eortí	kluvía	γí
Height dissimilation		iortí		
Glide formation	yatrós	yortí	kluvyá	
Palatalization				γ′i
Consonantality			kluvγ′á	yí
Softening	**žatrós**	**žortí**	**kluvžá**	**ží**

However, it is clear that the result would be precisely the same if we omitted to apply the consonantality rule, and that in either case the softening rule must be so formulated for Cretan as to convert [y] as well as [γ′] to [z]. In the dialect of Kalimnos softening affects only κλουβιά of the above items, which means that consonantality must necessarily apply there first to yield [yatrós], [yortí], [kluvγ′á], [yí] and that softening then acts in a version which affects [γ′] but not [y] (see 6.4).

The softening rule can now be formulated:

Softening I: A palatal stop is strident. (That is, [k′] > [č], [g′] > [ǰ].)
Softening II: A palatal stop or voiceless fricative is strident. (That is, in addition, [x′] > [š].)
Softening III: A palatal obstruent or glide is strident. (That is, in addition, [γ′] and [y] > [ž].)

(*c*) *Depalatalization.* This will convert [š] to [s], [ž] to [z], [č] to [t^s] and [ǰ] to [d^z]. It may be framed as follows:

Depalatalization: A strident obstruent is dental.

Depalatalization, as opposed to softening, exists in only one form. In addition to any effect it may have on stridents arising from /k, x, γ/, it may also operate on a [š] or [ž] from [sy] or [zy]. Compare, for example, the derivations of φύκια 'seaweed' and νησιά 'islands' in the dialect of Megara:

(2)	fíkia	nisía
Glide formation	fíkya	nisyá
Palatalization	fík'ya	nišyá
Postpalatal yod deletion	fík'a	nišá
Softening 1	fíča	
Depalatalization	**fít^sa**	**nisá**

In the dialects of northern Rhodes we may account for [t^serós], [séri] by assuming the following sequence:

(3)	kerós	xéri
Palatalization	k'erós	x'éri
Softening	čerós	šéri
Depalatalization	**t^serós**	**séri**

In the southern parts of the island depalatalization does not occur, so things do not develop beyond the [čerós], [šéri] stage and the same is true of Cypriot. It is also possible for a dialect to have both softening and depalatalization but to apply depalatalization first. Thus if softening and depalatalization were transposed in derivation (2) above we would get the following:

(4)	fík'a	nišá
Depalatalization		**nisá**
Softening	**fíča**	

This situation is found, for instance, in eastern Crete (see derivation (21) of 6.4).

(*d*) *Consonantality*. We have frequently had occasion to make use of this rule in order to convert [y] to [γ'] after a voiced consonant. Thus πόδια 'feet', καράβια 'boats' go first to [póδya], [karávya] by glide formation, and these then by consonantality to [póδγ'a], [karávγ'a]. The glide [y] in acquiring the audible fricativity of [γ'] has merely replaced the feature non-consonantal by consonantal. We have now noted that /γí/ goes first to [γ'í] and then [yí], so that we have in effect the converse of the process which changes [póδya] to [póδγ'a]. The net result of these two complementary processes is that after they have acted [y] and [γ'] are in non-contrastive distribution. [γ'] occurs only after voiced consonants and [y] elsewhere. A few Peloponnesian examples should suffice by way of illustration:

(i) [γ′] may arise from /γ/ by palatalization after a voiced consonant. Thus πύργοι 'towers' is derived /pírγi/ > [pírγ′i]; similarly φεύγει 'he leaves' develops /févγi/ > [févγ′i].

(ii) [γ′] may arise from /i/ (or [i] < /e/) by glide formation and consonantality after a voiced consonant. Thus χωριά 'villages', δόντια 'teeth' go from their respective intermediate forms [xoría], [δóndia] to [xoryá], [δóndya], then [xorγ′á], [δóndγ′a].

(iii) [y] may arise word-initially or intervocalically from /i/ (or [i] < /e/) by glide formation. Thus ἰατρός 'doctor', τσάϊα 'teas' develop by glide formation from /iatrós/, /tsáia/ to [yatrós], [tsáya].

(iv) [y] may arise from /γ/ by palatalization initially or intervocalically. Thus γέροι 'old men', μάγοι 'magicians' develop from /γéri/, /máγi/ to [yéri], [máyi].

(v) [y] may arise from /i/ (or [i] < /e/) by glide formation after a vowel when a consonant or word boundary follows. Thus from γάϊδαρος 'donkey' we get [γáyδaros] and from τσάϊ 'tea', [tsáy].

(vi) The sequences /γi/ and /γe/ before vowels will yield [y] if a vowel or word boundary precedes, and [γ′] after a voiced consonant. Thus τραγιά 'goats' develops /traγía/ > (glide formation) > [traγyá] > (palatalization) > [traγ′yá] > (postpalatal yod deletion) > [traγ′á] > (consonantality) > [trayá]; Γεῶργος 'George' undergoes height dissimilation to [γiórγos] and then develops in parallel fashion to [yórγos]. [γ′] arises from /γi/ in the genitive singulars and the plurals of πυργί 'small tower' and βεργί 'small stick'; thus the plural πυργιά derives /pirγía/ > [pirγyá] > [pirγ′yá] > [pirγ′á].

To complete the picture, we must add that in position after a voiceless consonant [y] goes to [x′]; in that position phonetic [x′] can arise either in this way, as in [mátx′a] 'eyes' from [mátya], or originate by palatalization of /x/, as in [efx′í] 'blessing' from /efxí/. In other positions it reflects only /x/.

The rule we require will have to state that [y] goes to [γ′] after a voiced consonant and to [x′] after a voiceless one; also that [γ′] goes to [y] initially and intervocalically. This can be accomplished by the following formulation:

Consonantality: A non-vocalic, non-strident, voiced, palatal, continuous segment agrees in consonantality and voice with any preceding consonantal segment; if no consonant precedes, it is nonconsonantal.

While, as we have suggested, palatalization as such occurs in all dialects, softening may occur in any one of three versions or may not occur at all, and if it does occur, its output may or may not be affected by depalatalization. This allows for seven combinations, which are listed, with their outputs for [k'], [x'], [γ'], in Table 5.

TABLE 5. *The reflexes of palatalized velars*

	Softening	Depalatalization	Output	Distribution
1	None	—	k' x' γ'	Peloponnesian–Ionian, northern, Elimbos
2	Type 1	No	č x' γ'	Ayassos, Plumari, Mesochori (Karpathos)
3	Type 1	Yes	tᷤ x' γ'	Old Athenian, Arachova, Lesbos, Cyclades, Chios
4	Type 2	No	č š γ'	Cyprus, Kos, Simi, S. Rhodes
5	Type 2	Yes	tᷤ s γ'	N. Rhodes, Kalimnos
6	Type 3	No	č š ž	Crete, Mani (with Cargese)
7	Type 3	Yes	tᷤ s z	?

As an illustration of the effects of softening and depalatalization, we may take the sentence ἐκεῖ ἔχει γῆ 'there is land there'. In Peloponnesian–Ionian, and in standard Athenian, this is unaffected by any form of softening and we accordingly have [ek'í éx'i yí] (with the conversion of [γ'] to [y] by consonantality). In the north with the known exceptions of Lesbos and the region of Arachova we find the same situation: [ik'í éx' yí]. Dialects which soften only [k'] tend then to depalatalize the [č] to [tᷤ], but in Ayassos and Plumari in southern Lesbos one finds [ičí éx' yí] and Dawkins (1904) reports the set [č, x', y] for a village in Karpathos. Much more commonly we get [etᷤí éx'i yí]. This pronunciation is found in Megara and Kimi of present-day Old Athenian dialects and used to be characteristic of the variety spoken in Aegina. In the Cyclades it is reported for at least Mikonos, Kithnos and Naxos. Most parts of Lesbos also have it, and it occurs near Delphi at Arachova.[1] [ečí eši yí], with softening of both [k'] and [x'] is found in the south east, as is its depalatalized version [etᷤí ési yí]. Finally Cretan and Maniot soften [γ'] as well, giving [ečí éši ží]. As far as is known, the final possibility, [etᷤí ési zí],

[1] It also occurred at Dimitsana and elsewhere in Arcadia according to Chatzidakis (1916), although I could find no evidence for it at Dimitsana in 1969.

does not occur, although the [ž] which may arise from [y] after voiced consonants in the south east can convert to [z] (as in Kalimnos, see 6.4).

We saw above that palatalization and consonantality convert /γ/ to [y], and that this often entails a merger at the phonetic level of /γ/ with /i/ or /e/. It might be thought at first sight, however, that softening and depalatalization should merely affect the pattern of positional variation within dialects; in a dialect with [š] for [x′], for instance, [š] would occur only before front vowels and [y], [x] only elsewhere, there being no need to set up a special phoneme /š/ in contrast with /x/. Now it is true that much regular alternation of this type arises. Thus the present tense singular of ἔχω 'I have' in a dialect of this type would run [éxo], [éšis], [éši], and of πλέκω 'I knit', [pléko], [pléčis], [pléči]. In addition, however, softening and depalatalization invariably have the effect of destroying at least some underlying contrasts; a [š] from [x′], for instance, will merge with the reflex of primary /s/ if depalatalized, and a depalatalized [č] will be in many dialects indistinguishable from the reflex of /ts/. Let us first consider the effects of softening /k/ to [č].

In a dialect of the type found in Cyprus a palatal /k/ goes to [č] and a palatal /kk/ to what may be written [čč], but in effect just differs from the simple affricate [č] in that the release of its stop element is somewhat delayed; a rough parallel to the [čč]:[č] distinction is provided by English 'white shoes' versus 'why choose?' Now in Cyprus [sy] goes to [š] (e.g. νησιά 'islands' > [nišá]), so that [tsy] is pronounced [tš] (e.g. παπούτσια 'shoes' > [papútša]). This [tš] from [tsy] is indistinguishable from the [čč] which arises by palatalization and softening from /kk/: /papútsia/ 'shoes' and /lákki/ 'wells' may be transcribed [papútša], [látši]. In Cypriot (and probably the other dialects with [č, š, γ′]) intermediate [k′, k′k′, tsy, ts] are realized [č, tš, tš, ts]. It may be noted that while [k′k′] and [tsy] merge, [č] remains distinct from them on the one hand (as being shorter) and from [ts] < /ts/ on the other as being both palatal and shorter. Thus /kilá/ 'it flows' and /tsillá/ 'he presses' are pronounced [čilá], [tsillá]. It may also be noted that /kukkí/ 'bean' and /kutsí/ 'lame' (fem. sing.) are distinguished as [kutší] versus [kutsí]. In Rhodes we again find that both [k′] and [x′] are softened, but in the north of the island depalatalization follows: [k′, k′k′, tsy, ts] there become [t^{s}, ts, tsk′, ts], and in Kalimnos and parts of Chios, where [sy] goes to [š], and then by depalatalization to [s], we find [t^{s}, ts, ts, ts]. The difference between [t^{s}] and [ts] is parallel to that between [č] and [tš] in Cyprus; thus in Rhodes we find [peát^{s}i] 'child' from /peδáki/ but [látsi] from

/lákki/ and [papútsi] 'shoe' from /papútsi/. In Kalimnos and those parts of Chios which convert [sy] to [s] the plural [papútsa] will have the same sound as [látsi] and [papútsi]. The dialects mentioned thus far have belonged to the south-eastern group, but when we move away from the area we find that the existence of the degemination rule reduces still further the system of contrasts. In Crete both [k′] and [k′k′] go to [č] ([peδáči], [láči]), and because [sy] goes to [s] in eastern Crete (to [sx′] in the west) we find that the reflexes of [ts] and [tsy] merge. While it is natural enough that [k′] and [k′k′] should lead to identical outputs in a dialect which does not in general distinguish long and short consonants, what is a little more surprising is that degemination apparently collapses any distinction between [ʦ] and [ts], which means that in a dialect with softening and depalatalization of [k′], replacement of [sy] by [s] and degemination, [k′, k′k′, tsy, ts] all lead to the same result, [ʦ]. Just as we normally assume that degemination neutralizes oppositions of long and short consonants in favour of the shorter term (asserting, for instance that /ll/ and /l/ both go to [l]), so we must apparently accept that another of its effects is to convert /ts/ to [ʦ]. To make this clear, let us consider the derivation in, say, Megarian of ἐκεῖ 'there', κουκκί 'bean', κουτσή 'lame' and κορίτσια 'girls':

(5)	ekí	kukkí	kutsí	korítsia
Glide formation				korítsya
Palatalization	ek′í	kuk′k′í		korítšya
Postpalatal yod deletion				korítša
Softening I	ečí	kutší		
Degemination		kučí	**kuʦí**	koríča
Depalatalization	**eʦí**	**kuʦí**		**koríʦa**

This situation, in which the reflexes of palatalized /k/ and of /ts/ come to coincide as [ʦ], is found, as we noted earlier, quite widely. It so happens, as we saw, that practically all dialects which apply softening I also apply depalatalization to its output. In Cretan, however, depalatalization does not apply to the output of the softening III rule which operates there (although, as we saw, in the east it acts on [š] from [sy]). Thus in Crete we find for the above items [ečí], [kučí], [kuʦí], [koríʦa] ([koríʦx′a] in the west).

One important isogloss in modern Greek is accordingly that which divides dialects which distinguish the reflexes of palatalized /k/ from those of /ts/ and those which do not do so. In Cretan, where [č] is not subsequently depalatalized, [čilá] from /kilá/ will remain distinct from [t̑ilá] from /tsillá/, and [činá] 'it moves' from /kiná/ is quite distinct from [t̑iná] 'it kicks'.[1] In Rhodes, although depalatalization applies, the absence of degemination still permits an opposition in terms of length: [t̑ilá]: [tsillá]. Only in Old Athenian and the Cyclades, parts of Lesbos, and Arachova do we find /k/: /ts/ neutralization before front vowels and yod. Although it is often used rather loosely, it is common practice to limit the term τσιτακισμός to these latter dialects.

While /k/ may merge after softening with the reflexes of /ts/, /x/ may develop in dialects which have the second or third type of softening in such a way as to merge with the reflexes of /s/. Merger may arise in two different ways:

(*a*) If /x/ undergoes palatalization and softening to [š], and /s/ is palatalized to [š], then a merger will result. In certain of the dialects which have [š] for /x/ in palatalizing environments, /s/ goes to [š] before [y] (not, as elsewhere, before [i] as well). This happens in Cypriot, as may be illustrated by deriving νησιά 'islands' and νύχια 'fingernails':

(6)	nisía	níxia
Glide formation	nisyá	níxya
Palatalization	nišyá	níx′ya
Postpalatal yod deletion	**nišá**	níx′a
Softening		**níša**

Similarly in Cypriot palatalized /xx/ and the sequence /ssi/ before vowel will both go to [šš]. Thus /víxxi/ 'he coughs' and /melíssia/ 'swarms of bees' go to [víšši], [melíšša]. Elsewhere in the south east, where /s/ is palatalized to [š] before [y], depalatalization subsequently acts, so that, for instance, ἴσιος 'straight' and ἴσως 'perhaps' both go to [ísos]. If this depalatalization precedes softening (see derivation (4) above), as in eastern Crete and Simi, while νησιά goes to [nisá], νύχια will yield [níša].

(*b*) If depalatalization follows softening then palatalized /x/ will go to [s] and merge with the outcome of /s/. Thus in Rhodes and Kalimnos ὄχι 'no' and ὅσοι 'as many as' are homophonous:

(7)	óxi	**ósi**
Palatalization	óx′i	
Softening	óši	
Depalatalization	**ósi**	

[1] The minimal pair [t̑iná]: [činá] is given by Pangalos (1955: 228).

In Rhodes /s/ does not palatalize before [y], and [sy] goes to [sk′], while in Kalimnos it goes to [ss]. A dialect which softened [x′] to [s], palatalized /s/ to [š] and then applied depalatalization, would have [s] for /x/ before front vowels, and for /s/ and /si/ before any vowel, but I do not know whether this possibility is realized anywhere.

As is the case with many other purely local rules, softening is subject to pressure from standardizing influence, and when it results in loss of underlying contrasts maintained elsewhere, hypercorrection is not uncommon. Thus in dialects with [tˢ] for standard [k′] and [tˢ], [k′] is sometimes reported for correct [tˢ]. In Megara [papúk′a] is said to be heard for [papútsx′a] (dialectally [papútˢa]), and in Mikonos villagers visiting the main town may reportedly address a Mr Kutsis as [k′írie kúk′i].[1] One would imagine some such phenomenon to have underlain the replacement of [tˢ] by [k′] in Delphi reported by Pernot (1912) rather than the elaborate rule sequence proposed by that scholar; as noted above, [k′] goes to [tˢ] still in nearby Arachova. Apart from instances of hypercorrection, softening may be resisted specifically in words of learned connotation; in Cyprus, for example, [k′] remains unsoftened in many common words, including [k′írie] 'Mr' (dialectal doublet [číris] 'father'), and the name of the island itself is in my experience always pronounced [k′ípros], not [čípros]. In Rhodes and Crete, though, speakers appear to use [tˢ] or [č] in all contexts. Although Cretans are sometimes reported to have [k′] in certain words such as κινῖνο 'quinine' I have found that villagers have [č] not only in the case of the 'exceptions' often alleged but in foreign names such as 'Kennedy', [čénedi], a pronunciation which Cypriot speakers find quite strange. Again, softening is inhibited for [k′] (but not [x′]) in verb paradigms in Cyprus. Thus we hear νὰ δώκω 'let me give' [naóko] but νὰ δώκῃ 'let him give' [naók′i], while Cretans appear to pronounce the latter [naδóči].

With regard to the ordering of velar palatalization we may assume that it will apply in general whenever its input conditions arise, that is, whenever /k/, /x/ or /γ/ come into contact with a following front vowel or yod within the same word. There do not appear to be any clear cases where the wrong output would result from the operation wherever applicable of velar palatalization – with one possible exception. In parts of Cyprus and Rhodes both /x/ and /θ/ in intervocalic position (whether medial or word-initial) go to [h]; now this rule must apply after palatal-

[1] See Manesis (1963).

ization and softening, for ἔχει 'he has' always goes to [éši], although ἔχω 'I have' may be heard as [ého]. But in at least Cyprus a velar rather than glottal fricative is heard when a word-initial /x/ or /θ/ is preceded by /s/ or /n/. Thus /δén+θélo/ 'I don't want' becomes [éxxélo] (where [θθ] does not go to [tt]) and /δén+tus+θélo/ 'I don't want them' may sound like [éndusxélo] rather than [éndushélo]. In such a case the conversion of the new [x] to [š] is unknown, and it is likely that it does not even go to [x'].

There is an interesting proof that velar palatalization must have been active historically over a considerable period of time. In the dialect of Ayassos (Lesbos) and certain other islands in the area (at least Limnos and Imbros) the third person plural present ending -ουν appears as [in] after consonant-final verb stems. The shift from [u] to [i] is to be explained as a result of high vowel loss followed by epenthesis of [i], the typical buffer vowel of modern Greek. Now consider the derivations for ἔχει 'he has' and ἔχουν 'they have':

(8)	éxi	éxun
Velar palatalization	éx'i	
High vowel loss	**éx'**	éxn
Vowel epenthesis		éxin
Velar palatalization		**éx'in**

Velar palatalization must have preceded high vowel loss historically, as otherwise /éxi/ would have gone to *[éx]. High vowel loss and epenthesis clearly occurred in that order, the fact that some northern dialects have [éxn] suggesting indeed that there may have been quite a long gap between the creation of the cluster and its destruction by the insertion of [i]. Once the new front vowel appeared, however, [x] immediately went to [x'] by velar palatalization.

We shall find evidence in the next section that the palatalization of /n, l, s, z/ is much more restricted in time and place than velar palatalization.

With softening and depalatalization, considerations of rule order become more complex. Softening, for example, does not normally apply in south-eastern dialects to the [k'] which arises via [x'] from [γ] after a voiceless obstruent, as in [alíθk'a] 'truth', which means that in fact it no longer represented an active trend when the [k'] arose by manner dissimilation. These problems are discussed in 6.4.

5.2 Dental palatalization

We saw in the last section that fronted variants of the velar obstruents /k, x, γ/ occur phonetically or in the intermediate stages of derivations in all dialects. The dental consonants /s, z, n, l/, and occasionally /t/, but not /θ, δ/, are also liable to acquire a typical palatal colouring before front segments. However, variation between dialects is more noticeable here than in the case of velar palatalization. Palatalization is a gradient phenomenon and from the phonetic point of view it is important to know in the case of a particular dialect what degree of palatality is induced in each dental consonant by each of the segments [i], [e] and [y]. For one striking feature of dental palatalization is that its grade is likely to differ according to the nature of the conditioning segment. While details may differ quite considerably, it is in general true that the strongest palatalizing effect is exerted by [y], the next strongest by [i], and the weakest by [e].

Much careful work must be done before a detailed and accurate survey of dental palatalization in Greek will be possible. The most this section can hope to do is to discuss certain phonological implications of the phenomenon.

The palatalization of /l/ and /n/ provides a good illustration of the way in which phonetic facts and phonological interpretations interlock. The palatal segments [l′], [n′] are referred to in the published literature in three basic contexts:

(*a*) It is often stated that the nasal of a word such as ἐννιά 'nine' [en′á] is palatal and similarly the liquid of, for instance, ἐλιά 'olive' [el′á].

(*b*) The dialect of Zakinthos is said to palatalize /l/ and /n/ before /i/ so markedly that the sequences /li/ and /ni/ have the sound of the last syllables of Italian *egli*, *ogni*. Similar pronunciations are attributed to /l/ and /n/ before both /i/ and /e/ in Thessaly.

(*c*) Northern dialects are said to have [l′] and [n′] for /l/, /n/ when a following unstressed /i/ has been deleted by high vowel loss. Thus the palatality of [ván′] 'he puts' from /váni/, [fíl′] 'friends' from /fíli/ will usually be carefully indicated. Let us consider these cases in turn.

(*a*) It is easy to see that attention is drawn to the [n′] of [en′á] because in prevocalic position [n′] may contrast with plain [n] (compare [éna] 'one'). In the case of [en′á] and [el′á] the palatal sonants derive from [ny] and [ly], and as we shall have occasion to observe in more detail in

6.1, what we require here is a rule palatalizing /n/ and /l/ before [y], followed by the loss of [y]:[1]

(9)	enéa	eléa	**éna**
Height dissimilation	enía	elía	
Glide formation	enyá	elyá	
Dental palatalization	en′yá	el′yá	
Postpalatal yod deletion	**en′á**	**el′á**	

While this is straightforward, it must be remembered that some palatality is triggered by /i/ and /e/, particularly the former, and that the description of an individual dialect must make it clear whether [y] has a stronger effect than [i]. As far as can be established this is almost always the case in southern dialects. Consider, for example, what appear to be the normal Peloponnesian pronunciations of νιοί 'young men' and χωνί 'funnel':

(10)	néi	**xoní**
Height dissimilation	níi	
Glide formation	nyí	
Dental palatalization	n′yí	
Postpalatal yod deletion	**n′í**	

The [xoní] may be assigned by a late phonetic rule some degree of palatality, but it must be less than that given to [n′í] by the rule of dental palatalization. Otherwise the final syllable of [xoní] would be homophonous with the word νιοί, and as far as my observations allow me to judge, this does not appear to be the case. However, when speakers do distinguish the reflexes of /ní/ and /níi/ (or /nií/), it is not necessarily a matter of palatality, for in the second sequence there may be at least some trace of the [y]. Cypriot speakers, for instance, palatalize /n/ and /l/ but slightly, and, phonologically speaking, such palatalization as exists is better attributed to the effect of late phonetic rules. Thus while the velars and sibilants before [y] in that dialect palatalize with the loss of the glide, /n/ and /l/ before [y] do not palatalize sufficiently to trigger postpalatal yod deletion. Thus [nisyá] 'islands' goes to [nišyá], then [nišá], while [enyá] 'nine' retains its [ny] with only slight palatalization.

(*b*) The Zakinthian pronunciation of /ni/, /li/ as [n′i], [l′i] is in all probability to be explained in terms of the assumption that in that dialect [i] and [y] trigger the same grade of palatality, and that this

[1] The true underlying form of [en′á] is /ennéa/ (cf. [ennéa] in Karpathos).

palatality, unlike that characteristic of Cypriot, is adequate to induce the loss of a following [y]. Thus in Zakinthian the required rule of dental palatalization will specify the environment as 'before high front non-consonantal segment' (i.e. vowel or glide), while the more usual rule will incorporate in addition reference to the feature 'non-vocalic' (i.e. glide). In Zakinthian, then, /néi/ and /xoní/ would derive thus:

(11)	néi	xoní
Height dissimilation	níi	
Dental palatalization	n'íi	**xon'í**
Glide formation	n'yí	
Postpalatal yod deletion	**n'í**	

Similarly in Zakinthian /paléi/ 'ancient' (nom. pl.) and /mallí/ 'wool' will rhyme as [pal'í], [mal'í]. The reason for placing the Zakinthian rules in the order of derivation (11) was mentioned in 2.7. Glide formation applies to stressed [í] in Zakinthos only after consonants which palatalize, and it is simpler to apply palatalization first and then state simply that glide formation applies in the environment 'after palatal segment'.

Thus in Zakinthos the outcomes of /n/ and /l/ before /i/ are identical with those of [ny], [ly] if the above account is correct. In Thessaly we find a similar collapse of /n/ and [ny], /l/ and [ly] before /e/ as well as before /i/. Thus /léγo/ 'I say', /kalí/ 'good' /leroménos/ 'dirty' are pronounced [l'éw], [kal'í], [l'iruménus], as if they were in fact /liéγo/, /kalií/, /lieroménos/.[1] In this dialect the rule of dental palatalization will occur in its most general form, the environment being 'before front non-consonantal segment' ([i], [e] or [y]). Here [pal'í] will rhyme with [mal'í], as in Zakinthian, and also [kal'és] 'good' (nom. pl. fem.) from /kalés/ with [pal'és] from /palées/ (which goes through the stage [palyés]). It may be noted that because this palatalization applies to primary /e/ as well as /i/, the ordering of this rule in relation to raising is not crucial, as is the case with dialects which palatalize only before /i/ (see below). Thus for ναί 'yes', νερό 'water', Νῖκος 'Nikos' the following is one possible derivation:

(12)	né	neró	níkos
Dental palatalization	**n'é**	n'eró	n'íkos
Raising		**n'iró**	**n'íkus**

But a transposition of our rules would not affect the outcome.

[1] That this is the correct account is suggested by the spellings such as λιέου for λέγω used by scholars who have described the phenomenon (e.g. Tzartzanos 1909).

(*c*) The general situation with regard to palatalization in northern dialects appears reasonably clear on casual inspection. In most of them /n, l, s, z/ are palatalized before underlying /i/ as well as before [y], and when unstressed /i/ is subsequently lost by the normal rule of northern high vowel loss they retain this palatal articulation. Thus in a dialect such as that of Etolia we find the following type of derivation for βάνει 'he puts', ἔβανε 'he was putting', χωνί /xoní/ 'funnel':

(13)	váni	évane	xoní
Dental palatalization	ván'i		xon'í
High vowel loss	**ván'**		
Raising		**évani**	**xun'í**

That the various publications on northern dialects normally fail to refer to the palatalization of dentals before stressed /í/, which does not drop, while specifically singling out palatalization before unstressed /i/, is presumably to be explained by reference to the phonetic contrasts which result. While an item such as [n'íkos] cannot contrast with a *[níkos], the final segment of [ván'] contrasts with that of [pán] 'above' from /pánu/ (cf. also learned πᾶν 'all'). Contrast is also possible before consonants: /fílisa/ 'I kissed' > [fíl'sa], /élusa/ 'I washed' > [élsa]. It is important to notice that in a dialect such as that of Etolia the palatalization rule required to account for the [n'] of [ván'] is crucially ordered before the rule raising unstressed /e/ to [i]. If we transposed these rules, palatalization would act on the secondary [i] of [évani], and this ordering is not apparently found in any core dialect of the northern type (see, however, 7.2 for a possible exception in Cappadocian). (In Thessaly, as we saw above, the relative ordering of dental palatalization and raising is immaterial, as [ván'], [évan'i] would result under either arrangement.) Similarly for /l/, we find that primary /i/ but not secondary [i] from /e/ triggers palatalization. Thus /líkos/ 'wolf', /varéli/ 'barrel' and /lemóni/ 'lemon' go first to [l'íkos], [varél'i], [lemón'i] and then by high vowel loss and raising to [l'íkus], [varél'], [limón']. Finally, as an example for the sibilants, /síko/ 'fig', /θa+filísi/ 'he will kiss' and /fílise/ 'he kissed' go by dental palatalization to [šíko], [θafilíši], [fíl'ise], and then by high vowel loss and raising to [šíku], [θafl'íš], [fíl'si].

It is obvious that a dialect of the above type will not palatalize the dentals before /e/ at all, or if it does so the palatalization will be less than that induced by /i/ and of little phonological significance. In Thessalian it is equally clear that /i/, /e/ and [y] palatalize to an identical degree a preceding /n, l, s, z/. What is more difficult to determine is whether dialects other than Thessalian are of the Zakinthian type, and palatalize /n/ and /l/ to the same extent before /i/ as before [y], or of the Peloponnesian type and have three grades of palatality, associated in descending order of intensity with [y], /i/ and /e/ respectively. If a northern dialect were found with such a threefold scale of palatalization this would presumably be manifested at the phonetic level in certain theoretically possible cases. Consider for example the items λίμνη 'lake', λίμνιοι, the nominative plural masculine form of the adjective derived therefrom, and ὕμνου 'hymn' (gen. sing.). If a higher grade of palatality affected /n/ before [y] than before /i/, we would move from the typical southern output [límn'i] (medium palatality), [límn''i] (high palatality), [ímnu] (zero palatality) to [límn'], [límn''], [ímn]. While in southern dialects the difference between the [n'] of [límn'i] and the [n] of [ímnu] is non-contrastive (subphonemic), it would become phonemic in a northern dialect. If, on the contrary, a northern dialect has the Zakinthian type of palatalization then the first two items will be homophonous. In fact I believe this to be the actual situation in Etolia, Acarnania and southern Epirus, where μαλλί 'wool' and παλιοί 'ancient' appear to rhyme, as they do in Zakinthos. However, the general tendency of informants to maximize the contrastive possibilities of their language in the context of an interview (and pronounce, for instance, [pal'yí]), make it difficult to draw a firm conclusion, and it is unfortunate that the question appears to have been ignored by students of modern Greek.

Before we leave the topic of sonant palatalization in the north, it may be mentioned that in parts of Epirus only [y] appears to convert /n/ and /l/ to [n'] and [l']. North of Ioannina neither segment palatalizes before /i/, so that /fílu/ 'friend' (gen. sing.) and /fíli/ 'friends' both go to [fíl]; I have noted for an informant from the Zagori region [bólko], [ambél], [líγu] for /bóliko/ 'plenty', /ampéli/ 'vineyard', /líγo/ 'a little', and in Zitsa I noted pronunciations such as [θilkó] for /θilikó/ 'female' instead of the usual [θil'kó]. While /l/ resists palatalization before /i/ only in the northerly parts of Epirus, /n/ fails to go to [n'] in the same position as far south as Arta. Thus /váni/ 'he puts', /γitónisses/ 'neighbours' are widely heard as [ván], [γ'tónsis] for the normal [ván'], [γ'tón'sis]. One obvious result of this is that certain distinctions are lost. It is reported, for example, that in the region of Kastoria φέρνει 'he brings' and φέρνουν 'they bring' collapse into [férn]:[1]

[1] See Georgiou (1962).

(14)	férni	férnun
High vowel loss	**férn**	férnn
Geminate reduction in clusters		**férn**

That this loss of contrast is to be attributed to failure of dental palatalization rather than to some process of depalatalization in final and preconsonantal position is shown by the fact that there is no perceptible palatalization when the /i/ remains (as in [líγu] cited above).

The sibilants /s/ and /z/ go to [š] and [ž] in many dialects, usually under the same circumstances as /l/ and /n/ are palatalized. The items κρασιά 'wines', κρασί 'wine', βρύση 'spring', μισές 'half' (fem. pl.) are pronounced as follows in various dialects:

krasx'á	krasí	vrísi	misés	(W. Crete, Corfu)
krašá	krasí	vrísi	misés	(Peloponnese, Cyprus)
krašá	krasí	vrís	msés	(Epirus)
krašá	kraší	vríš	msés	(Samothraki, Ayassos)
krašá	kraší	vríš	mšés	(Thessaly, Ímbros)

The treatment of /z/ follows exactly that of /s/. That is, βυʒιά 'breasts', βυʒί 'breast', βρίʒει 'he curses', χαʒές 'silly' (fem. pl.) are pronounced in the dialects listed above respectively as follows:

vizγ'á	vizí	vrízi	xazés
vižá	vizí	vrízi	xazés
vžá	vzí	vríz	xazés
vžá	vží	vríž	xazés
vžá	vží	vríž	xažés

The first line in each case shows the pronunciations found not only in western Crete and Corfu, but the rest of the Ionian Isles, and most mainland urban dialects as well as various insular dialects (which, however, usually convert the [sx'] to [sk']); in all these there is no contrastive palatalization of the sibilants, although some degree of subphonemic palatalization may affect them before [y] (often converted to [x'] by consonantality) and [i]. The second and third lines are typical of dialects which palatalize the sibilants to [š] and [ž] before [y], with subsequent loss of the glide by postpalatal yod deletion. It is noteworthy that in the Peloponnese and Epirus the palatalization of /n/ and /l/ occurs in just this environment, although in Cyprus, as we saw, palatalization of the sonants before [y] is slight. As will be shown later (see 6.1) the dialects which have [s], [z] for [sy], [zy] are most simply accounted for by the assumption that they went through the [š], [ž] stage, and were then subject to depalatalization. Such cases are found in the Peloponnese, in Old Athenian, in western Crete and in the Cyclades, and in certain northern dialects including those of Arachova, Skiros, Samos and Lesbos. In Samothraki and in the Lesbian village of Ayassos [š] and [ž] are generated before /i/ and [y], but not before /e/.[1] Thus in Ayassos κρασί, βρύση, μισές and φίλησε 'he kissed' derive thus:

(15)	krasí	vrísi	misés	fílise
Dental palatalization	**kraší**	vríši		fíl'ise
High vowel loss		**vríš**	**msés**	fíl'se
Raising				**fíl'si**

As we noted in the case of /l/ and /n/, dental palatalization does not affect the [i] arising from /e/ in northern dialects. It may also be noted at this point that it does not affect the epenthetic [i] which breaks up the final clusters resulting from the action of high vowel loss on the third plural active forms of verbs (see derivation (8) above). Thus in Ayassos βάζει 'he puts', θέλει 'he wants', βάζουν 'they put', θέλουν 'they want' develop as follows:

(16)	vázi	θéli	vázun	θélun
Dental palatalization	váži	θél'i		
High vowel loss	**váž**	**θél'**	vázn	θéln
Vowel epenthesis			**vázin**	**θélin**

Apart therefore from differences of phonetic content, dental and velar palatalization differ formally in that dental palatalization is crucially ordered in respect to at least two other rules, while velar palatalization acts whenever the appropriate conditions arise.

This palatalization of sibilants before /i/ and [y] appears to be common in the north outside Epirus (but see below) and Thessaly. Thus θὰ χαλᾶς 'you will be spoiling' was said by informants to contrast with θὰ χαλάσῃ 'he will spoil' as [θaxalás] versus [θaxaláš] (or with slightly

[1] The statement in Kretschmer (1905: 151) is that /s/ goes to [š] 'vor hellen Vokalen'; yet his own data indicate that only primary /i/ and yod trigger palatalization. For reasons unclear to me /s/ is not palatalized at Ayassos after /t/. I found, for instance, [t^sit^{s}íδyimnus] 'stark naked', [papút^s] 'shoe', [papút^{s}x'a] 'shoes' for /tsitsíδiγimnos/, /papútsi/, /papútsia/. [t^sípa] 'crust' < /tsípa/ contrasts with [čípa] 'and I said' < /ke + ípa/.

palatal [s′]) at most points except for two southerly towns (Etoliko, Arachova) and the island of Skiros, where [θaxalás] was given for both.[1]

One also hears [š], [ž] before /i/ as well as for [sy] occasionally in the Peloponnese; thus in Messenia /íkosi/ 'twenty', /krasí/ 'wine', /krasía/ 'wines' go to [íkoši], [kraší], [krašá], the main phonological implication here as elsewhere being the neutralization of /si/ and /sii/ at the phonetic level as [ši]. A rather interesting development was reported for certain villages in Laconia by Koukoules (1908). There, when an /i/ had palatalized a preceding sibilant it was rounded to [ü]. Thus /krasí/ 'wine' went via [kraší] to [krašǘ]. The genitive of this word, /krasíu/, presumably went to [krašú] as elsewhere in the Peloponnese.

In Thessaly, just as /l/ and /n/ go to [l′], [n′] before /i/, /e/ and [y], so /s/ and /z/ go to [s′] and [z′] (somewhat less 'hushing' sounds than [š] and [ž]). This is the situation depicted in the last lines of the data presented above.

It remains to mention briefly one problem relating to sibilant palatalization in Epirus. It was stated that in Epirus, as in the Peloponnese and Cyprus, the sibilants go to [š], [ž] only before [y]. However, one puzzling feature of Epirot dialects is that underlying /si/, /zi/ appear to convert by palatalization and high vowel loss to [š], [ž] when a velar obstruent follows. Thus for συκώτι 'liver', ἀφύσικος 'ugly', σηκώνει 'he raises' we may set up the following derivations:

(17)	sikóti	afísikos	sikóni
Dental palatalization	šikóti	afíšikos	šikóni
High vowel loss	**škót**	afíškos	**škón**
Raising		**afíškus**	

The last item now contrasts minimally with [skón] from /skóni/ 'dust'. The voiced counterpart of /s/ behaves in a similar fashion: /ziγós/ 'yoke' > [žiγós] > [žγós]. Yet palatalization fails to occur when another consonant follows or the /i/ is final. Thus /símera/ 'today' goes to [símira], /simáδi/ 'mark' to [smáδ], /zimía/ 'damage' to [zmn′á]. What is particularly curious is that sibilants palatalize before a stressed /í/ followed by a velar obstruent: /síka/ 'figs' > [šíka], /síko/ 'get up!' > [šíku], /zíγose/ 'he yoked' > [žíγusi]. The only explanation that I can suggest would be that (*a*) all sibilants palatalized before stressed

[1] In Etoliko /s/ is palatalized only before [y] as in Epirus, and in Arachova and Skiros [s] is found for [sy], which suggests palatalization followed by depalatalization ([sy] > [šy] > [š] > [s]).

or unstressed /i/, (*b*) high vowel loss occurred, (*c*) depalatalization affected all sibilants except before velar obstruents or vowels other than [i], (*d*) these palatal sibilants before velar obstruents were generalized to members of the paradigm with stressed /i/. The forms σημάδι 'sign', σῦκα 'figs', συκόφυλλα 'fig leaves' would have developed as follows on this hypothesis:

(18)	simáδi	síka	sikófilla
Degemination			sikófila
Dental palatalization	šimáδi	šíka	šikófila
High vowel loss	šmáδ		**škófla**
Depalatalization	**smáδ**	síka	
(Analogical generalization)		**šíka**	

Similarly [zíγusi] would have been repalatalized on the basis of forms such as [žγónu] < /ziγóno/ 'I yoke'. There are various problems still: /sitári/ 'wheat', for instance, goes to [štár] rather than the *[stár] our rules predict, but the only alternative seems to be to set up some unnatural rule such as that proposed by Hoeg, to the effect that /s/ goes to [š] 'in the cases where [i] has been lost between [s] and [k]'.[1]

Turning finally to the dental stops [t] and [d], we find again that attention tends to be drawn to their palatalization when either (*a*) it results in a collapse of the distinction between /t/ on the one hand and some other unit segment or cluster or (*b*) it gives rise to a plain versus palatal contrast in the reflexes of /t/ itself.

(*a*) In the dialect spoken in Siatista (Macedonia) [t] and [d] are said to develop what appear to be palatal affricate variants before front vowels and yod. Thus /γiatí/ 'why' > [yačí], /patéras/ 'father' > [pačéras], /péfti/ 'he falls' > [péfč]; as is the case with the other palatalizations noted above, this one occurs before high vowel loss, as otherwise the last item would be *[péft]. That this affricate also reflects /ts/ is suggested by the occurrence of hypercorrect forms such as [katíka] for /katsíka/ 'goat', [tiγáro] for /tsiγáro/ 'cigarette'. However, Tsopanakis (1952) is unclear on the point.

A rather more interesting case of /t/ palatalization occurs in Plumari, Lesbos (and Mesta, Chios according to Pernot 1907). There a [t] in the environment before /i/ or [y] becomes [k'], and [d], [g']. Examples are /máti/ 'eye' > [mák'], /mátia/ 'eyes' > [mák'a], /aftí/ 'she' > [afk'í], /mantíli/ 'handkerchief' > [mag'íl']. While this [k'], [g'] are homo-

[1] See Hoeg (1925/6: 130).

phonous with the reflexes of /k/ in standardizing pronunciations, there is no merger of /t/ and /k/ in the dialect, for the latter undergoes palatalization and softening to [č] or (after nasal) [ǰ] in the same circumstances as /t/ goes to [k′] or [g′]. This implies the following derivation for λύκοι 'wolves', σπίτι 'house':

(19)	líki	spíti
Velar palatalization	lík′i	
Softening 1	líči	
Dental palatalization	l′íči	spík′i
High vowel loss	**l′íč**	**spík′**

This example confirms our earlier observation that velar and dental palatalization differ formally as well as phonetically. In Plumari, as elsewhere in the north, dental palatalization does not occur before secondary [i] from /e/; thus, if my information is correct, /teNPélis/ 'lazy' goes to [tibél′s], not *[k′ibél′s]; compare τεμπέλης and τυρί 'cheese':

(20)	teNPélis	tirí
Postnasal voicing etc.	tebélis	
Dental palatalization	tebél′is	**k′irí**
High vowel loss	tebél′s	
Raising	**tibél′s**	

It is clear from this that dental palatalization does not act on the output of raising (see also derivation (13) above for /n/). We have now in derivation (19) a further constraint: dental palatalization must follow softening.

It might be useful to summarize at this point the ordering constraints linking the two forms of palatalization to other rules, and to one another, as these may be determined for Plumari. These are represented in Figure 3. Lines are used to represent the obvious fact that phonological processes are not from the historical point of view instantaneous, but take place over more or less extended periods of time. In the present instance there is one rule, velar palatalization, which can actually be shown to have come into operation before another (high vowel loss) and to have been still active when the process described by the second rule had come to an end (see on derivation (8) above).

Figure 3 may be read as follows:

(1) Velar palatalization began before softening ceased, for /líki/ went to [lík′i] and only then to [líči]. This is shown by the broken line (1) linking the beginning of the solid line which stands for velar palatalization and the end of the one which stands for softening.

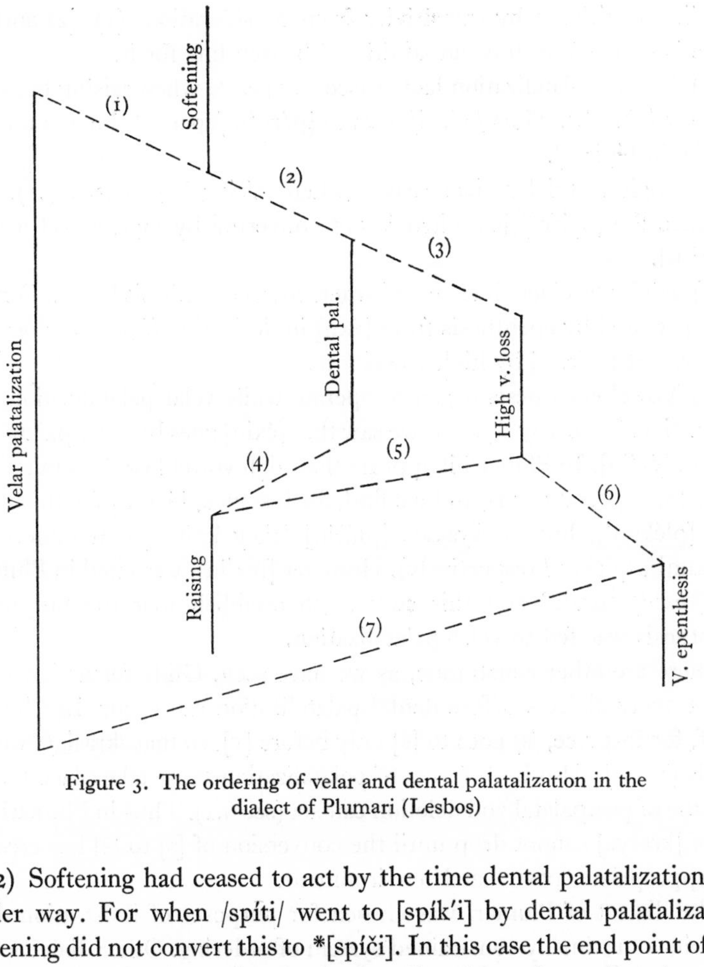

Figure 3. The ordering of velar and dental palatalization in the dialect of Plumari (Lesbos)

(2) Softening had ceased to act by the time dental palatalization got under way. For when /spíti/ went to [spík'i] by dental palatalization softening did not convert this to *[spíči]. In this case the end point of the softening rule is shown by the broken line (2) to be earlier than the initial point of the solid line for dental palatalization.

(3) Dental palatalization must have begun to operate before high vowel loss began to operate, whence broken line (3). The evidence for this is that for items such as /varéli/ 'barrel', /pérni/ 'he takes', /spíti/ 'house' we find [varél'], [pérn'], [spík']. If high vowel loss had come into operation first, it would have removed the /i/ which triggers dental palatalization. It may be added that velar palatalization is similarly linked to high vowel loss, for if high vowel loss removed the final vowel of /líki/ 'wolves' before palatalization had converted it to [k'], the output for Plumari would be *[l'ík] rather than the correct [l'íč]. But because

this linkage follows by transitivity from considerations (1), (2) and (3) there is no need to draw an additional broken line for it.

(4) Dental palatalization had ceased to operate when raising began to convert /e/ to [i]. Thus /pérni/ goes to [pérn′], /éperne/ 'he was taking' results in [épirni].

(5) High vowel loss had ceased when raising began (see 7.1). For instance the [épirni] just cited is not converted by high vowel loss to *[épirn].

(6) High vowel loss had ceased when vowel epenthesis began. For the [éxin] created by epenthesis from [éxn] in derivation (8) above does not then revert to [éxn] by high vowel loss.

(7) Vowel epenthesis began to operate while velar palatalization was still active. In nearby Ayassos we saw that [éxin] goes by velar palatalization to [éx′in]. In Plumari it appears that high vowel loss does not affect these third plural forms, and we find, for instance, [éxun′] for this item, and [plékun′], but in Ayassos [pléčin] 'they knit' (from underlying /plékuni/, /plékun/ respectively). However [téx′in′] was cited in Plumari for /téxni/ 'trade' and this suffices to establish that the output of epenthesis was fed to velar palatalization.

There are other constraints, as we have seen. Glide formation must act in many dialects before dental palatalization can occur. In Plumari itself, for instance, /s/ goes to [š] only before [y], so that /krasía/ 'wines' yields [krašá]. Also both forms of palatalization must take place before the rule of postpalatal yod deletion can act (see 6.1). Thus in Plumari the [y] of [krasyá] cannot drop until the conversion of [s] to [š] has created the appropriate 'postpalatal' environment.

The dialect of Plumari was chosen for purposes of illustration as it exhibits a maximally constrained system of ordering. Other dialects will be more simply ordered in one respect or more. In numerous cases, for example, there is no need to separate velar from dental palatalization by the interposition of the softening rule, and in southern dialects it is usually possible to apply dental as well as velar palatalization whenever its input conditions arise.

(*b*) Returning now to /t/ palatalization, we find that while in most northern dialects only /n, l, s, z/ of the dental consonants palatalize before /i/ in such a way as to enter into plain:palatal oppositions when unstressed /i/ drops, in Thessaly, Macedonia and Thrace this palatalization affects /t/. Thus we find that throughout this area /kátu/ 'down' contrasts with /káti/ 'something' as [kát] versus [kát′]; compare also [δónd′]

(Thessaly, W. Macedonia), [δód′] (E. Macedonia, Thrace) for /δónti/ 'tooth'. Although Thessaly and Macedonia palatalize all consonants before /i/ (see 5.3, 7.2) there are grounds for not treating the palatalization of /t/ as an instance of this general palatalization. Firstly it behaves like the velar consonants and /n, l, s, z/ in retaining this palatality before following consonants. Thus /triótikos/ 'three years old' > [triót′kus] just as /sináxi/ 'cold' > [s′náx′]. Secondly in Thracian dialects /t/ palatalizes although there is no general palatalization rule. Thus /káti/ > [kát′] but /níNfi/ 'bride' > [n′íf], not [n′íf′] as in Thessaly. Thirdly, in at least the dialect of Velvendos, the palatalization of /t/ shares with that of /n, l, s, z/ conditioning by /e/ as well as /i/.

5.3 Palatality assimilation

When a cluster of two palatalizing consonants (whether velar or dental) is followed by a front vowel or glide the question arises as to whether the palatalization of the second member of the cluster can be transmitted to the first member.[1] We shall consider in turn (*a*) geminate clusters, (*b*) other clusters with a velar in initial position, (*c*) clusters with an initial /n/ or /l/ and (*d*) clusters with an initial sibilant.

(*a*) We have already observed that one ground for regarding geminate consonants as long counterparts of simple consonants is that rules which apply to simple consonants usually apply equally well to geminates. If we wish to adopt the cluster analysis, however, we must set up, among other special rules of assimilation, one which will assimilate the first of a sequence of two identical consonants to the second in respect of palatality. On this interpretation λάκκοι 'wells' would be derived as follows in a typical south-eastern dialect:[2]

(21)	lákki
Palatalization	lákk′i
Palatality assimilation	lák′k′i
Softening	**láčči**

(*b*) Those clusters consisting of velar consonant followed by palatalizing consonant which are actually found are [ks, kn, kl, xn, γn, γl] and there appears to be no evidence that the palatalization of the second term can

[1] Palatality assimilation is implied in Zakinthian [voxθáo], [vóγδi] for βοηθάω, βόϊδι (see chapter 3, p. 65, n. 1).

[2] Pernot (1907: 439) prefers this method of arriving at Chian [ál′l′i] 'other', [mít′t′i] 'nose' from /álli/, /mítti/.

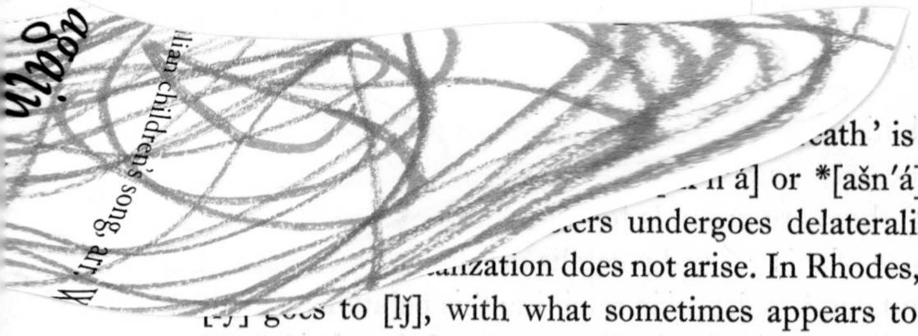

[illegible] eath' is always, so far as can [illegible] á] or *[ašn'á].

[illegible] ers undergoes delateralization to [r] and the [illegible] ization does not arise. In Rhodes, though, the sequence [illegible] goes to [lǰ], with what sometimes appears to be a palatalized [l′]. Now if we assume that the /l/ is palatalized by the [y] it is not clear why the yod does not immediately drop by postpalatal yod deletion. If we accept the possibility of a late rule of palatality assimilation, however, then we can derive, say, βασιλιάς 'king' as follows:

(22)	vasiléas
Height dissimilation	vasilías
Glide formation	vasilyás
Consonantality	vasilγ′ás
Manner dissimilation	vasilg′ás
Softening	vasilǰás
Palatality assimilation	**vasil′ǰás**

It can perhaps be indicated in favour of this interpretation that Rhodian is one of the few dialects which does not palatalize /s/ before [y] either, so that [sy] goes to [sx′] and then, by manner dissimilation, to [sk′].

The nasal /n/ is eliminated before continuants in all dialects by nasal assimilation, so that the cases which concern us are /nk/ and, in the few dialects where /t/ palatalizes, /nt/. However, whether nasal assimilation I occurs (yielding [ŋg], [nd]) or nasal assimilation II (yielding [g], [d]), no special assumption of palatality assimilation is required. Consider first the items ἀγγειά 'pots', μαντήλι 'handkerchief' in the dialect of Plumari:

(23)	aNKía	maNTíli
Postnasal voicing	aNgía	maNdíli
Nasal assimilation II	aggía	maddíli
Degemination	agía	madíli
Glide formation	agyá	
Velar palatalization	ag′yá	
Postpalatal yod deletion	ag′á	
Softening	**aǰá**	
Dental palatalization		mag′íl′i
High vowel loss		**mag′íl′**

In dialects which assimilate nasals to following stops only in respect of point of assimilation, this assimilation itself renders superfluous the assumption of a specific rule transferring palatality. Thus the [n′] of Cypriot [an′ǯá] is easily accounted for by assuming that once the /k/ has palatalized, nasal assimilation can convert the /n/ to [n′]. Similarly Cypriot [δón′g′a] 'teeth' owes its [n′] to the assimilation of /n/ to [g′] (see 6.5).

(*d*) Palatalizing clusters with initial sibilant are limited to [st] and [sk]. The conversion of [st] to [s′t′] in a dialect which includes dental stops in the domain of dental palatalization is reported for Thrace and Velvendos. The Thracian form [n′is′kós] 'with an empty stomach' shows one way in which the occurrence of palatality assimilation can create phonetic contrast. Compare in this dialect βοσκός 'shepherd' and the item νηστικός:

(24)	**voskós**	nistikós
Dental palatalization		n′ist′ikós
Palatality assimilation		n′is′t′ikós
High vowel loss		n′is′t′kós
Cluster simplification		**n′is′kós**

For [sk] evidence of palatality assimilation is plentiful. In the north it is likely that all dialects which palatalize the sibilants at all, even if only before [y], will assign the same grade of palatality to /s/ when it is followed by palatal [k′]. Whence the common pronunciations of σκυλί 'dog', ἄσχημος 'ugly' in northern dialects:

(25)	skilí	ásximos
Manner dissimilation		áskimos
Palatalizations	sk′il′í	ásk′imos
Palatality assimilation	šk′il′í	ášk′imos
High vowel loss	**šk′l′í**	ášk′mos
Raising		ášk′mus
Cluster simplification		**ášmus**

The reason for placing palatality assimilation before high vowel loss is that in general secondary clusters arising from the action of the latter are not affected by it. Thus /kukkí/ 'bean', /túrkika/ 'Turkish' go to [kk′i], [túrk′ka] (see 7.5).

Palatality assimilation, as we saw in the cases of [n′is′kós] and [ášmus], may give rise to plain : palatal contrast when cluster simplification removes the consonant in which the palatality originated. Another source lies in the subsequent depalatalization of this latter. In the dialect of the nomadic Sarakatsans, for instance, [k′] goes to [k] before [l] or [s], so that σκυλάκι 'puppy' develops as follows:

(26)	skiláki
Velar palatalization	sk′ilák′i
Palatality assimilation	šk′ilák′i
High vowel loss	šk′lák′
Palatality assimilation	**šklák′**

The details of Sarakatsan (for which I rely heavily on Hoeg 1926) are often obscure, but it looks here as if palatality assimilation may act, exceptionally, after high vowel loss, and that, among other things, it converts [k′s] to [ks], [sk′] to [šk′] and [k′l] to [kl]. I have here supposed that it acts whenever its input conditions arise; the alternative would be to apply it at one point after high vowel loss had yielded [sk′l], but that it should assimilate the first term to the second and then the second to the third is intrinsically rather implausible. Finally in Zagori (Epirus) /vríski/ 'he finds' goes to [vríšk′] and the [š] is then generalized throughout the paradigm, so that /vrísko/ 'I find' comes to be pronounced [vríšku], this again providing a source of contrast (cf. [θrískus] 'religious' from /θrískos/).

Outside northern dialects [sk′] and its softened derivative [sč] are not normally subject to noticeable palatality assimilation even in dialects with [š] for [sy]. Thus in the Peloponnese and Ionian Isles we find 'dog' pronounced [sk′ílos], in Crete [sčílos], in Rhodes [sčíllos], and in Lesbos [st^sílus]. However, in certain Chian dialects and in Cypriot, which have [č] for palatal /k/, /sk/ in a palatalizing environment becomes [šš]; in the variety of Old Athenian spoken in the Kimi region, as well as in the dialect of Kalimnos, both of which have [t^s] for palatalized /k/, it develops to [ss]. The following derivation would be appropriate for Kimi and Kalimnos (ἐκεῖ 'there' is provided for comparison):

(27)	skíllos	ekí
Velar palatalization	sk′íllos	ek′í
Softening	sčíllos	ečí
Palatality assimilation	ščíllos	
Deaffrication	ššíllos	
Depalatalization	**ssíllos**	**et^sí**

In Chios and Cyprus the derivation stops at [ššíllos].

It is not clear whether the deaffrication rule can be formulated more generally than to state [šč] > [šš]. One point of interest is that it is not found outside the 'geminating' dialects; it is particularly striking that while Kimi has [ssíllos], the closely related dialects of Megara and Aegina, which degeminate, have [stᷤílos].

In dialects with [šš] or [ss] for [sk′] the same outcome is found for [sx′]. This can be accounted for quite easily by applying manner dissimilation before softening; indeed for Chios and Kimi we have no alternative, for these dialects have the first form of softening, which acts on /k/ but not /x/. The required sequence is therefore /sx/ > [sx′] > [sk′] > [sč] > [šč] > [šš] > [ss]. Here are various dialectal forms of σκύλος 'dog', ἀσκιά 'flasks', σχίζω 'I tear', ἄσχημος 'ugly':

/skíllos/	/askía/	/sxízo/	/ásximos/	
sk′ílos	ask′á	sk′ízo	ásk′imos	(Peloponnese)
šk′ílus	ašk′á	šk′ízu	ášmus	(Epirus)
sčílos	asčá	sčízo	ásčimos	(Crete)
stᷤíllos	astᷤá	stᷤízzo	ástᷤimos	(Rhodes)
stᷤílos	astᷤá	stᷤízo	ástᷤimos	(Megara)
ššíllos	aššá	ššízzo	áššimos	(Cyprus)
ssíllos	assá	ssízzo	ássimos	(Kimi)

6 *Consonant and Yod Sequences*

6.0 Most studies of individual dialects of modern Greek, particularly if the dialect belongs to the south-eastern group, devote a special section to the reflexes of consonant + yod clusters; these clusters appear to undergo a bewildering variety of metamorphoses as one moves eastward from the mainland and it is easy to get the impression that they are subject to a self-contained network of idiosyncratic phonological processes. For reasons of general convenience I shall follow the usual practice of examining these clusters in a special section, but attempt at the same time to show that what at first sight might appear to be isolated phenomena represent in general the natural outcome of straightforward and familiar rules. Instead, for instance, of assuming some special rule to account for the development of /peδía/ 'children' to [pedzá] in Kalimnos, I shall show that the rules already at our disposal are perfectly adequate to the task; in this case, for instance, we can set up the derivational sequence: /peδía/ > (glide formation) > [peδyá] > (consonantality) > [peδγ'á] > (softening) > [peδžá] > (depalatalization) > [peδzá] > (manner dissimilation) > [pedzá].

Postconsonantal yod can derive only from an original /i/ or from an /e/ which has been acted on by height dissimilation. Thus the [y] of intermediate [peδyá] above came from /í/; the source of [y] in [elyá] 'olive' is the /é/ of /eléa/. Because the consonantality rule specifies that [γ'] or [x'], but not [y], can occur phonetically after a consonant, /γ/ cannot yield yod in postconsonantal position, although it can do so, as we saw in 5.1, elsewhere: /γéros/ 'old man' may go to [yéros] but /arγí/ 'he is late' cannot move to *[aryí] at any stage of its derivation, only to [arγ'í]. An intermediate [aryí] can come only from /areí/ 'sparse' (nom. pl. masc.). This will go by consonantality to [arγ'í] and once consonantality has taken place the rules make no distinction between [γ'] from /y/ and [γ'] from /γ/.

We shall begin by showing that in all dialects consonant + yod clusters are subject either to the rules of palatalization and postpalatal yod deletion or, failing that, to consonantality. Section 6.2 will describe how in certain northern dialects manner dissimilation may act on the [x′] or [γ′] arising by consonantality from [y] and 6.3 introduces a rule of 'fricativity assimilation' which accounts for the development in some dialects of [ty] to [θx′] or (with manner dissimilation) [θk′]. In 6.4 certain features of the south-eastern dialects are handled separately for ease of exposition; it is in these dialects that the most striking developments occur. Finally in 6.5 certain observations are made relating to sequences of two consonants and yod.

6.1 The three basic rules

Outside the south-eastern and Cretan dialects perhaps the commonest set of reflexes for consonant + yod sequences is that attributed in Table 6 (see over) to Zitsa and the Peloponnesian dialects of the first type. A glance at the data will suggest immediately that postconsonantal yod may develop in one of two ways:

(*a*) It may palatalize the consonant which precedes it and then drop. This is always the case with such consonants as have a velar point of articulation (i.e. /k/, /x/, /γ/) and, among the dental consonants, with /l/ and /n/ (except for the cases to be noted below of Cyprus, Rhodes and Santorini). In various dialects such as that of Zitsa /s/ also palatalizes to [š] before [y] and /z/ to [ž]. Thus, for [ky, xy, γy, ly, ny, sy, zy] we find there [k′, x′, γ′, l′, n′, š, ž]. The [γ′] goes in the normal way to [y] by the consonantality rule of 5.1, which, among other things, converts intervocalic [γ′] to its glide counterpart [y]. Consider the derivations of νύχια 'finger-nails', τραγιά 'goats', νησιά 'islands' and γωνιά 'corner' in a Peloponnesian dialect of the first type:

(1)	níxia	traγía	nisía	γonía
Glide formation	níxya	traγγyá	nisyá	γonyá
Palatalization	níx′ya	traγ′yá	nišyá	γon′yá
Postpalatal yod deletion	**níx′a**	traγ′á	**nišá**	**γon′á**
Consonantality		**trayá**		

Similarly /vizía/ 'breasts' > [vizyá] > [vižyá] > [vižá], /peδákia/ 'children' > [peδákya] > [peδák′ya] > [peδák′a], /eléa/ 'olive' > [elía] > [elyá] > [el′yá] > [el′á]. Because in at least some dialects the palatalization of /s/ to [š] is triggered by [y] but not [i], and this is often true of /n/ and /l/ (see 5.2), the rule of dental palatalization must refer specifically to [y] and accordingly follows that of glide formation; as there is no reason

TABLE 6. *Consonant + yod sequences in certain northern, Ionian, Peloponnesian and Old Athenian dialects*

	py	fy	vy	ty	θy	δy	ky	xy	γy	sy	zy	my	ny	ly	ry
Zitsa / Peloponnese (1)	px′	fx′	vγ′	tx′	θx′	δy′	k′	x′	y	š	ž	mn′	n′	l′	rγ′
Peloponnese (2)	px′	fx′	vγ′	tx′	θx′	δγ′	k′	x	y	s	z	mn′	n′	l′	rγ′
Corfu	px′	fx′	vγ′	tx′	θx′	δγ′	k′	x′	y	sx′	zγ′	mn′	n′	l′	rγ′
Megara / Lesbos (1)	px′	fx′	vγ′	tx′	θx′	δγ′	tᷤ	x′	y	s	z	mn′	n′	l′	rγ′
Lesbos (2)	px′	fx′	vγ′	tx′	θx′	δγ′	č	x′	y	š	ž	mn′	n′	l′	rγ′
Lesbos (3)	px′	fx′	vγ′	k′	θx′	δγ′	č	x′	y	š	ž	mn′	n′	l′	rγ′
Velvendos	px′	fk′	vγ′	tx′	θk′	δγ′	k′	x′	y	s′k′	?	mn′	n′	l′	rγ′

to place velar palatalization *before* glide formation in any dialect (except perhaps Zakinthian, see 2.7), we may most conveniently place both types together after glide formation, and barring some special circumstance such as we find in Plumari (Lesbos, see 5.2), lump them together under the label 'palatalization' *simpliciter*.

(*b*) If the consonant does not palatalize, then consonantality applies and the [y] converts to [γ′] or [x′] according as the consonant is voiced or voiceless. Thus /peδía/ 'boys' goes to [peδyá] by glide formation, then to [peδγ′á] by consonantality; /mátia/ 'eyes', /alíθia/ 'truth' go to [mátya], [alíθya], then [mátx′a], [alíθx′a].

Reference to the derivation of [trayá] in (1) above will show that palatalization must occur before consonantality. That is, the phonetic [y] of this word derives from [γ′] by the action of consonantality and the [γ′] arises from the original /γ/ by palatalization. Furthermore, postpalatal yod deletion, which obviously must follow palatalization, is most conveniently ordered before consonantality. For the assumption of this sequence enables us to state the consonantality rule in a maximally simple manner: it applies to [y] after any consonant. Compare, for instance, the derivations of μαγειά 'spell', κλουβιά 'cages' and κουπιά 'oars' using the same rule sequence as in (1) above:

(2)	maγía	kluvía	kupía
Glide formation	maγyá	kluvyá	kupyá
Palatalization	maγ′yá		
Postpalatal yod deletion	maγ′á		
Consonantality	**mayá**	**kluvγ′á**	**kupx′á**

If we place consonantality immediately after palatalization we must stop it from acting on, e.g., the sequence [γ′y], which means adding to our formulation 'except when the previous consonant is palatal'. In any case there is no reason to suppose that historically palatalization and postpalatal yod deletion represented two discrete stages; it is quite possible that the most faithful historical statement would be rather [γy] > [γ′], [xy] > [x′] etc. One difference between the approach used in this book and a strictly historical one lies in the fact that we can allow ourselves to 'unpack' a single event into its theoretical components.

One development we have not yet had occasion to mention involves the conversion of [my] to [mn′]. This can be handled by simply adding to our formulation of the consonantality rule that the [y] or [γ′] following a consonant agrees with it in nasality (as well as in consonantality and voice). The full formulation is therefore as follows:

> **Consonantality:** A non-vocalic, non-strident, voiced, palatal, continuant segment agrees in consonantality, voice and nasality with any preceding consonantal segment; otherwise it is non-consonantal.

The consonantality rule, as is the case with many other rules, may be resisted to a greater or lesser degree in careful speech (i.e. the fricativity which it introduces may be barely perceptible); many speakers, for instance, will pronounce [myá] (or perhaps [mγ′á]) rather than [mn′á] for /mía/ 'one' (fem.) and it is possible that some vernacular dialects apply it less vigorously than others. In Lesbos, for instance, it was held by Kretschmer[1] that [y] does not go to [x′] after voiceless consonants, although he recorded [mn′] for [my]; my own impression on the matter is that we are faced with what is phonetically a gradient phenomenon. In the case of Lesbian some fricativity seems to be present. The problem is rather one of phonological interpretation: some dialects convert both [fx′] from primary /fx/ before a front vowel to [fk′] (as /efxí/ 'blessing' > [efx′í] > [efk′í]) and [fx′] from [fy] (as /ráfia/ 'shelves' > [ráfya] > [ráfx′a] > [ráfk′a]), while others, such as Lesbian, apply manner dissimilation only to primary /fx/. If it could be shown that dialects which do not convert [fy] to [fk′] have only a slight degree of fricativity in their postconsonantal yod, then we might wish to say that they did not apply the consonantality rule at all, but applied manner dissimilation to [fx′] without restriction. I do not possess such evidence and have preferred rather to assume that all dialects possess the consonantality rule, but in

[1] See Kretschmer (1905: 153).

some cases (as in Lesbos, Zitsa and the Peloponnese) do not apply manner dissimilation to its output (do not convert to [fk′] the [fx′] arising from [fy]).

The other data in Table 6 illustrate some of the ways in which dialects may depart from the pattern described for Zitsa and part of the Peloponnese. In Corfu we find that [sy] and [zy] become [sx′] and [zγ′] rather than [š] and [ž]. What this means is simply that in that particular dialect the sibilants do not palatalize before [y]. This pronunciation is also found in the urban centres of the Peloponnese and is normal in Athens, although it is often quite difficult to determine whether what the speaker has is in fact [sx′] or [s′]; that is, it is not always clear whether what we have is non-palatalization of sibilants and consonantalization of the [y], or mild palatalization followed by postpalatal yod deletion.

Still another reflex of [sy] is found in rural Peloponnese, as well as Old Athenian, Arachova (near Delphi) and most islands: [s] (and [z] for [zy]). The clue to the interpretation of this apparent loss of [y] after [s] may be found, I believe, in the dialects in which softening is followed by depalatalization. We saw (in 5.1) that the [č] arising by softening from /k/ may be depalatalized to [t͡s]. Now if a dialect of this type also palatalized [s] before [y] we would expect derivations such as the following (for κρασιά 'wines' and κῦμα 'wave'):

(3)	krasía	kíma
Glide formation	krasyá	
Palatalization	krašyá	k′íma
Postpalatal yod deletion	krašá	
Softening		číma
Depalatalization	**krasá**	**t͡síma**

Precisely these outputs for /krasía/ and /kíma/ are found in Lesbos, Arachova, parts of Chios, Santorini (as described by Georgakas 1934) and Kalimnos (except that there [sy] goes to [ss]). What I would like to suggest is that all dialects with [s], [z] for [sy], [zy] derive these via [š], [ž] irrespective of whether they also affricate /k/ to [t͡s] before front vowels. It is significant that where [s] and [z] occur for [sy] and [zy], neighbouring dialects often have [š] and [ž], suggesting that both types are to be accounted for by the assumption of palatalization and post-palatal yod deletion. The resultant [š], [ž] is in some dialects then depalatalized. This representation of the phonological relations does not imply a strict parallelism in the historical sequence of events. A dialect with [nisá] 'islands', for instance, may have generalized its rule of dental palatalization from /n/ and /l/ to the sibilants, but the threatened [š] was never actually realized; it converted to [s] instantaneously by the existing phonological rule specifying sibilants as having a dental point of articulation.

In the Peloponnese [s] and [z] for [sy], [zy] are found in the north west and the hinterland of Patra, as well as around Tsakonia on the east coast, while many villages have [š], [ž]. In Lesbos the village of Ayassos has [š] and [ž], with [č] for palatalized /k/, while [s], [z], [t̑ˢ] are usual elsewhere in the island. This again suggests that the second dialect type differs in having an additional rule of depalatalization.

In Cyprus /s/ goes to [š] before [y] (and not before /i/ as at Ayassos), and /x/ is softened before front vowels and [y], so that phonetic [š] can arise from either /s/ or /x/. Compare the derivations of νύχια 'finger-nails' and νησιά 'islands':

(4)	níxia	nisía
Glide formation	níxya	nisyá
Palatalization	níx'ya	nišyá
Postpalatal yod deletion	níx'a	**nišá**
Softening	**níša**	

The reader will note finally that opposite the specification 'Lesbos (3)' Table 6 gives [k'] for /ty/. This development, which is found in Plumari, is a natural consequence, however, of the palatalization of /t/ to [k'] before primary /i/ and before [y] characteristic of that particular dialect (see 5.2). Thus μάτια 'eyes', φύκια 'seaweed' and ἴσια 'straight on' are derived in Plumari as follows:

(5)	mátia	fíkia	ísia
Glide formation	mátya	fíkya	ísya
Velar palatalization		fík'ya	
Softening		fíčya	
Dental palatalization	mák'ya		íšya
Postpalatal yod deletion	**mák'a**	**fíča**	**íša**

6.2 Manner dissimilation and yod

In the dialect of Velvendos (see Table 6) the reflexes of /fy/, /θy/, /sy/ are [fk'], [θk'] and [s'k']. In the other dialects for which data are provided in this table /fy/ goes to [fx′] and /θy/ to [θx′], so that what we have in Velvendos is the further conversion of these outputs to [fk′] and [θk′] by manner dissimilation. While all dialects apply manner dissimilation to underlying sequences of voiceless non-strident fricatives, so that, for example, /efxí/ 'blessing' goes to [efk′í] in all true vernaculars (and this occasionally to [efčí] by softening), it is not normal outside the south east for the secondary [fx′] and [θx′] arising from /fy/ and /θy/ to be affected by it. We may describe this point of variation as a matter of relative rule order. Consider first the derivation of εὐχή 'blessing' and κούφιοι 'hollow' (nom. pl. masc.) in a typical Peloponnesian dialect:

(6)	efxí	kúfii
Glide formation		kúfyi
Palatalization	efx′í	
Manner dissimilation	**efk′í**	
Consonantality		**kúfx′i**

In such a dialect the output of the consonantality rule is immune to the action of manner dissimilation (i.e., from the historical point of view, manner dissimilation was no longer active when the consonantality trend set in). Now consider the derivation of these forms in the dialect of Velvendos:

(7)	efxí	kúfii
Glide formation		kúfyi
Palatalization	efx′í	
Consonantality		kúfx′i
Manner dissimilation	efk′í	**kúfk′i**

The first item also undergoes raising at some point, so that what we actually get is [ifk′í]. Now while the simplest synchronic explanation of the relation between our two dialect types is based on the concept of rule transposition there is no reason to suppose that the dialects with [fk′] for /fy/ did not go through the stage represented by Peloponnesian dialects. That is, the historical events may very well have included the following sequence:

(8)	efx′í	kúfyi
Manner dissimilation	**efk′í**	
Consonantality		kúfx′i
Manner dissimilation		**kúfk′i**

One point worth noting is that while /fy/ goes to [fk′], /vy/ does not go to [vg′], nor does /δy/ to [δg′] or /ry/ to [rg′]. The reason is not far to seek. Manner dissimilation occurs in three versions (see 4.5), two of which are relevant to the point at issue. One acts on voiceless fricatives when another fricative precedes and the other on all fricatives after a fricative or liquid irrespective of voice state. It turns out that where manner dissimilation acts on the fricative arising from [y] in post-consonantal position it affects only [x′] where the former version of the rule occurs, and where the latter, both [x′] and [γ′]. Thus a dialect which changes [efx′í] to [efk′í] but has [avγó] for /avγó/ 'egg' will change [fy], [θy] to [fk′], [θk′] but [vy], [δy] to [vγ′], [δγ′] and [ry] to [rγ′]; one which has [avgó] will also have [vg′], [δg′], [rg′].

In the case of [sy] we have a parallel situation in that dialects which order consonantality before manner dissimilation may also convert this to [sk′]. However, we have already seen that /s/ palatalizes to [š] in many dialects, so that the following [y] drops by the rule of yod elision before consonantality and manner dissimilation can take effect. Thus in Cyprus νησιά 'islands' develops to [nišá] as in derivation (4) above; in parts of Rhodes the /s/ of this word remains unpalatalized so that while the development of γωνιά 'corner' parallels that of νησιά in Cyprus, νησιά itself goes to [nisk′á]:

(9)	γonía	nisía
Glide formation	γonyá	nisyá
Palatalization	γon′yá	
Postpalatal yod deletion	**γon′á**	
Consonantality		nisx′á
Manner dissimilation		**nisk′á**

The [s′k′] of Velvendos appears at first sight to provide a counter-instance to the general principle that [y] drops once a previous consonant is palatalized. However, the palatalization of the sibilant in a form such as [kras′k′á] 'wines' from /krasía/ is probably not to be attributed to the normal palatality rule which converts, e.g., /l/ to [l′], but rather to the rule of palatality assimilation which operates widely in northern dialects to sharpen sibilants before a following palatal obstruent (see 5.3). Indeed the picture is further complicated by the fact that palatalization itself appears to have occurred in two stages, the first affecting only the velars, /l/ and /n/. σκυλλιά 'dogs', κρασιά 'wines' and κρασί 'wine' seem to have developed in Velvendos somewhat as follows:

(10)	skilía	krasía	krasí
Glide formation	skilyá	krasyá	
Palatalization (1)	sk'il'yá		
Postpalatal yod deletion	sk'il'á		
Consonantality		krasx'á	
Manner dissimilation		krask'á	
Palatalization (2)			**kras'í**
Palatality assimilation	s'k'il'á	**kras'k'á**	
High vowel loss	**s'k'l'á**		

To summarize the discussion thus far, we may say that northern, Peloponnesian–Ionian and Old Athenian dialects differ but little in their treatment of consonant + yod clusters. In all cases we find that palatalization, postpalatal yod deletion and consonantality apply in that order, and in practically all dialects manner dissimilation is crucially ordered before consonantality, so that sequences such as [fx'] from [fy] are unaffected by the former. The softening of /k/ to [č] before front vowels and [y] in Old Athenian and Lesbian and the depalatalization of this to [t͡s] in Megara and Kimi, as well as much of Lesbos, belong rather to the study of palatalization and softening and do not raise any special problems. Perhaps the most noticeable area of variation lies in the development of [sy] and [zy], and this variation, as we have seen, results from the differential scope of the rule of palatalization. While [š] and [ž] (or, in Thessaly and Macedonia, [s'] and [z']) are found in most of northern Greece including Samothraki, Imbros and part of Lesbos, as well as much of rural Peloponnese, [s] and [z] were provided by informants at most villages in N.W. Peloponnese, at Arachova (near Delphi) and in the northern islands of Thasos and Skiros. Urban dialects everywhere show [sx'] or [sy] for [si] or [sí] before vowel although it is not clear what the vernacular basis for this pronunciation is; only in Corfu and western Crete does [sx'] appear to be truly dialectal (i.e. to be used consistently at all educational levels). Stamatelos, writing in 1874, declared that [y] dropped after [s] 'everywhere in Greece' (πανταχοῦ τῆς Ἑλλάδος) outside the Ionian Isles and he recommended the spellings δροσά, ἐκκλησά for δροσιά 'coolness', ἐκκλησιά 'church'. This might perhaps suggest that the adoption of [sy] or [sx'] in the modern standard represents a recent revival of learned origin. Alternatively we might suppose that the urban dialects of the Peloponnese, which provide the base for standard demotic, never succumbed to the rural tendency to replace [sy] by [s] or [š].

Outside Crete and the south east, then, yod normally develops after consonants other than /k/ and the sibilants as follows:

(11)	py	fy	vy	ty	θy	δy	xy	γy	my	ny	ly	ry
Palatalization							x'y	γ'y		n'y	l'y	
Postpal. yod del.							x'	γ'		n'	l'	
Consonantality	px'	fx'	vγ'	tx'	θx'	δγ'			mn'			rγ'

The sequences /ky, sy, zy/ develop in different ways according to whether the particular dialect possesses the following rules:

(*a*) /s/ goes to [š] before [y] (and /z/ to [ž]).
(*b*) /k/ is softened before front vowel or [y] to [č].
(*c*) Any [š], [ž] or [č] resulting from (*a*) or (*b*) is depalatalized.

Dialects with (*a*) alone show the following derivations:

(12)	ky	sy	zy
Palatalization	k'y	šy	žy
Postpalatal yod deletion	k'	š	ž

This situation is found in parts of the Peloponnese and of the north. When (*c*) occurs in addition, we get [k', s, z], as in N.W. Peloponnese. Dialects with (*a*) and (*b*) may be represented thus:

(13)	ky	sy	zy
Palatalization	k'y	šy	žy
Postpalatal yod deletion	k'	š	ž
Softening	č		

This possibility is realized in Lesbian dialects of types (2) and (3). In most of Lesbos (*c*) also occurs, as it does in Megara, giving [t͡s, s, z]. In Corfu none of our three rules occurs, so that we get [k', sx', zγ']. Dialects with (*b*) but not (*a*) would have [č, sx', zγ'] but this possibility does not appear to be realized outside western Crete and the south east.

6.3 Fricativity assimilation

While the normal reflex of /ty/ is given as [tx'] in all the dialects of Table 6 it is reported by Boundonas[1] that in Velvendos the single item τέτοιος 'such' could be pronounced [téθk'us], and this replacement of [ty] by [θk'] is general in Tyrnavos (Tzartzanos 1909). Furthermore Phavis (1909) reports that [ty] goes to [θy] in one village near Kimi, but

[1] See Boundonas (1892: 45).

in view of the virtual universality of the consonantality rule we are fairly safe in interpreting him to mean [θx′]. Outside these dialects the replacement of [ty] by [θx′] or [θk′] is common. [θx′] is found in all parts of Crete and in southern Rhodes, while northern Rhodes, Kos, Chios and Ikaria have [θk′]. Thus for /mátia/ 'eyes' we find [máθx′a] or [máθk′a], and for /kutía/ 'boxes', [kuθx′á] or [kuθk′á]. It is significant that the dialects with [θk′] all belong to the group which apply manner dissimilation to the output of consonantality (e.g. convert /alíθia/ 'truth' to [alíθk′a]), while Cretan and the dialect of Phavis' village near Kimi, which have [θx′] for [ty], do not apply manner dissimilation to [θx′] from [θy]. Because the present phenomenon, but not manner dissimilation, affects postconsonantal yod in these latter dialects we may suppose it to represent a special process of 'fricativity assimilation' rather than an incipient form of the general rule of manner dissimilation. Its effect will be to convert a dental stop to its fricative counterpart before [x′] or [γ′]. Taking advantage of the fact that no other non-sibilant fricative occurs after dental stops we may formulate the rule thus:

Fricativity assimilation: A dental obstruent is continuous in the environment before a continuous non-sibilant obstruent.

That is, before any fricative other than [s] or [z] we can have [θ] or [δ] but not [t] or [d]. On the present assumption μάτια 'eyes' and αλήθεια 'truth' will derive thus in a dialect such as that of Ikaria or Tyrnavos:

(14)	mátia	alíθia
Glide formation	mátya	alíθya
Consonantality	mátx′a	alíθx′a
Fricativity assimilation	máθx′a	
Manner dissimilation	**máθk′a**	**alíθk′a**

Dialects such as Cretan which do not apply manner dissimilation to the output of consonantality will have [máθx′a], [alíθx′a].

One obvious effect of fricativity assimilation is to eliminate at the phonetic level the contrast between underlying /t/ and /θ/ before yod. In most cases, however, the occurrence of morphophonemic alternation ensures the persistence of underlying contrast. Thus Cretan [spíθx′a] 'houses' matches a singular [spíti], thus implying /spítia/, and [kráθx′e] 'he was holding' must derive from /krátie/ (κράτειε) rather than */kráθie/ as in positions other than before yod we find [t] ([kratό] 'I hold')

It remains to note that [ty] goes to some voiced cluster in various south-eastern dialects. Thus Kos has for /mátia/ [máδg'a], and Kalimnos [mádza]; in the Paphos area of Cyprus we find [máδγ'a], as well as [máδg'a]. It is not clear how we can account in a simple way for the change in voice state from [t] to [δ] which all these outcomes require. Perhaps the clue lies in the observation that our consonantality rule as we have framed it converts [ty] to [tx'] 'in one move', whereas in actual fact two steps are involved, consonantalization and devoicing: [ty] > [tγ'] > [tx']. Now voice assimilation, as we saw in 4.4, is regressive in modern Greek, so that we would expect a [tγ'] to go to [dγ']. If we then suppose that the consonantality rule simply converts [y] to [γ'], the [máδγ'a] form of μάτια can be derived somewhat as follows:

(15)	mátia
Glide formation	mátya
Consonantality (*special*)	mátγ'a
Voice assimilation	mádγ'a
Fricativity assimilation	**máδγ'a**

The resultant [máδγ'a] is acted on by manner dissimilation (type III) in dialects which have this form of the rule (e.g. Kos) and becomes [máδg'a]. In Kalimnos it is acted on by softening and depalatalization and then manner dissimilation:

(16)	máδγ'a
Softening	máδža
Depalatalization	máδza
Manner dissimilation	**mádza**

That these forms went through a stage with [dγ'] is perhaps supported by the existence of a pronunciation reported for the village Menites in Karpathos by Dawkins (1904). There /mátia/ was realized as [mádya] (i.e. [mádγ'a]?). Indeed he also found cases of [mbž] for [py], although his cases are confined to initial position (e.g. [mbžós] for ποιός 'who?'); but, as he observes, this suggests strongly that the voicing occurs here as a result of the nasal prothesis common in dialects, by which a nasal is transferred by a process of 'false analysis' onto a following noun or adjective from an accusative article. Thus τὸν ὦμο 'the shoulder', phonetically [tonómo], is sometimes interpreted (in dialects with de-gemination) as the output of /ton+nómo/, so that the nominative comes to be ὁ νῶμος.

Whatever the most appropriate account of this phenomenon, its effect is to collapse the [ty]:[δy] distinction. Again morphophonemic alternation ensures the maintenance of underlying distinctions: [máδg′a] has a singular [máti], while [láδg′a] 'oils' corresponds to singular [láδi] or [lái]. In central Cyprus, where the rule of 'devoicing' applies, so that [δy] from /δi/ goes to [δg′] and then [θk′], there is a threefold neutralization. The simplest way to relate the subdialects of Cypriot is to suppose that they all went through the [máδγ′a] stage; some then applied manner dissimilation and some of these in turn devoicing. Thus central Cypriot καλάθια 'baskets', μάτια 'eyes', λάδια 'oils' will be accounted for thus:

(17)	kaláθia	mátia	láδia
Glide formation	kaláθya	mátya	láδya
Consonantality (special)	**kaláθx′a**	mátγ′a	**láδγ′a**
Voice assimilation		mádγ′a	
Fricativity assimilation		**maδγ′a**	
Manner dissimilation	**kaláθk′a**	**máδg′a**	**láδg′a**
Devoicing		**máθk′a**	**láθk′a**

6.4 Crete and the south east

Although most of the phenomena manifested in the development of consonant + yod sequences as they appear in Crete and the south east represent familiar rules, this dialect group as a whole stands out in exploiting more fully the available phonological processes, and a further dimension of apparent idiosyncrasy is provided by the operation of the various forms of the softening rule on the [x′], [γ′], [k′] and [g′] which arise by consonantality and manner dissimilation from [y]. The dialects listed in Table 7 illustrate the main features found in the area.

The palatalizing consonants (/k, x, γ, s, z, n, l/), which do not behave very differently before yod in these dialects than they do in others, may be left aside for the moment. The remainder are subject to four main rules:

(i) Consonantality
(ii) Softening
(iii) Manner dissimilation
(iv) Depalatalization

Consonantality acts first in all south-eastern dialects, as everywhere, to convert yod to [x′] or [γ′]. This fricative may then be fed to either the

TABLE 7. *Consonant + yod sequences in Crete and the south east*

	py	fy	vy	ty	θy	δy	ky	xy	γy	sy	zy	my	ny	ly	ry
E. Crete	pš	fš	vž	θx′	θx′	δγ′	č	š	ž	s	z	mn′	n′	l′	rž
S. Rhodes	pš	fš	vγ′	tx′	θx′	δγ′	č	š	y	sx′	zγ′	mn′	n′	lǰ	rγ′
N. Rhodes	px′	fk′	vg′	tx′	θk′	δg′	$\overset{s}{t}$	s	y	sk′	zg′	mn′	n′	lg′	rg′
Chios	pk′	fk′	vg′	θk′	θk′	δg′	$\overset{s}{t}$	x′	y	s	z	mn′	n′	l′	rg′
Cyprus	pk′	fk′	fk′	θk′	θk′	θk′	č	š	y	š	ž	my	nny	lly	rk
Kos	pk′	fk′	vg′	δg′	θk′	δg′	č	š	y	sk′	zγ′	mn′	n′n′	l′l′	rg′
Kalimnos	ps	fs	vz	dz	ts	dz	$\overset{s}{t}$	ss	y	ss	zz	mn′	n′	l′	rz
Santorini	ps	fx′	vγ′	ts	ts	dz	$\overset{s}{t}$	x′	y	s	z	mn′	n′	ldz	y

softening rule (converting it to [š] or [ž]) or to that of manner dissimilation (giving [k′] or [g′]), or to both, in which case it is important to know which comes first. To illustrate the various possibilities, let us consider the sequences [θx′] and [fx′]. They may develop, given these two rules, in one of five different ways:

(1) Neither softening nor manner dissimilation occurs (that is, after consonantality has acted to yield [θx′] from [θy] and [fx′] from [fy]); output: [θx′], [fx′]. This situation is not apparently found in true Cretan or south-eastern dialects.

(2) Softening occurs; output: [θš], [fš]. This is characteristic of Crete and southern Rhodes, although after [θ] and the other dentals softening is impeded. Thus we find, for /kupía/ 'oars', /ráfia/ 'shelves', [kupšá], [ráfša]. In Crete [vy] goes to [vž], giving [karávža] for /karávia/ 'boats'.

(3) Manner dissimilation occurs; output: [θk′], [fk′]. This situation occurs in Chios, N. Rhodes, Kos and Cyprus, where we find [alíθk′a] for /alíθia/ 'truth', [ráfk′a] for /ráfia/, [karávg′a] for /karávia/. We saw that [fy] and [θy] convert to [fk′], [θk′] in Thessaly, but it is worth observing that while Thessalian dialects do not possess a softening rule at all, the south-eastern dialects do apply softening to primary /k/ and /x/ in palatalizing environments. What we have then in the case of the dialects of Chios, N. Rhodes, Kos and Cyprus is not the absence of softening but its failure to operate on the output of the consonantality rule. Consider, for instance, the words λάφια 'kids', χέρι 'hand', εὐχή 'blessing' in one of these dialects:

(18)	láfia	xéri	efxí
Glide formation	láfya		
Palatalization		x′éri	efx′í

Manner dissimilation			efk′í
Softening		**šéri**	**efčí**
Consonantality	láfx′a		
Manner dissimilation	**láfk′a**		

We must assume that manner dissimilation operated historically over a fairly long stretch of time. It acted on [fx′] from original /fx/ to yield [fk′] and this was then softened to [fč]. By the time the consonantality rule became active, converting [láfya] to [láfx′a], the softening process was no longer active, although manner dissimilation still operated.

(4) Manner dissimilation and softening occur in that order; output: [θč], [fč]. This particular output is not found in the dialects listed. However, while the general rule is for dialects which apply both processes to the output of consonantality to order softening first, there is sporadic evidence that the present ordering is possible. Dawkins (1904), for instance, reported [karávǰa] 'boats' for /karávia/ in a village on Karpathos, and this, as he suggests, implies the sequence [karávya] > [karávγ′a] > [karávg′a] > [karávǰa]. Similarly τὰ δόντια 'the teeth' may occasionally be heard as [taón′ǰa] in Cyprus. This means that the [n′g′] which arises by, among other rules, manner dissimilation (see 6.5) is then subjected to softening. Finally the sequence manner dissimilation – softening is implied by the [xorďó] reported for /xorío/ 'village' in Astipalea (see below).

(5) Softening and manner dissimilation occur in that order; output: [tš], [fš]. This situation is found in Kalimnos and Santorini; in both islands, however, the [š] is subsequently depalatalized. Similarly the [δγ′] arising from [δy] is in both dialects converted by softening and manner dissimilation to [dz], as is the [δγ′] arising from [ty] in Kalimnos (see derivation (16) above). In southern Rhodes some informants provided [džó] for /δío/ 'two' and [karidžá] for /kariδéa/ 'walnut tree', although [δγ′o], [kariδγ′á] appear to be commoner. In Crete also [džó] is reported by Pangalos[1] for one village, as is [afedžá] for /afentía/ '(your) honour'. These last two are presumably to be accounted for in some such manner as the following:

(19)	afeNTía	δío
Postnasal voicing	afeNdía	
Nasal assimilation II	afeddía	
Degemination	afedía	

[1] See Pangalos (1955: 207).

Glide formation	afedyá	δyó
Consonantality	afedγ'á	δγ'ó
Fricativity assimilation	afeδγ'á	
Softening	afeδžá	δžó
Manner dissimilation	**afedžá**	**džó**

In Kalimnos, while the [γ'] arising by the action of consonantality on [y] is softened to [ž] (as in Crete) and then depalatalized to [z], yet the [γ'] which results from the palatalization of primary /γ/ before front vowels goes to [y] as normally in Greek dialects, and not to the [ž] which occurs in Cretan. The simplest explanation is that initial [γ'] goes to [y] by consonantality in Kalimnos as in Crete (see 5.1) but that softening in Kalimnos applies only to the palatal obstruents [k', x', γ'], not to the glide [y]. Thus γέρος 'old man', παιδιά 'children', θεῖος 'uncle' would develop as follows in Kalimnos:

(20)	γéros	peδía	θíos
Glide formation		peδyá	θyós
Palatalization	γ'éros		
Consonantality	**yéros**	peδγ'á	θx'ós
Softening		peδžá	θšós
Strident depalatalization		peδzá	θsós
Manner dissimilation		**pedzá**	**tsós**

The data for Santorini, as they stand, pose a more serious problem. There secondary [x'] from [y] goes to [s], while palatalized /x/ is not acted on by the softening rule; thus we get [psós] for ποιός 'who?' but [x'éri] for χέρι, 'hand'. Any process which assibilated a secondary [x'] would also, one would imagine, have a similar effect on a primary one. However, there is considerable doubt as to the facts for Santorini; the set of reflexes presented in Table 7 is based on enquiries among young speakers at the southern village of Emboryo, and elsewhere on the island a much more conservative situation appears to exist ([px', tx', θx', δγ', l', rγ']). There are good reasons to suppose that while the replacement of [y] by [s] or [z] after consonants represents a survival from an earlier situation in which softening affected /k/ and /x/ in a regular fashion, [x'] for /x/ is a recent standardizing innovation for [s]. Indeed even [tˢ] for /k/ is nowadays very rare, although it is reported by Georgakas (1934).[1]

1 My informants at Emboryo labelled their dialect [tsevδá], and if it were not for the fact that the rules which it implies are also found in Crete, Kalimnos and elsewhere in the area, I would be tempted to dismiss it as some sort of special language rather than a true if strongly adulterated dialect.

It will thus be seen that much of the variation affecting consonant + yod clusters may be attributed to the interplay of the rules of manner dissimilation, softening and strident depalatalization. If we ignore one or two miscellaneous restrictions (e.g. that softening tends not to affect [x′] or [γ′] after a dental consonant), the basic patterns found in the south east result from the ordering possibilities offered by these rules. The situation may be summarized as follows:

(1) Consonantalization is followed by manner dissimilation in the dialects of northern Rhodes, Kos, Kalimnos, Chios, Santorini and Cyprus; in Crete and southern Rhodes the order is reversed. This accounts for facts such as that northern Rhodes, Chios and Kos have [láδg′a] 'oils' corresponding to the [láδγ′a] of southern Rhodes.

(2) Consonantalization is followed by softening in Crete, southern Rhodes, Kalimnos and Santorini; elsewhere the order is reversed. Thus, while [py] goes to [px′] and then [pš] in the islands listed, elsewhere primary /k/ goes to [č] or [t̑] and often /x/ to [š] or [s], but the [x′] originating in [y] is unaffected. Crete, for instance, has [pšós] for ποιός 'who?' and [rífša] for ρίφια 'kids', while Chios has [pk′ós], [rífk′a]. It may be noted that where [x′] from [y] is unaffected by softening in south-eastern dialects, it undergoes conversion to [k′] in at least some environments.

(3) Softening is followed by strident depalatalization in northern Rhodes, Chios, Kalimnos and Santorini; in eastern Crete the [š] arising from [sy] is depalatalized, but not that arising from either /x/ or [y]. This means that softening in eastern Crete occurs after strident depalatalization. Consider eastern Cretan χέρι 'hand', βυʒιά 'breasts', καράβια 'boats':

(21)	xéri	vizía	karávia
Glide formation		vizyá	karávya
Palatalization	x′éri	vižyá	
Postpalatal yod deletion		vižá	
Consonantality			karávγ′a
Depalatalization		**vizá**	
Softening	**šéri**		**karávža**

Finally in Kos, Cyprus and southern Rhodes, which apply softening to [k′] and [x′], depalatalization does not occur at all. In Kos and Cyprus, softening precedes consonantality, giving us [vračá], [níša] for βρακιά 'trousers', νύχια 'finger-nails' but [rífk′a], [alíθk′a] for ρίφια 'kids', ἀλήθεια 'truth'; in Cyprus, where /s/ goes to [š] before [y] we find [nišá] for νησιά 'islands'. In southern Rhodes softening follows consonantality, so that the derivation there for ρίφια, βρακιά, νύχια, νησιά is as follows:

(22)	rífia	vrakía	níxia	nisía
Glide formation	rífya	vrakyá	níxya	nisyá
Palatalization		vrak'yá	níx'ya	
Postpalatal yod deletion		vrak'á	níx'a	
Consonantality	rífx'a			**nisx'á**
Softening	**rífša**	**vračá**	**níša**	

We conclude this section by considering various phenomena with rather restricted distribution.

The data listed in Table 7 for central Cyprus show [fk'] for [vy] as well as for [fy], and [θk'] for [δy], [θy] and also [ty]. The simplest assumption is that the rule of devoicing (see 4.5), which specifies that a cluster consisting of fricative or liquid followed by a stop is voiceless throughout, applies to the [vg'] arising by consonantality and manner dissimilation from [vy], and to the [δg'] originating in [δy]. Indeed, as we noted above (see derivation (17)), [ty] and [δy] are also represented in Cypriot by [δγ'] (in subdialects which order manner dissimilation before consonantality) and by [δg'] (where the devoicing rule is lacking), so that we may assume that phonetic [θk'] went through the [δγ'] stage whether it represents [δy] or [ty]. A similar situation is reported for a village in Kos by Karanastasis (1963), where καράβια 'boats', χωριά 'villages', αὐγό 'egg' derive thus:

(23)	karávia	xoría	avγó
Glide formation	karávya	xoryá	
Consonantality	karávγ'a	xorγ'á	
Manner dissimilation	karávg'a	xorg'á	avgó
Devoicing	**karáfk'á**	**xork'a**	**afkó**

Although Karanastasis does not mention the fact, comparison with Cypriot suggests that the [r] in [xork'á] is voiceless.

In central Cyprus we find [karafk'a], [afkó], but [xor̥ká] (with a velar stop). We assume here a rare rule converting [γ'] to [γ] between [r] and back vowel:

Velarization: A voiced non-strident fricative with a non-front point of articulation is velar between liquid and back vowel.

This states that of [γ] and [γ′] only the former can occur between a liquid (in fact always [r]) and a back vowel. That the appropriate rule acts on [γ′] rather than on the [g′] which develops from this by manner dissimilation is suggested by the fact that [ry] is realized directly as [rγ] before back vowels in at least one other region (Kastelli, western Crete).[1]

Altogether we find nine reflexes of [ry] in south-eastern dialects. They can be accounted for entirely in terms of the action of various combinations of the normal rules of manner dissimilation, softening, strident depalatalization, velarization and devoicing on [rγ′], the output of the consonantality rule. Abbreviating our rules 'MD, S, SD, V, D' we may represent the facts as follows:[2]

(No rule)	xorγ′ó (S. Rhodes)
MD	xorγ′ó > xorg′ó (N. Rhodes, Kos, Chios)
MD – S	xorγ′ó > xorg′ó > xorǰó (Menites in Karpathos)
MD – S – SD	xorγ′ó > xorg′ó > xorǰó > xorď^{z}ó (Astipalea)
V	xorγ′ó > xorγó (Kastelli in Crete)
V – MD	xorγ′ó > xorγó > xorgó (one village in S. Rhodes)
V – MD – D	xorγ′ó > xorγó > xorgó > xor̥kó (Cyprus, parts of Rhodes and Kos)
S	xorγ′ó > xoržó (Crete)
S – SD	xorγ′ó > xoržó > xorzó (Kalimnos)

The [lǰ], [lg′], [lď^{z}] found in southern Rhodes, northern Rhodes and Santorini respectively presumably arise from the failure of [l] to palatalize before [y] and the consequent persistence of the latter, with the result that it converts by consonantality to [γ′] and becomes subject to the usual rules of manner dissimilation, softening and strident depalatalization. In S. Rhodes, βασιλιάς 'king' could derive somewhat in this manner:

(24)	vasiléas
Height dissimilation	vasilías
Glide formation	vasilyás
Consonantality	vasilγ′ás
Manner dissimilation	vasilg′ás
Softening	**vasilǰás**

[1] See Kondosopoulos (1960).

[2] My source for Astipalea is Pandelidis (1929) and for Rhodian [xorgó], Tsopanakis (1940).

While the processes cited seem to account for the particular outcome [lǰ] there are various difficulties in relating this derivation to the general framework underlying S. Rhodian: it is odd, for instance, that [lγ′] should go to [lg′] while [vγ′] and [δγ′] are unaffected by manner dissimilation. Furthermore softening almost always precedes manner dissimilation, so it might be preferable to go from [vasilγ′ás] to [vasilžás] and then insert a 'buffer' [d] by the same rule as converts [θéls] to [θélts] in the north (see 7.4). One clear principle of ordering does emerge: the rule of delateralization, which converts [l] to [r] before a consonant, must precede the action of consonantality, as the converse order would yield [vasilyás] > [vasilγ′ás] > *[vasirγ′ás].[1]

In Kimolos and Siphnos [ly] is reported to go to [y],[2] presumably by a rule similar to the one converting [l′] to [y] found in Spanish dialects and in French (cf. *fille* [fíy] from [fíl′a]). The development in these dialects of the item βαρέλια 'barrels' would be:

(25)	varélia
Glide formation	varélya
Palatalization	varél′ya
Postpalatal yod deletion	varél′a
[l′] > [y]	**varéya**

The change [ry] to [y] in Santorini has a quite different origin: there [r] drops in all positions.

An interesting situation arises in two Naxian villages.[3] Apparently there (*a*) primary /l/ is lost intervocalically before back vowel and (*b*) [ly] is replaced by [l]. ἔλα 'come!' and ἐλιά 'olive' would develop according to this information thus:

(26)	éla	elyá
/l/ deletion	**éa**	
Palatalization		el′yá
Postpalatal yod deletion		el′á
[l′] *depalatalization*		**elá**

The conventional historical account would probably claim that the rule of /l/ deletion had ceased to operate when [l′] went to [l], so that the new [elá] remained intact. Emellos, however, claims that the /l/ of new words introduced into the dialect from outside is still deleted according

[1] Some speakers seem to have [l′ǰ]; see 5.3.
[2] By Vogiatzidis (1925).
[3] The facts are described in Zevgolis (1956) and Emellos (1964).

to the same rule as reduced /éla/ to [éa], which might appear to lend support to the view sometimes held which denies that sound change always operates directly on the phonetic form of words. In this case, it might be argued that the /l/ deletion rule was still active, but affected not all cases of [l], only those which reflected underlying /l/, not those stemming from [ly]. On the other hand it is not clear whether the new items referred to by Emellos actually possess the intervocalic liquid when introduced into the dialect which replaces [ly] by [l], for the rule deleting intervocalic primary [l] is widely distributed in the island, and it may be that the newly introduced items are better regarded as not having an /l/ from the start.

There are still many unexplained features in the data; it is unclear, for instance, why [θx′] is exempt from softening in Crete, and indeed in general whether immunity to otherwise regular processes has a phonological basis or represents standardizing influence. The conversion of [xy] and [sy] to [ss] in Kalimnos clearly involves some lengthening process; the underlying distinction between [nny] and [ny] as well as between [lly] and [ly] is collapsed in both Cyprus and Kos, but there appears to be no obvious link between this and the Kalimnos phenomenon. It is worth noting that in various geminating dialects other than that of Kalimnos the item νησί is pronounced [nissí], and its plural [nissá], but in this case the geminate must be attributed to the underlying form. The present account represents at most a tentative outline of the main phonological processes found to operate in the area on post-consonantal yod.

6.5 Sequences of two consonants and yod

It remains to consider briefly cases in which a yod is preceded by two consonants. There are three cases worth distinguishing for our purposes:

(*a*) Sequences of consonant + [r].
(*b*) Other heterogeneous clusters.
(*c*) Geminate sequences.

(*a*) *Sequences of consonant* + [r]. To this group belong items such as /γréa/ 'old woman', /kréas/ 'meat', /tría/ 'three', /ovréos/ 'Jew', /ávrion/ 'tomorrow', /krío/ 'cold'. In many dialects, including at least some northern and perhaps some Peloponnesian ones, as well as in standard Athenian, glide formation is blocked in such cases (see 2.7), and in the north at least a hiatus-stopping [y] may subsequently develop: thus in Vourbiani (Epirus)[1] we find [kríyo], [ávriyo]. More relevant to our present topic are dialects in which glide formation in fact occurs after a consonant + [r] sequence. In Peloponnesian dialects in which this situation is found there is little to add to our previous observations: consonantality applies, as it does to [y] after [r] alone, and we find forms such as [krγ'ó], [ávrγ'o], [γrγ'á], [krγ'ás]. In the island dialects we find, however, the forms [križó] (Crete) and [kriyó] (Lesbos), [krikó] (Cyprus) and [krió] (Rhodes, Simi, Karpathos). Now while the northern [kríyo] can be explained on the basis of straightforward epenthesis, this is not easy with Lesbian [kriyó], for it is not clear how the assumption of epenthesis can be reconciled with the observed shift of stress. The only way in which stress can be shifted is by glide formation, but this cannot occur once epenthesis has converted /krío/ to [kríyo]. The probable line of development was rather as follows:

(27)	krío
Glide formation	kryó
Vowel epenthesis	**kriyó**

This derivation is confirmed by Cypriot [krikó] 'cold', [krikás] 'meat', [r̥ká] 'old woman', [triká] 'three', [ár̥kon] 'tomorrow'. It will be recalled that in Cypriot /xorío/ 'village' goes to [xor̥kó] (see 6.4) by various rules, and we may assume that these same rules account for the [k] in [krikó] etc.: κρύο 'cold' and γριά 'old woman' would then develop thus:

(28)	krío	γréa
Height dissimilation		γría
Glide formation	kryó	γryá
Consonantality	krγ'ó	γrγ'á
Velarization	krγó	γrγá
Manner dissimilation	krgó	γrgá
Devoicing	kr̥kó	γr̥ká
Initial [γ] *deletion*		**r̥ká**
Vowel epenthesis	kr̥ikó	

The voiceless [r̥] of [kr̥ikó] would then be revoiced by a late phonetic rule.

This epenthesis rule, if the above account is correct, is also found in

[1] The dialect of Vourbiani is described by Anagnostopoulos (1930).

Crete. We may suppose that there a sequence [Crγ′] converted to [Criγ′] and the [γ′] went by the normal Cretan softening to [ž]. The deletion of initial [γ] in Cypriot from [γr̥ká] represents an alternative method of dealing with the phonetically inadmissible [Crk] cluster. That [γ] but not [k] should be deletable is not surprising, as intervocalic [γ] is lost frequently, while the stops are among the most stable sounds. Forms such as [krió], [triá], [kriás], which are found in the area, can be explained on the assumption that epenthesis was followed by the usual south-eastern rule of voiced fricative deletion.

It may be worthwhile at this point to summarize the derivations in various dialects of the word κρέας 'meat'. There seem to be at least eleven possibilities. In the dialects which do not apply glide formation to the [i] which follows a sequence of consonant + [r], height dissimilation may or may not occur. It occurs in Zakinthos, giving [krías], and in parts of the north west this goes by a version of /γ/ epenthesis to [kríyas]. In the north east and Crete height dissimilation is replaced by contraction, giving [krä́s] in the former area, [krés] in western and [krás] in eastern Crete. In standardizing idiolects and always in Athenian Greek none of these rules applies. We thus obtain the following picture for dialects which do not apply glide formation to this form:

(29)	kréas	kréas	kréas	kréas	kréas	**kréas**
Fronting	kréäs	kréäs	kréäs	—	—	—
Contraction	**krä́s**	**krás**	**krés**			
Height dissimilation				krías	**krías**	—
/γ/ epenthesis				**kríyas**	—	—

In dialects which apply glide formation at least the following five developments are found:

(30)	kréas	kréas	kréas	kréas	kréas
Height dissimilation	krías	krías	krías	krías	krías
Glide formation	kryás	kryás	kryás	kryás	kryás
Consonantality	krγ′ás	krγ′ás	krγ′ás	krγ′ás	**krγ′ás**
Velarization	krγás	—	—	—	—
Manner dissimilation	krgás	**krg′ás**	—	—	—
Devoicing	krkás	—			
Vowel epenthesis	**krikás**	—	kriγ′ás	kriγ′ás	—
Voiced fricative deletion			**kriás**	—	
Consonantality				**kriyás**	

[krikás] is found in Cyprus, as noted; northern Rhodes has [krg′ás], southern Rhodes and various other islands [kriás]. [kriyás] is found in the Cyclades and Lesbos and [krγ′ás] is common in rural Peloponnese. It is also likely that dialects with [xorǰó], [xord^{z}ó], [xorzó] for /xorío/ 'village' (see 6.4) will also have [krǰás], [krd^{z}ás], [krzás].[1]

(*b*) *Other heterogeneous clusters.* Many heterogeneous clusters other than those in [r] end in one of the palatalizing consonants, in which case palatalization is followed by loss of the [y] in the normal way. Thus ἀρνιά 'sheep', παπούτσια 'shoes' in a dialect where [s] palatalizes before [y] (as in eastern Crete) will derive as follows:

(31)	arnía	papútsia
Glide formation	arnyá	papútsya
Palatalization	arn′yá	papútšya
Postpalatal yod deletion	**arn′á**	papútša
Depalatalization		**papútsa**

When the consonant immediately preceding [y] does not palatalize, the [y] will convert in the usual way to [x′] or [γ′], thus yielding a sequence of three consonants. /karδía/ 'heart', /omorfía/ 'beauty', will go to [karδγ′á], [omorfx′á], for instance. While in most dialects this leads to no further development, in dialects in which the [x′] and [γ′] are subject to manner dissimilation, softening or both, as is the case with south-eastern dialects, the middle consonant tends to drop by the rule of cluster simplification. Thus in Crete, southern Rhodes and western Cyprus we find [omoršá], which suggests this derivation:

(32)	omorfía
Glide formation	omorfyá
Consonantality	omorfx′á
Softening	omorfšá
Cluster simplification	**omoršá**

In Crete and western Cyprus αὐτιά 'ears' is pronounced [afšá], which seems to imply the loss of a [t] between two continuants, although the rule of cluster simplification does not normally affect stops in this circumstance. However, in these dialects fricativity assimilation operates

[1] Unfortunately the Ἱστορικὸν Λεξικόν does not go as far as this item and I have no record of these forms in my notes; however the work mentioned does give in the article on αὔριο 'tomorrow' spellings such as αὔρτʒο (Nisyros), αὔιρʒο (Kalimnos).

and we may suppose it to take effect before simplification. Cretan [afšá] will accordingly derive as follows:

(33)	aftía
Glide formation	aftyá
Consonantality	aftx'á
Fricativity assimilation	afθx'á
Cluster simplification	afx'á
Softening	**afšá**

After /r/ the loss of [θ] and [δ] does not appear to occur in Crete, and thus καρδιά 'heart' and χαρτιά 'cards' appears there as [karδγ'á], [xarθx'á]. It will be recalled that softening does not occur after dental consonants in Cretan, so that in the case of [afšá] we must assume the prior application of cluster simplification. Where softening does affect [x'] and [γ'] after dentals, [δ] and [θ] may be acted on by manner dissimilation, as in the case of Kalimniot [kardzá], or the [kardžá] found in parts of southern Rhodes. In dialects where manner dissimilation, but not softening, follows consonantality [δ] drops between a consonant and [y]. Thus in Chios, Kos and northern Rhodes /karδía/ develops via [karδγ'á] to [karδg'á] and the cluster is then reduced to yield [karg'á]. In central Cyprus devoicing takes effect, giving [kar̥k'á] (usually 'stomach', 'heart' being [karδía]).

Apart from [rf] and [rδ], [sp], [Np] and [rp] are found before [y], as well as various clusters with [t] as second member. One important point of ordering which emerges from the study of [Np] and [Nt] clusters is that postnasal voicing must precede consonantalization. Consider, for instance, κουμπιά 'buttons' in a dialect such as Cretan:

(34)	kuNpía
Postnasal voicing	kuNbía
Nasal assimilation II	kubbía
Degemination	kubía
Glide formation	kubyá
Consonantality	kubγ'á
Softening	**kubžá**

The first three rules are ordered in the usual manner as are the last three; the crucial constraint linking the two triples is that postnasal voicing must precede consonantality. If it followed consonantality we would get [px′] for [py] and it would not be possible to convert this to [bγ′]. The principle applies also to more conservative dialects, e.g. those with [kumbγ′á] or [kubγ′á]. The derivation of δόντια 'teeth' in Cretan will parallel that of κουμπιά, and again it is crucial that postnasal voicing should precede consonantality. The application of the rules required to yield [kubγ′á] will give us [δódγ′a], whereafter fricativity assimilation acts to convert this to [δóδγ′a]. Thus, just as the singular [máti] 'eye' alternates with plural [máθx′a] in Cretan, [δódi] matches plural [δóδγ′a]. The [δódza] of Santorini and the [δóndza] of Kalimnos again depend on an intermediate step [dy] > [δγ′], the [γ′] then going by softening and depalatalization to [z].

One of the problems with regard to postconsonantal yod concerns the reflex [k′] for [ty] which occurs in the dialects of Chios, Kos and Cyprus after another consonant: /aftía/ 'ears' > [afk′á], /xartía/ 'cards' > [xark′á], /aróstia/ 'illness' > [arósk′a], /aδráxtia/ 'spindles' > [aδráxk′a]. Pernot[1] assumed a rule palatalizing [t] to [k′] in the environment between consonant and [y]:

(35)	aftía
Glide formation	aftyá
[ty] > [k′y]	afk′yá
Postpalatal yod deletion	**afk′á**

The difficulty with this account is that there is no independent evidence in these particular dialects for the palatalization of [t]. Where [t] does go to [k′] in Plumari (Lesbos) the relevant environment is before [i] or [y] so that /aftía/ goes to [afk′á] there by the same rule as converts /mátia/ 'eyes' to [mák′a], and /aftí/ 'ear' to [afk′í]. But in Chios and Cyprus /mátia/ is pronounced [máθk′a]. Indeed it seems highly probable that the [k′] in an item such as [afk′á] is of just the same origin as the [k′] in [máθk′a]; there is no reason whatever to invoke a special rule. αὐτιά, χαρτιά, ἀρρώστια, μάτια may be derived as follows:

(36)	aftía	xartía	aróstia	mátia
Glide formation	aftyá	xartyá	aróstya	mátya
Consonantality	aftx′á	xartx′á	aróstx′a	mátx′a
Fricativity assimilation	afθx′á	xarθx′á	arósθx′a	máθx′a
Manner dissimilation	afθk′á	xarθk′á	arósθk′a	**máθk′a**
Cluster simplification	**afk′á**	**xark′á**	**arósk′a**	

[1] See Pernot (1907: 264 ff.).

In these same dialects [nty] goes to [n′g′]: δόντια 'teeth' is pronounced [δón′g′a]. There is again no reason to make any *ad hoc* assumption:

(37)	δóntia
Postnasal voicing	δóndia
Glide formation	δóndya
Consonantality	δóndγ′a
Fricativity assimilation	δónδγ′a
Manner dissimilation	δónδg′a
Cluster simplification	δóng′a
Nasal assimilation	**δón′g′a**

Pernot mentioned, only to reject, this possibility of deriving [δón′g′a] via [δónδγ′a]; his objection was that such an intermediate stage would have gone to [δóδδγ′a] by nasal assimilation, and that there is no way to derive the phonetic [n′] from this. In actual fact he himself cites [δóδg′a] as possible in some villages, and this, far from invalidating the derivation offered here for [δón′g′a], may be held rather to support it, for the difference between the two subdialects can now be reduced to one of variation in rule order: both dialects derive intermediate [δónδg′a] and then proceed as follows:

(38)	δónδg′a		δónδg′a
Nasal assimilation	δóδδg′a	*Cluster simplification*	δóng′a
Cluster simplification	δóδg′a	*Nasal assimilation*	δón′g′a

(*c*) *Sequences of geminate consonant + yod.* The development of sequences of geminate consonant + yod does not appear to raise any important problems. Again the distinction between palatalizing and non-palatalizing consonants is crucial. Palatalizing segments undergo the same processes when geminate as when simple and the normal outcomes of /kk, xx, nn, ll/ before yod are [k′k′, x′x′, n′n′, l′l′], and of the geminate sibilants in dialects which palatalize them, [šš, žž]. Softening converts [k′k′] and [x′x′] to [čč] and [šš]. μελίσσια 'swarms' as it develops in some Chian dialects illustrates the essential features:

(39)	melíssia
Glide formation	melíssya
Palatalization	melíššya
Postpalatal yod deletion	melíšša
Depalatalization	**melíssa**

Dialects which palatalize /s/ but lack the rule of depalatalization, such as Cypriot, will have [melíšša].

Where the yod following a nonpalatalizing geminate such as [ff] or [θθ] converts by manner dissimilation to [k'], the rule of 'geminate reduction in clusters' (4.7) shortens the geminate, so that, e.g., contrast is lost between [θθy] and [θy]. Consider, for example, the derivations of ἀνθιά 'blossoms' and βαθειά 'deep' in Chian:

(40)	anθía	vaθéa
Height dissimilation		vaθía
Glide formation	anθyá	vaθyá
Nasal assimilation	aθθyá	
Consonantality	aθθx'á	vaθx'á
Manner dissimilation	aθθk'á	**vaθk'á**
Geminate reduction	**aθk'á**	

This may lead to alternation between a geminate in the singular of neuter nouns and a corresponding single consonant in the plural: /xáppin/ 'pill' and its plural /xáppia/ appear as [xáppin] and [xápk'a] in Cyprus; similarly [aŋgáθθi] 'thorn', plural [aŋgáθk'a].

Where softening affects the secondary [x'] or [ɣ'] from [y] it again appears that the length contrast is neutralized, although the facts are not absolutely clear. In S. Rhodes, the outcomes of [ppy] and [py] sound homophonous but since in this dialect (as in general in geminating ones) [p], [t] and [k] are pronounced tense before sibilants, we may have in this case a lengthening of [pš] rather than a shortening of [ppš].

7 Northern Dialects

7.0 Many of the phonological processes described in earlier chapters occur in northern as much as in southern dialects, and in dealing with them we have often had occasion to refer to the northern rules of high vowel loss and mid vowel raising. In this chapter we look specifically at these rules and in particular at their relations to those which are found in all dialects. The first section considers the circumstances which tend to impede high vowel loss, in so far as these can be identified in phonological terms at all. Section 7.2 examines certain cases in which high vowel loss apparently acts on the secondary [i] and [u] produced by raising from /e/ and /o/, and then the relation of both rules to palatalization and certain other processes. Some problems relating to stress are discussed in 7.3. Much of the apparent strangeness of northern pronunciations results from the way in which the clusters produced by high vowel loss are subsequently acted on by various rules to which primary clusters are subject. Thus [mátsa] 'I plucked' exhibits the result of applying voice assimilation and manner dissimilation to [máδsa], which itself comes from /máδisa/. Rules such as these, which apply to the secondary clusters resulting from high vowel loss, are discussed in 7.4. Others, such as nasal assimilation and degemination, are found no longer to operate after high vowel loss, so that a word such as /mprómita/ 'prone' goes to [brómta] rather than *[brónda]; these are dealt with in 7.5.

7.1 The conditions of high vowel loss and raising

It is by no means the case that all unstressed high vowels are deleted and all unstressed mid vowels raised in northern Greek dialects. For one thing, there is a group of dialects, the so-called 'semi-northern' ones, in which high vowel loss occurs, but not raising.[1] These are spoken in Thrace and the island of Skiros, and present little of special interest; it may be suggested, however, that they represent a stage through which

[1] The isogloss for semi-northern dialects is located by Andriotis (1944).

all northern dialects must have passed, for the prior occurrence of high vowel loss in the synchronic rule sequence (see 7.2) almost certainly reflects the historical sequence of events. But apart from such 'moderate' dialects, it is still not true that a dialect which possesses high vowel loss and raising will exploit both rules to the full. While much fluctuation is doubtless fairly unpredictable, certain general factors may be singled out as militating against the occurrence of at least loss. Some are essentially phonological while others would traditionally be thought of as rather 'grammatical' in nature.

Turning first to phonological constraints on high vowel loss, we may start by examining what is perhaps the hypothesis most commonly formulated in the literature – that high vowel loss fails to occur when the consonant cluster which would thereby result is 'difficult to pronounce' (δυσεκφώνητον). Now if 'difficult to pronounce' means 'not found as the reflex of a primary cluster' the statement is factually mistaken. We find in northern dialects a large number of clusters which are 'impermissible' in this sense: /to kukkí/ 'the bean' appears as [tukk'í] with a sequence of velar and palatal stop impossible as the outcome of a primary cluster and never found in southern dialects; /fánika/ 'I appeared' is pronounced [fán'ka] with the sequence nasal + voiceless stop, /simáδi/ 'sign' as [smáδ] or [šmáδ], with an 'impossible' cluster of voiceless sibilant + nasal. If on the other hand 'difficult to pronounce' is simply used of those clusters whose threatened appearance inhibits high vowel loss the statement becomes circular. What is required is a systematic study for each dialect of the precise segmental conditions which impede loss, and no one seems to have done this.

As far as resultant dyadic clusters are concerned there indeed appears to be no unambiguous evidence that the nature of the cluster in itself plays any role in determining the occurrence of high vowel loss. The most detailed listing available of clusters which allegedly inhibit high vowel loss is in Anagnostopoulos (1915) for the dialect of Zagori (Epirus). It is there implied, for instance, that /lipíθika/ 'I was sorry' and /kirá/ 'madam' retain their first [i], becoming [l'ipíθka] and [k'irá], because [k'r] and [l'p] are difficult clusters; but yet /alepú/ 'fox' becomes [al'pú] and the preservation of the vowel of [k'irá] could equally well be attributed to its relation to [k'írie] 'Mr'. Nor is it at all clear that /kseróvixas/ 'dry cough' and /xeliδóni/ 'swallow' go to [ksiróvixas] and [x'il'iδón'] rather than the [ksirófxas], [x'il'δón'] we find elsewhere because of the difficulty of [fx] or [l'δ].

What is perhaps true for many dialects is that word-final clusters tend to be avoided. In the dialect of Saranda Ekklisies (Thrace), for instance, the occurrence of a dyadic cluster in word-final position is avoided in one of two ways. In some cases high vowel loss is simply impeded, so that while /sitári/ 'wheat' goes to [štár], /vukéntri/ 'goad' goes to [fk′édri]. The alternative solution is to apply high vowel loss and then delete the final consonant, so that /péfti/ 'he falls' goes to [péft] and then [péf]. Indeed this type of specifically word-final cluster simplification is quite widespread. Various dialects drop the final [n] resulting from the third plural verbal ending -ουν when the stem terminates in a consonant: /θa+párun/ 'they will take' > [θapár] (Etolia, Imbros). Where the consonant preceding the [n] of third plural verb forms is of the palatalizing group an interesting alternation may occur between singular and plural. Thus in, e.g., Thasos while /pézun/ 'they play' goes via [pézn] to [péz], the singular /pézi/ is realized as [péž]; similarly, in such dialects, we get [éx′] 'he has' from /éxi/ versus [éx] 'they have' from /éxun/. Again the final [n] of certain nouns is sometimes lost by the application of this principle: /skepárni/ 'adze' > [sk′ipár] in Zagori. Still a third device for avoiding final clusters is provided by vowel epenthesis (7.4). In Lesbos /éxun/ 'they have' goes to [éxn] and then [éx′in], while dialects such as that of Etolia which have a final /e/ on the third plural morpheme convert their /éxune/ to [éxni], never *[éx′ini]. In spite of all this final clusters are widely tolerated: many dialects have [éxn], [sk′ipárn′], [péft], [fk′éndr].

We are on somewhat firmer ground when we claim that the probability of high vowel loss decreases as the resultant cluster becomes longer than dyadic. The only case I have found of loss resulting immediately in a four-member cluster is /xristós/ 'Christ', and names such as /xristóδulos/ formed from it. But the resultant [xrstós] is always reduced by cluster simplification to [xstós], where things remain, or manner dissimilation acts to yield [kstós] (as in Lesbos). In other items loss is impeded: /vurtsízo/ 'I brush' > [vurt͡sízu], /sfixtós/ 'tight' (itself from /sfinktós/) > [sfixtós], /pastrikós/ 'clean' > [pastrikós], /éskuksa/ 'I howled' > [éskuksa].

While in general the threat of a dyadic cluster never in itself impedes loss, and the threat of one of more than triadic length does impede it, a triadic cluster may or may not have an inhibitory effect. We saw earlier that a small number of triadic clusters occur phonetically for underlying consonant sequences (4.7); it would be natural to suppose that when such a cluster would result from high vowel loss, loss takes place, and this is in fact found. Thus /skulíki/ 'worm' goes to [skl'ík'] (compare σκληρός 'hard'), /proskunó/ 'I adore' goes to [prosknó] (compare σκνίπα 'midge'). We also noted that there is a rule of cluster simplification which deletes the middle consonant of a triadic cluster unless the second and third terms form one of three exempt sequences: (*a*) sibilant + any consonant, (*b*) stop + sibilant or liquid, (*c*) any consonant + palatal fricative (see 4.7). If these conditions are met, then high vowel loss occurs and the resultant cluster survives intact. If not (i.e. if the resultant cluster meets the conditions for simplification), then one of two things might happen: high vowel loss might fail to occur or it might occur and be succeeded by simplification. To clarify this, let us consider a few examples.

(*a*) The resultant cluster is of a type exempt from simplification; high vowel loss occurs and the outcome survives intact. As examples in which the resultant cluster has a sibilant as middle term we may take /persinós/ 'last year's' and /meθizménos/ 'drunk'. These go to [piršnós] (or [pirsnós]) and [meθzménus], [miδzménus], [midzménus]. Although in the second instance the resultant [θzm] may be affected by voice assimilation or even manner dissimilation, there is no loss. For instances with stop as second and liquid or sibilant as third term we have /éstila/ 'I sent' and /ániksa/ 'I opened'; here again high vowel loss occurs, giving [án'ksa] and [éstla] and the clusters remain. It may be observed that in these and many other cases, although the clusters meet the conditions for exemption from simplification, they are not found as reflexes of primary clusters. Neither [n'ks] nor [stl] can arise otherwise than by high vowel loss, and are accordingly not found in southern dialects. The item ἀνιψιός 'cousin' also meets the conditions for loss without simplification, although the derivation of its common northern form [ampšós] is a little complex:

(1)	anipsiós
Glide formation	anipsyós
Dental palatalization	anipšyós
Postpalatal yod deletion	anipšós
High vowel loss	anpšós
Nasal assimilation	**ampšós**

(*b*) The resultant cluster meets the conditions for simplification; high vowel loss fails to act, or it acts and is followed by simplification. The simplification conditions are met by the [plt], [krv], [xtp], [ftk] which would result were high vowel loss to affect /áplitos/ 'unwashed', /ékriva/ 'I was hiding', /ktipáo/ 'I hit', /paNTrévθika/ 'I married'. What we find is that loss is impeded in the first two cases, giving [ápl'itus], [ékriva], while in the others it and simplification take effect:

(2)	paNTrévθika	ktipáo
Postnasal voicing	paNdrévθika	
Voice assimilation	paNdréfθika	
Nasal assimilation	pandréfθika	
Manner dissimilation	pandréftika	xtipáo
High vowel loss	pandréftka	xtpáo
Raising		xtpáu
Cluster simplification	**pandréfka**	xpáu
Weak glide formation		**xpáw**

It may be observed in passing that because manner dissimilation takes place before high vowel loss (see 7.4) it may under certain circumstances have the effect of preserving from simplification clusters otherwise subject to this. In the case of the /fθik/ above we would still obtain the correct result if we failed to apply manner dissimilation before loss, for both /fθk/ and /ftk/ meet the conditions for simplification. But consider /ésxisa/, 'I tore'. Palatalization converts this to [ésx'isa], and if we now apply high vowel loss we obtain [ésx'sa], which is now reducible by simplification to *[éssa]. Here the prior action of manner dissimilation is crucial to the correct output: /ésxisa/ > [ésx'isa] > [ésk'isa] > [ésk'sa], this in many dialects going by palatality assimilation to [éšk'sa] (see 5.3). There is a general tendency for high vowel loss to be inhibited when the middle term of a resultant triadic cluster would be a sonant. Thus /ksetripóno/ 'I unearth' > [ksitripónu], /almirós/ 'salty' > [armirós], /akrivós/ 'expensive' > [akrivós]. However there are exceptions: /kriθári/ 'barley' often goes via [krθár] to [kθár] and /arsenikós/ 'male' is found widely as [asirkós], implying first metathesis to [asernikós], then high vowel loss and simplification.

The most specific statement on the factors inhibiting high vowel loss which has emerged so far would be to the effect that it tends to be blocked when the resultant cluster would be either longer than triadic or would be triadic with a sonant as middle term. There are two other classes of constraint commonly cited in the relevant literature. The first concerns the occurrence of high vowels in successive syllables and the second the effects of 'analogy'. A brief discussion is in order.

When unstressed high vowels occur in two successive syllables before stress, it appears to be a general rule that only the second one drops. Thus /puliménos/ 'sold' > [pul'ménus] (but [pl'iménus] 'washed' < /pliménos/), /pisinós/ 'rear' > [pišnós], /vissinéa/ 'sour cherry tree' > [višn'á], /sinnimfáδes/ 'wives of brothers-in-law' > [šinfáδis]. The only example known to me with more than two such unstressed high vowels is /δimitriáris/ 'October', which appears in Lesbos as [δimtriárs] (suggesting that the rule can be generalized to delete alternate high vowels starting with the first counting from stress to qualify). But exceptions are not hard to find. While most northern informants gave [θil'kó] for /θilikó/ 'female', for instance, I found [θl'ikó] in Thasos and a village in southern Thessaly. Kretschmer, from whom the above examples are drawn, found that κυνηγῶ 'I hunt' appeared in Lesbos as [čniγó] (but [k'inγáw] in Epirus).[1]

The blocking of high vowel loss is often attributed to 'analogy' with allomorphs in which the particular high vowel occurs in stressed position. Any such account must rely on the fact that because stress shifts occur within paradigms and between derivationally related forms, one essential condition for high vowel loss, viz. that the vowel be unstressed, may not be met in all the given alternants of a given morpheme. As may be seen from the following typical examples, this often results in alternation between a stressed /i/ or /u/, and zero:

σῦκο, συκόφυλλο	'fig, figleaf'	[síku], [škóflu]
μῆλο, χαμόμηλο	'apple, camomile'	[mílu], [xamómblu]
πίττα, βασιλόπιττα	'pie, new year's cake'	[píta], [vašlópta]
βούτα, βουτῶ	'dip!, I dip'	[vúta], [vtó] (or [ftó])
ἀκούω, ἄκουσα	'I hear, I heard'	[akúw], [áksa]
πήδηξα, πηδῶ	'I jumped, I jump'	[píδiksa], [bδó]
δούλεψα, δουλέψετε	'I worked, you worked'	[δúlipsa], [δlépsiti]

While such alternation is common, it is sometimes suggested that high vowel loss may be inhibited in the unstressed forms through the influence of the stressed ones. A speaker, it is claimed, will avoid saying [ftó] for /vutó/ 'I dip' because he associates this form with other members of the paradigm such as /vúta/ 'dip!' in which loss cannot occur. In more modern but equivalent terms, where alternation occurs

[1] See Kretschmer (1905: 93). His first example, repeated in Papadopoulos (1927: 16), is unfortunate. [vul'kós] surely represents βολικός 'handy' rather than his βουλικός, for which there appears to be no authority in available dictionaries.

the speaker knows that there is an underlying form with a high vowel, and he is therefore at liberty to apply or not apply the rule of high vowel loss. Where high vowel loss has affected a morpheme at a point where a stressed counterpart of the vowel in question does not occur in any variant, this knowledge is not available. This thesis is supported by facts such as that κουβεντιάζω 'I converse' tends to be heard everywhere as [kvindγ'ázu] or [gvindγ'ázu], for no other members of the paradigm with [kúv] exist to inform the speaker what, if anything, has dropped. But κουράζω 'I tire' is perhaps always [kurázu], never *[krázu], for the existence of [kúrasa] 'I tired', and various other forms with stressed [ú] indicate an underlying stem /kuraz/.

Now while it may be true that the existence of stressed alternants favours resistance to high vowel loss, the cases listed above indicate that it by no means blocks it automatically. Indeed alternation between unstressed high vowel and zero is so characteristic of verb paradigms that it is sometimes wrongly introduced through a mistaken reconstruction of the underlying form. Thus [kapnízu] is interpreted in Zagori to represent not /kapnízo/, which standard [kapnízo] requires, but */kapinízo/, so that the aorist is derived /kapínisa/ > [kapín'sa] rather than normal /kápnisa/ > [kápn'isa]. Similarly the underlying form /pníγo/ 'I drown' yielding [pníγu] is restructured as /piníγo/, which would give the same result; the aorist, however, is now derived /píniγsa/ > [pín'ksa] instead of /épniγsa/ > [épn'iksa]. In cases such as these it would appear that the pattern of alternation provided by verbs such as φιλῶ 'I kiss', which in Zagori has the first singular present and aorist forms [fláw]:[fíl'sa] from /filáo/:/fílisa/, has been generalized.

We have mentioned some of the specific factors which may militate against the regular operation of high vowel loss; what makes a proper assessment of these suggestions difficult, if not impossible, however, is that we are not able for at least contemporary speakers to separate out what is indubitably the most powerful inhibiting factor of all – that northern speakers will have a knowledge of the southern vowel structure of a word (in all but a few purely local items), derived from contact with speakers of southern dialects, or more probably nowadays from exposure to the standard language. Speakers of northern dialects seem to exert deliberate control over the degree to which they allow northern phonological rules to affect their speech. As a Greek scholar has pointed out, βουτῶ 'I dip' may be pronounced [vutó], [v^{w}tó], [vtó] or [ftó], and the reason is that 'the image (ἴνδαλμα) of each word lives in the speaker's mind in its intact shape, and from this proceed all the forms produced on individual occasions; they approximate more or less closely to it according to the varying inclinations of the speaker'.[1]

7.2 The position of high vowel loss and raising in the rule sequence

Apart from questions relating to stress and the secondary clusters which arise from high vowel loss, various problems emerge with regard to (*a*) the relative ordering of high vowel loss and raising themselves, (*b*) their relation to palatalization, (*c*) their relation to glide formation and (*d*) their relation to the rule lowering /i/ to [e] before /r/. These are discussed in the present section.

(*a*) The essential constraint governing the relative ordering of high vowel loss and raising is by now familiar: high vowel loss precedes, with the result that any high vowel created later by the raising rule is no longer subject to loss. This crucial feature can be illustrated by comparing the derivations for ἔμεινε 'he remained' (aorist) and ἔμενε 'he used to remain' (imperfect):

(3)	émine	émene
High vowel loss	émne	
Raising	**émni**	**émini**

Clearly a transposition of these rules would cause /émene/ to go to [émini] and then *[émn]. This synchronic ordering suggests the inference that loss preceded raising historically, and indeed the assumed first stage, with loss alone, is found nowadays, as we observed above, in the dialects of Skiros and eastern Thrace.

It is clear from this that the northern speaker must be able to distinguish those occurrences of [i] and [u] which derive from underlying /i/ and /u/ from those which reflect raised mid vowels; for only the former are subject to high vowel loss. As we saw, this knowledge depends to a large extent on the occurrence of alternation; the speaker hears [épisa] 'I fell' and [áfisa] 'I left', let us say, but while he may repeat the latter as [áfsa], he never says *[epsa]. For while the [i] of [épisa] alternates with [é], as in [θapésu] 'I shall fall', the [i] of [áfisa] alternates with [í], as in [θafísu] 'I shall leave'. But suppose there exists no common stressed variant of a given morpheme; does the speaker then sometimes interpret

[1] Phavis (1951: 5).

an unstressed [i] or [u] as deriving from /i/ or /u/ when in fact either rare stressed allomorphs or the practice of speakers of southern dialects imply /e/ or /o/? The answer appears to be that this in fact happens. The word παιδί 'child' is pronounced [peδí] in southern dialects and when its stressed allomorph does appear in the north it shows an [é]: ψυχο-παίδι 'godchild' is in northern dialects [pšixupéδ] (or [pškupéδ]). And yet the pronunciation [pδí] or [bδí] is not known. If we assume that in this and similar cases the lack of common alternation has resulted in restructuring of the underlying form, then the derivation of παιδί may be compared to those of παιδεύω 'I torment' and παίδεψα 'I tormented' as follows:

(4)	/peδí/	/peδévo/	/péδepsa/
Raising	piδí	**piδévu**	**péδipsa**
(Restructuring)	/piδí/		
High vowel loss	pδí		
Voice assimilation	**bδí**		

While [piδévu] is consistently assigned the underlying structure /peδévo/ because of the existence of [péδipsa] (and, for the /o/, perhaps of verbs with stressed personal ending such as [buró] 'I can'), [piδí] has no obvious matching alternant with [péδ] and is subject to reinterpretation as /piδí/. Other examples showing loss of secondary [i] or [u] are as follows:

περιστέρι	'pigeon'	[pl′istér]
ἀλεπού	'fox'	[al′pú]
ἀγελάδα	'cow'	[γ′láδa]
νερό	'water'	[n′ró]
μεδούλι	'marrow'	[mδúl′]
γομάρι	'load'	[γmár]
βοτρύδι	'bunch of grapes'	[ftríδ]
χωνί	'funnel'	[xn′í]
φιλενάδα	'girl friend'	[fil′náδa]

The transcriptions on which the above data rely (mostly in Andriotis 1931) do not make it clear whether the sonants in [al′pú], [n′ró], [fil′náδa] have the same grade of palatality as occurs when a primary /i/ has dropped; if they have not, then an account which assumes restructuring of the underlying form loses much of its plausibility.

Andriotis, in the work just cited, has shown that secondary high vowels preceded or followed by liquid or nasal are particularly vulnerable to loss: γελῶ 'I laugh', for instance, appears quite widely as [γ′ló] or [γ'láw]. He also suggests that such loss is characteristic of dialects which show other 'extreme' features such as the application of manner dissimilation to the output of high vowel loss, entailing, for instance, the pronunciation of /kutí/ 'box' as [xtí]. If this is correct, it is the breakdown of ordering constraints rather than the possession of unusual rules which determines the degree of aberrance in northern dialects.

There are various other cases in which northern dialects delete what in the south is a mid vowel, but which are to be carefully distinguished from the loss of secondary high vowels just described. For instance, the words πάνω 'above', κάτω 'below' are pronounced [pán], [kát], but the prior raising of /o/ to [u] in these words is found in the Peloponnese and elsewhere and is unrelated to northern raising (see 2.2). Again the reduction of -ετε to -τε in the second plural aorist imperative is common in southern dialects (πάρτε 'take!', δόστε 'give!') and even when the same morpheme is reduced in the second person plural active indicative, a peculiarly northern development, we probably have an extension of this same process of syncopation. The same applies to the loss of the first vowel of the homophonous third singular passive morpheme -εται, as in [xriázte] for /xriázete/ 'he needs'. That all three verbal endings are subject to loss in eastern Thrace, which has a semi-northern dialect, and does not raise /e/ to [i], confirms that what we have is some process of syncope.[1] Finally it must be kept in mind that a considerable number of ancient cases of ο or ω are reflected by [u] in southern dialects, so that northern forms such as [gδún'] for southern [kuδúni] 'bell', ancient κώδων, simply imply underlying /u/, /i/ (see derivation (3) of 2.2).

(*b*) The relation of palatalization to high vowel loss and raising was discussed in chapter 5 (see especially 5.2). While northern dialects differ in the scope and phonetic description of their palatalization rules they all agree in the possession of two crucial ordering constraints:

(i) High vowel loss cannot act until the dialect has applied whatever palatalization rules it possesses.

(ii) Any palatalization conditioned by [i] but not [e] cannot apply after raising, i.e. it affects primary /i/ but not the [i] arising from /e/. These points will be examined in turn.

To show that high vowel loss cannot occur before all palatalization rules have acted we may take any word in which the final syllable

[1] See Psaltis (1905: 21). Again details of palatality are sorely needed. I assume his χρειάʒ.ται represents [xriázte] and not [xriážte]; certainly δόστε is [δósti] and not [δóšti] in northern dialects which palatalize sibilants before /i/.

consists of a palatalizing segment + unstressed /i/. Consider ράχη 'back', μέλι 'honey', βαπόρι 'boat' in the dialect of Velvendos:

(5)	ráxi	méli	vapóri
Palatalizations	ráx'i	mél'i	vapór'i
High vowel loss	**ráx'**	**mél'**	**vapór**

This dialect not only palatalizes the velars before /i/ and /e/, which is universal, and the dentals /s, z, t, n, l/ before /i/, which is common in the north, it also palatalizes these dentals before /e/ and all other consonants before /i/. The dialects of northern Epirus palatalize only velars, but our basic principle applies equally to both sets of dialects. In Epirus we find [ráx'], [mél], [vapór], not because high vowel loss precedes the palatalization of /l/ and /r/, but because non-velar segments do not palatalize at all before /i/. In the dialects of Thessaly and Macedonia, in which all consonants palatalize before /i/, the effect of this principle of rule ordering is to create a plain: palatal contrast in word-final position throughout the whole consonantal system. Thus, while all northern dialects contrast the exclamation [óx] with [óx'] 'no' from /óxi/, and most contrast [róz] 'pink' with [róž] 'corns' from /rózi/, in Thessaly and Macedonia the recently borrowed [spór] 'sport' contrasts with [spór'] 'seeds' from /spóri/, and [kát] 'down' from /kátu/ contrasts with [kát'] 'something' from /káti/; compare also the final syllable of [pal'üpéδ'] 'rascal' from /paleopéδi/ with [k'éδ] the abbreviation of Κέντρον 'Εκπαιδεύσεως Διαβιβάσεων 'School of Signals'. This plain: palatal contrast may also arise before consonants by the same processes of palatalization and high vowel loss. Thus in all dialects κινῶ 'I move' and κουνῶ 'I shake', if they coexist, will contrast as [k'nó]: [knó] or [k'náw]: [knáw]. Compare also, for contrast in the dentals, [tfílt] 'of his friend' from /tu + fílu + tu/ and [ifíl't] 'his friends' (nom.) from /i + fíli + tu/.

The constraint which orders palatalization before raising can be established only on the evidence of consonants which palatalize before [i] and [y], that is, for most dialects /s, z, n, l/. The Lesbian dialect of Ayassos provides an excellent illustration for the sibilants. There the words βάʒει 'he places' and ἔβαʒε 'he was placing' derive as follows:

(6)	vázi	évaze
Dental palatalization	váži	
High vowel loss	**váž**	
Raising		**évazi**

The output of the raising rule, [évazi], is no longer subject to the rule which converted original /vázi/ to [váži]. In this dialect sibilants are palatalized only before [i] and [y], not [e], as is the case in, e.g., Thessaly, and, as in all northern dialects for which published data are available, this palatalization precedes raising. Another example may be taken from Etolia, where /n/ and /l/ palatalize before high front non-consonantal segments but not the mid [e]. Let us take τέχνη 'trade' and ἔχουν 'they have':

(7)	téxni	éxune
Dental palatalization	téxn'i	
High vowel loss	**téxn'**	éxne
Raising		**éxni**

Again original, but not secondary, [ni] sequences undergo palatalization. It is therefore possible for [n] to contrast with [n'] not only finally and preconsonantally (e.g. [ván'] 'he places' from /váni/ versus [pán] 'above' from /pánu/) but before [i]. The word /nistikós/ 'not having eaten' will in this and similar dialects become [n'istkós] or, with cluster simplification, [n'iskós], for, as we saw in 7.1, when high vowels occur in successive syllables, only the one adjacent to stress is deleted; but /neró/ 'water' will appear as [niró]. Similarly for /l/: [θal'ipθó] 'I shall be sorry' from /θa+lipiθó/ but [liruménus] 'dirty' from /leroménos/.

That dental palatalization does not act on the output of the raising rule might be thought to follow automatically from the facts that (*a*) dental palatalization must precede high vowel loss in order that, for instance, /váni/ might go to [ván'] and (*b*) high vowel loss must precede raising, so as to ensure that secondary [i] and [u] remain intact. However, the argument from transitivity does not apply to this situation. Not only can we imagine the sequence [ni] going to [n'i] every time it arose historically, just as [xi] always goes to [x'i] (see derivation (8) in 5.1), but precisely this situation can be inferred for the obsolete dialect of Silli in Cappadocia. We are told that there /n/ and /l/ 'before all *i* sounds, old and new, are pronounced *mouillée*'; thus we find for ἡ γυναίκα του φορτώνεται 'his wife dresses', [enékatufortón'iti].[1] As both high vowel loss and raising also occurred in Silli (although under grammatically restricted conditions) and palatalization appears to have preceded high vowel loss as in northern dialects, we may suppose that the item /éline/ 'he was loosening' would have been derived in Silli as follows:

[1] See Dawkins (1916: 45, 298).

(8)	éline
Dental palatalization	él′ine
High vowel loss	él′ne
Raising	él′ni
Dental palatalization	**él′n′i**

But there is no evidence within the core dialects, as has been stated already, that palatalizations which are triggered by /i/ but not /e/ can also be brought about by secondary [i]. That [él′n′i] is possible in Thessaly and Macedonia is a consequence of the fact that there /i/ and /e/ induce equivalent grades of palatality in the dentals.

(*c*) Glide formation, as was shown in 2.7, is ordered before high vowel loss: /póδia/ 'feet', for instance, converts first to [póδya], so that what was originally /i/ is no longer subject to loss. However, we have also seen that the [i] and [u] generated by raising is converted in postvocalic position to [y], [w], as the case may be. Thus we found that /éleγe/ 'he was saying' develops by various rules to [éliyi], the yod drops, yielding [élii], and this finally goes by 'weak glide formation' to [éliy] (see derivation (10) in 3.3). The relation between glide formation, high vowel loss and weak glide formation may be further illustrated by a consideration of typical northern forms for φιλιά 'kisses', φιλάει 'he kisses', φιλάω 'I kiss', φίλαγε 'he was kissing'. We start from the stage at which /γ/ epenthesis has occurred:

(9)	filía	filáγi	filáγo	fílaγe
Glide formation	filyá			
Palatalizations	fil′yá	filáγ′i		fílaγ′e
Postpalatal yod deletion	fil′á			
Consonantality		filáyi		fílaye
High vowel loss	**fl′á**	fláyi	fláγo	
Raising			fláγu	fílayi
Intervocalic yod deletion		flái	fláu	fílai
Weak glide formation		**fláy**	**fláw**	**fílay**

The [γ] of [filáγo] is deleted by analogy with members of the paradigm in which /γ/ converts to [y] before front vowel (see 3.3). The reason for setting up a special rule of weak glide formation rather than allowing the normal rule of glide formation to act a second time was given in 3.3. It is that normal glide formation acts on stressed [í] and converts a sequence [ii] to [yi], while once intervocalic yod deletion has occurred [í] remains intact and [ii] goes to [iy].

(*d*) It is in general true that all those ancient vowels and diphthongs which normally go to [i] in unstressed position are represented in southern dialects by [e] when an /r/ follows. Thus for standard γυρεύω 'I seek', μοιράζω 'I share', πληρώνω 'I pay', ξηρός 'dry', σκληρός 'hard', θηρίο 'wild animal' we find [yerévo], [merázo], [pleróno], [kserós], [sklerós], [θeryʹó]. Now stressed vowels are unaffected by this 'preliquid lowering' (μοῖρα 'fate' > [míra], πῆρα 'I took' [píra]) so that we would expect cases of alternation between [er] and [ír]. Such alternation may indeed be found in a few sets of derivationally related items, as in Cypriot [číris] 'father' < κύριος versus [čerkačí] 'Sunday', [čerá] 'mother-in-law' < Κυριακή, κυρία. But apart from such marginal cases analogical pressure has generalized the [e], or in some cases the [í]. Thus we find that the aorists of [pleróno], [merázo] are [plérosa], [mérasa] rather than the expected [plírosa], [mírasa], and μοιρολόγι 'dirge' is pronounced [mirolóyi] under the influence of [míra] 'fate'. Thus preliquid raising has little relevance to the synchronic phonological structure of the dialects, although, like many other historical processes, it serves to account for certain demotic:katharevusa correlations.

We may accordingly take the underlying vowel in such cases to be /e/ rather than /i/, and this applies equally well to northern dialects. There, for southern [pleróno]:[plérosa], [merázo]:[mérasa] we find [plirónu]:[plérusa], [mirázu]:[mérasa]. Apart from considerations of alternation we may note that the [l] of [plirónu] appears to possess the grade of palatality associated with /e/ (or secondary [i]), not that found before /i/. Similarly in the dialect of Ayassos (Lesbos), which palatalizes /s/ to [š] before /i/, we find [ksirós] not *[kširós]. If we did wish to set up a rule of preliquid lowering it would have to be very early in the rule sequence. The derivations of (θὰ) πληρώσῃ 'he will pay', πλήρωσε 'he payed' would then run somewhat as follows:

(10)	plirósi	plírose
Preliquid lowering	plerósi	
(Generalized)		plérose
Dental palatalization	pleróši	
High vowel loss	pleróš	
Raising	**pliróš**	**plérusi**

The word τυρί 'cheese' is always [tirí] in northern dialects, never *[trí], and this might suggest that preliquid lowering applied historically and converted an original /tirí/ to [terí]. Similarly πειράζει 'it matters' is always [piráz] (or [piráž]), never *[práz]. But that the correct explanation is rather that high vowel loss fails to affect an underlying /i/ in both cases is suggested by two considerations: in stressed allomorphs there is no shift to [é] ([pírazi] 'it mattered'), and these items show [i] in the south.

7·3 The northern rules and stress

Stress, as we have seen, plays a crucial role in the operation of both high vowel loss and raising; neither can occur on a stressed syllable. It is important to note in this connexion that phonetic stress, with which we are concerned, is not completely coextensive with graphic stress, and that in particular the various forms of the definite article, the proclitic pronouns μέ, σέ, τόν, τήν, τό, τοῦ, τῆς, τούς, τίς, the conjunction καί and various short prepositions such as μέ, ἀπό, are phonetically unstressed and accordingly undergo the northern rules of high vowel loss and raising:

μὲ θέλει	'he wants me'	[miθél']
τῆς νύφης	'of the bride'	[dznífs]
ἀπὸ τὸ κουτί	'from the box'	[aputuktí]
νὰ σὲ πῶ	'let me tell you'	[nasipó]

The two categories of stress which we have been distinguishing in this book are 'primary' and 'enclitic'. Primary stress is placed on verbs in accordance with the three mora rule: /afise/ 'he left' takes stress on the third mora from the end, giving us [áfise] and the same applies to /afinī/ 'he leaves', which becomes [afínī], for [ī] is worth two moras. In the case of nouns and adjectives we have been assuming an inherent stress which, however, is subject to shift in accordance with the restriction imposed by the three mora rule. Thus /ánθropos/ 'man' (nom.) has an underlying genitive /ánθropū/ which undergoes stress shift to [anθrópū].

The placing of primary stress on verb forms and its shifting in the case of other grammatical classes precedes high vowel loss and raising. Thus:

(11)	ánθropū	ánθropos
Stress placement	anθrópū	
High vowel loss	**anθróp**	
Raising		**ánθrupus**

If stress placement were ordered after high vowel loss and raising we would get /ánθropū/ > *[ánθrup]. In the case of verbs the effect of this transposition would be that no verb would ever appear with a stressed mid vowel. Thus /θelome/ 'we want' would convert by raising to [θilumi] and this by stress placement to *[θílumi], while what we actually find is [θélumi]. That stress placement, which was inherited from ancient Greek, should apply in modern Greek before the historically much later rules of high vowel loss and raising seems natural enough. Yet it would be equally natural to make a similar assumption regarding enclisis, although, as we shall now see, this assumption would be incorrect.

Because the possessive του 'his' is enclitic in modern dialects (except or Cypriot and certain dialects formerly spoken in Asia Minor) τὸ γόνατό του 'his knee' /to+γónato+'tu/[1] is pronounced in southern dialects [toγónatótu]. The object pronoun τόν 'him' throws back its stress in a similar manner: σκότωσέ τον 'kill him' /skótose+'ton/ [skótoséton]. Now in order to predict the northern forms of these phrases it is obviously crucial to know whether raising or enclisis occurs first. The outputs we actually find, [tuγónatót], [skótusétun], imply the following derivations:

(12)	to+γónato+'tu	skótose+'ton
Enclisis	to+γónató+tu	skótosé+ton
High vowel loss	to+γónató+t	
Raising	**tu+γónató+t**	**skótusé+tun**

There does not appear to exist any dialect which applies raising before enclisis, yielding, for instance, from /skótose+'ton/, [skótusi+'tun] and finally *[skótusítun]. Consider now, though, the phrase οἱ γειτόνισσές μας 'our neighbours'. The application of enclisis, high vowel loss and raising in that order would yield the following result:

(13)	i+γitónisses+'mas
Palatalizations etc.	i+yitón'ises+'mas
Enclisis	i+yitón'isés+'mas
High vowel loss	i+ytón'sés+mas
Raising	(inapplicable)

This would ultimately go to [iγ'tón'sézmas], and is in fact sometimes found. We also find [iγ'tón'sizmas] which implies a different ordering:

[1] The preposed stress sign indicates enclitic elements.

(14)	i+γitónisses+'mas
Palatalizations etc.	i+yitón'ises+'mas
High vowel loss	i+ytón'ses+'mas
Enclisis	i+ytón'ses+mas
Raising	i+ytón'sis+mas

Because high vowel loss has had the effect here of converting /γitónisses/ into a paroxytone form, enclisis results in the complete loss of enclitic stress (see derivation (17) of 2.7). Exactly the same fluctuation between the relative orderings of high vowel loss and enclisis affects constructions with the imperative verb form and enclitic pronoun. Thus in Tyrnavos /afike+'ton/ 'leave him!' may be realized as [áfk'étun] or [áfk'itun]. As in all dialects primary stress placement acts first to convert this to [áfike+'ton] and palatalization yields [áfik'e+'ton], whereafter one of two things may happen:

(15*a*)	áfik'e+'ton
Enclisis	áfik'é+ton
High vowel loss	áfk'é+ton
Raising	**áfk'é+tun**

(15*b*)	áfik'e+'ton
High vowel loss	áfk'e+'ton
Enclisis	áfk'e+ton
Raising	**áfk'i+tun**

We thus find that two results are possible, [áfk'étun] or [áfk'itun].

Thus, while high vowel loss and enclisis on the one hand always precede raising on the other, they may themselves occur in either of the two possible orders. This fluctuation acquires particular significance in northern dialects because these, in company with Cretan, Ionian and certain other dialects, often allow paradigmatic pressures to shift primary stress further back than the three mora rule permits. Thus many northern dialects shift on to the previous syllable the stress of the present passive endings of the first and second persons plural, so that while Peloponnesian dialects have [erxómaste] 'we come', [erxósaste] 'you come', possible northern counterparts might be [érxumasti], [érxusasti] (cf. [érxumi] 'I come'). The same applies to imperfect forms such as [érxumastan], [érxusastan]. This shifting of stress to the syllable fourth from the end is also characteristic of certain Thessalian aorist and imperfect active forms. Thus the stress of [éfaγa] 'I ate' is generalized to [efáɣaman] 'we ate' and [efáyetan] 'you ate'. Now when this happens, most dialects, northern and southern, avoid violation of the three mora rule by adding a second stress on the next-but-one syllable, giving [érxumásti], [érxusásti], [éfaɣáman], [éfayétan].[1] The net effect of this addition of a second stress is quite similar to that of enclisis, in that it preserves the three mora rule intact; furthermore the parallelism extends to the matter of ordering. Consider first the Thessalian [ékuvétan] 'you were cutting':

(16)	ekovetan
Stress placement	ekóvetan
(Analogical shift)	ékovetan
Second stress	ékovétan
Raising	**ékuvétan**

Second stress placement, like enclisis, always precedes raising, so that we never find pronunciations such as *[ékuvítan]. Again, however, the placement of second stress resembles enclisis in that it may precede or follow high vowel loss. Thus, in Vourbiani (Epirus) standard τραβήξατε 'you pulled' is matched by either [trávksiti] or [trávkséti]. After primary stress placement has acted on /traviksete/ to yield [travíksete], and this has undergone analogical stress shift, we find that two orderings are possible:

(17*a*)	tráviksete
Second stress	trávikséte
High vowel loss	trávkséte
Raising	**trávkséti**

(17*b*)	tráviksete
High vowel loss	trávksete
Second stress	(no change)
Raising	**trávksiti**

[1] My main sources for this section are Hoeg (1925/6), Tzartzanos (1913), Georgiou (1962). What I call 'second' stress is usually referred to by Greek scholars as 'secondary' (δευτερεύων), but my observations do not confirm the implication that the second stress is weaker. A northern speaker's [érxumástan] has to my ears the same stress and intonation pattern as [élapézmas], ἔλα, πές μας 'come, tell us!', and the Cretan's [érxomástene] resembles [élafílatin] ἔλα, φίλα την 'come, kiss her!'

7.4 Secondary clusters: rules following high vowel loss

While there is no rule which applies invariably to the secondary clusters arising from the loss of unstressed high vowels, six are found to act on them with some degree of regularity. Three involve assimilatory or dissimilatory feature change. They are (*a*) voice assimilation, (*b*) manner dissimilation and (*c*) palatality assimilation, all of which have been discussed in connexion with primary clusters (4.4, 4.5, 5.3). Three others involve epenthesis or deletion and are (*d*) cluster simplification (see 4.7), (*e*) vowel epenthesis and (*f*) buffer consonant epenthesis.

(*a*) *Voice assimilation.* The rule of voice assimilation applies in the case of primary clusters to obstruent sequences and to sibilant + sonant sequences. We shall consider first secondary sequences with stop as first member, and then those with fricative as first member.

As voiced stops are in general found only after nasals it is obvious that in dialects with nasal assimilation I (in which /nt/, for instance, goes to [nd]), both stops of a secondary dyadic cluster will be voiceless (e.g. /kutí/ 'box' > [ktí]), and the question of voice assimilation will not arise. Where the second type of nasal assimilation is found, as in Thrace and Lesbos, it will be possible for stops of different voice state to come into contact and we then find that voice assimilation is normal. Consider κουμπί 'button', κουντῶ 'I push', ποντικός 'mouse' in the dialect of Thasos:

(18)	kuNPí	kuNTó	poNTikós
Postnasal voicing	kuNbí	kuNdó	poNdikós
Nasal assimilation II	kubbí	kuddó	poddikós
Degemination	kubí	kudó	podikós
High vowel loss	kbí	kdó	podkós
Voice assimilation	**gbí**	**gdó**	potkós
Raising			**putkós**

Voice assimilation is also found to affect secondary clusters of stop + fricative. The following examples are taken from various northern dialects:[1]

πηγάδι	'well'	[bγáδ]
κουδούνι	'bell'	[gδún']
κουβαλῶ	'I carry'	[gvaló]

[1] Tzartzanos (1909), from whom I take most of these items, does not mark any palatality in [urtágδis], [rágzan], although the depalatalization before sibilant thus implied is usually attributed only to the Sarakatsans. The use of /ti/ for /tu/ (gen. sing. masc., neut.) is common in the north.

πηδῶ	'I jump'	[bδó]
τηγάνι	'frying pan'	[dγán']
ὀρτάκηδες	'partners'	[urtágδis]
ράκιζαν	'they were drinking ouzo'	[rágzan]
ὅτι δίνεις	'whatever you give'	[od'δín'ts]
τοῦ βασιλιά	'of the king'	[d'vasl'á]

These examples showed the voicing of [p, t, k] before voiced fricatives. In dialects of the Thracian type [b, d, g] will be devoiced before voiceless fricatives. Thus κολύμπησα 'I swam', ἔντυσα 'I dressed' develop as follows in Ayassos, Lesbos:

(19)	éNTisa	kolíNPisa
Postnasal voicing	éNdisa	kolíNbisa
Nasal assimilation	éddisa	kolíbbisa
Degemination	édisa	kolíbisa
High vowel loss	édsa	kolíbsa
Voice assimilation	**étsa**	kolípsa
Raising		**kulípsa**

The [ts] of [étsa] is distinct from the [t͡s] arising from primary /ts/, and this is commented on further in 7.5. Where nasal assimilation I operates it appears that voice assimilation overrides the effect of postnasal assimilation in cases such as this, so that we find, e.g., [éntsa], [kulímpsa]. This is just what one would expect from an ordering which places postnasal voicing before high vowel loss, but allows voice assimilation to act whenever applicable. In the case of the first two items of derivation (18) the conditions for voice assimilation do not arise and [kmbí], [kndó] are heard. When the sequence nasal + stop + stop arises in such a dialect as in [pundkós] 'mouse' I believe that voice assimilation again takes precedence, giving [puntkós], but my data are fragmentary. One would expect cluster simplification to be possible, yielding [punkós].

Like stops, fricatives also tend to assimilate in voice to a following obstruent, although not with quite the same degree of regularity. The following are typical for fricative + stop sequences:

λαδικό	'oil-press'	[laθkó]
δικός μου	'mine'	[θkósim]
ἀνέβηκα	'I went up'	[anéfka]
συμπαθῶ	'I pity'	[žbaθó]
βουτῶ	'I dip'	[ftó]
γράφονταν	'it was being written'	[γrávdani]

The last example implies an underlying /γráfuNTane/;[1] its derivation and that of [žbaθó] are as follows:

(20)	γráfuNTane	sinPaθó
Postnasal voicing	γráfuNdane	sinbaθó
Nasal assimilation II	γráfuddane	sibbaθó
Degemination	γráfudane	sibaθó
Dental palatalization		šibaθó
High vowel loss	γráfdane	šbaθó
Voice assimilation	γrávdane	**žbaθó**
Raising	**γrávdani**	

Cases involving sequences of two fricatives where voice assimilation occurs without manner dissimilation are somewhat difficult to find, but one does occasionally come across them in the literature. Σαράφηδες 'money-changers', for example, is said to be pronounced [sarávδis] in Zagori and ἔφυγε 'he left' as [évγ'i] in a village near Velvendos;[2] θὰ φοβηθῶ 'I shall fear' sometimes appears as [θafufθó]. But such agreement does not appear to be automatic by any means unless accompanied by manner dissimilation. Thus a form such as /ampóδisa/ ἀμπόδησα 'I prevented' is usually found as either [ampóδsa] or [ambótsa], although [ambóθsa] is possible. μεθυσμένος 'drunk' tends to appear as [midzménus], with both manner dissimilation and voice assimilation, or as [meθzménus] with neither. There is some evidence that analogical influence may play some role in inhibiting the action of voice assimilation. Thus τραγούδησε 'he sang' often remains [trayúδsi], perhaps because the existence of forms such as [trayδísami] 'we sang' reinforces the identification of its underlying form as /trayuδise/; δισάκκι 'saddle-bags' usually appears as [tsák'], presumably because there is no common alternant with [δís]:

(21)	δisákki
Degemination	δisáki
Palatalization	δisák'i
High vowel loss	δsák'
Voice assimilation	θsák'
Manner dissimilation	**tsák'**

[1] [γrávdani] is from Papadopoulos (1927: 16).

[2] Katafigio, according to Boundonas (1892: 18). The first person is also cited as [ívγa] for Chalkidiki (Papadopoulos 1923).

Finally we may observe that [s] does not assume the voice state of a following sonant in secondary clusters arising from high vowel loss, in spite of the fact that a sibilant is predictably voiced before a sonant in underlying clusters, whether word-medial (κόσμος 'world' [kózmos]) or straddling a word boundary (τῆς νύφης 'of the bride' [tiznífis], northern dialects [dzn'ífs]). Thus in Epirus and most Lesbian dialects σημάδι 'mark', συνάχι 'cold', συλλογή 'collection' take the shapes [smáδ], [snáx'], [sluí], and in dialects which palatalize sibilants before /i/ such as that of Ayassos (Lesbos) [šmáδ], [šnáx'], [šluí].

We may conclude that secondary dyadic consonant clusters resulting from high vowel loss normally undergo voice assimilation where both members are obstruents, but that /s/ is not voiced before sonants, as happens with primary clusters. Exceptions are frequent, and may be particularly likely when there occur allomorphs with intervening stressed vowels. Perhaps more important are considerations of 'stylistic' level. In Lesbos /vutína/ 'barrel' was always given by informants as [vtína], while /rakovutína/ 'raki barrel, ouzo addict' seems to exist only in the form [rakuftína].

(*b*) *Manner dissimilation.* The only secondary clusters to be affected at all commonly by manner dissimilation appear to be those consisting of non-labial fricative and /s/. Thus /méθise/ 'he got drunk', /traγúδise/ 'he sang' often go to [métsi], [traγútsi] and /xristós/ 'Christ' (particularly when it occurs in names such as /xristóδulos/) is prone to go to [kstós]. In this latter case high vowel loss yields [xrstós], in spite of the normal blocking of the rule when clusters of more than triadic length result, and cluster simplification reduces it to [xstós]. /ávγustos/ 'August' develops in Thrace, Thessaly and parts of Lesbos to [ákstus]; that [áxstus] is found in certain places supports our decision to treat voice agreement as a rule which applies immediately its input conditions are met, for by placing it before manner dissimilation we can generate both these dialectal forms:

(22)	ávγustos
High vowel loss	ávγstos
Voice assimilation	áfxstos
Raising	áfxstus
Cluster simplification	**áxstus**
Manner dissimilation	**ákstus**

Although there is not enough evidence to determine how the cluster simplification rule should be extended to cover the loss of [f] above, we may compare the dialectal [aksáno] 'I increase' for standard [afksáno] (see 4.7). Voice assimilation is shown here, as occasionally elsewhere, to act iteratively (i.e. to assimilate all members of an obstruent cluster to their final term). The sequence /xis/ normally appears as [x′s], as in /vréxis/ 'you wet' > [vréx′s], but the common /éxis/ 'you have' is reported as [ék′s] in Tyrnavos.[1]

That /s/ can occlusivize a following fricative after loss of an intervening high vowel is shown by the forms [ždérs] 'Sideris' and [ždiručéfalus] 'iron-head' found in Ayassos (Lesbos). The latter develops /siδero-kéfalos/ > [šiδeročéfalos] > [šδeročéfalos] > [žδeročéfalos] > [žδiru-čéfalus] > [ždiručéfalus]. Similarly /siδerosíni/ 'iron tray' goes to [ždirušín′].

The action of manner dissimilation on secondary clusters other than those containing /s/ is almost unknown. [θafuftó] is reported for /θa+foviθó/ 'I'll be afraid' and the Sarakatsans are claimed to pronounce /kutávia/ 'puppies' as [xtávγ′a]. Certainly the normal situation (and the only one recognized as possible by most informants) can be represented by a comparison of the typical pronunciations of ἑπτά 'seven' and μηλόπιττα 'apple pie':

(23)	eptá	milópitta
Degemination		milópita
Manner dissimilation	eftá	
High vowel loss		**mlópta**
Raising	**iftá**	

(*c*) *Palatality assimilation.* We saw that in the case of primary clusters palatality assimilation affects the cluster [sk′], converting it to [šk′] in many dialects, including northern ones, but that in general palatalization affects only the final member of a cluster. When a plain and a palatal consonant come into contact as a result of high vowel loss, palatality assimilation again seems not to occur. It may be observed that in secondary as opposed to primary clusters the palatal element may precede. Thus /sikóni/ 'he raises' goes to [škón′] in dialects which palatalize /s/ to [š] before primary /i/, thus contrasting with [skón′]

[1] See Tzartzanos (1909: 32). It is not clear from his spellings whether we have the pronunciations cited, or [éks], [vréxs]. The change [k′s] > [ks] is usually attributed to the Sarakatsans (see below).

'dust' from /skóni/; similarly for /θilikó/ 'female', /γinéka/ 'woman', /kitázo/ 'I look' we find [θil'kó], [γ'néka], [k'tázu]. Even where one of the consonants is a palatalized counterpart of the other, we do not find assimilation: /kukkí/ 'bean' > [kk'í], /túrkika/ 'Turkish' > [túrk'ka].

However, I have found several cases where some sort of palatality assimilation affects the output of high vowel loss, depalatalizing in each case the first member of the cluster.

(i) While γυναίκα 'woman' usually goes to [γ'néka], it is reported as [γnéka] by an informant from N. Epirus.

(ii) A palatalized /n/ seems occasionally to go to velar [ŋ] before /k/ in Epirus, but usually when postnasal voicing also applies. Thus γίνηκα 'I became' may be found as [yíŋga] rather than the commoner [yín'ka]. But this process is perhaps better regarded as an instance of nasal assimilation.

(iii) In the dialects of Thessaly and Macedonia, in addition to velar and dental palatalization we find a rule of 'general palatalization' which affects all consonants. Any consonant palatalized by this latter rule (but not the others) loses its palatality when brought into contact with a following plain consonant.[1] The forms found in Velvendos for λύπη 'grief', λύπης (the genitive of this) and χελώνης 'tortoise' (gen.) will accordingly develop as follows:

(24)	lípi	lípis	xelónis
Palatalizations	l'íp'i	l'íp'is	x'elón'is
High vowel loss	**l'íp'**	l'íp's	x'elón's
Raising			**x'ilón's**
Palatality assimilation		**l'íps**	

(iv) In the dialect of Plumari (Lesbos), the [k'] which arises from /t/ before /i/ and [y] is depalatalized to [k] when it comes into contact with a following /s/; thus, while an original /kis/ is realized as [čs], /tis/ goes to [ks]. Compare the derivations of προίκισα 'I dowered' and πάτησα 'I stepped':

(25)	príkisa	pátisa
Velar palatalization	prík'isa	
Softening	príčisa	
Dental palatalization		pák'isa
High vowel loss	**príčsa**	pák'sa
Palatality assimilation		**páksa**

[1] I imagine that when the second consonant is palatal this effect is not found, but my data are not sufficiently detailed on the point to warrant a definite conclusion.

(v) When [k′s] arises from /kis/ in the dialect spoken by the Sarakatsans the stop converts back to [k] by palatality assimilation. Thus the name /kostákis/, pronounced [kusták′s] throughout most of northern Greece, will appear in their dialect as [kustáks].

(*d*) *Cluster simplification*. If a triadic cluster arises as a result of high vowel loss the middle term is deleted by cluster simplification unless this and the third term represent one of the exempt sequences (see 4.7, 7.1). This cluster simplification may be followed by voice assimilation, as may be seen by considering the form of κλέφτηδες 'thieves' which is reported for Saranda Ekklisies (Thrace):

(26)	kléftiδes
High vowel loss	kléftδes
Raising	kléftδis
Cluster simplification	kléfδis
Voice assimilation	**klévδis**

Miscellaneous illustrations showing the effect of cluster simplification are as follows:

χτυπῶ	'I hit'	[xpó]
κάρβουνα	'coal'	[kárna]
κριθάρι	'barley'	[kθár]
νηστικός	'fasting'	[niskós]
στουπί	'tow'	[spí]
δέχτηκα	'I received'	[δéxka]
κουράστηκα	'I got tired'	[kuráska]
παντρεύτηκα	'I married'	[pandréfka]
τὰ ἀφεντικά	'the master and mistress'	[tafiŋká]
ἔρχουνται	'they come'	[érdin] (Thasos)

The last item appears to have an underlying /érxuNTen/, in which case it derives thus:

(27)	érxuNTen
Postnasal voicing	érxuNden
Nasal assimilation II	érxudden
Degemination	érxuden
High vowel loss	érxden
Raising	érxdin
Cluster simplification	**érdin**

Cluster simplification does not in general apply across word boundaries. Thus μᾶς χτύπησε 'he hit us' never, it seems, goes to [mastípsi]. The definite article constitutes an interesting exception, and while the details vary considerably, readers may form some impression of what may occur by examining the development of στὴν κόρη 'to the girl' and στὴν πόρτα 'to the door' in Lesbos:

(28)	stinkóri	stinpórta
Postnasal voicing	stingóri	stinbórta
Nasal assimilation II	stiggóri	stibbórta
Degemination	stigóri	stibórta
High vowel loss	stgór	stbórta
Voice assimilation	zdgór	zdbórta
Cluster simplification	**zgór**	**zbórta**

(*e*) *Vowel epenthesis*. High vowel loss, in addition to bringing single consonants into final position, may also create final clusters. Sometimes a final /i/ has been lost as in [ríxt] 'he throws' from /ríxti/ or [sk'iparn'] 'adze' from /skepárni/, or more rarely a final /u/ as in [t'kózm] 'of the world' from /ti + kózmu/. In other cases the high vowel is lost from the position before final consonant: /éxun/ 'they have' > [éxn], /tis + níNfis/ 'of the bride' > [dznífs]. When the second (or third) consonant of the resultant cluster is a liquid or nasal an epenthetic [i] may develop before this.[1] The conditions under which this epenthesis occurs can only be defined for a given dialect in terms of certain grammatical restrictions. There are three main cases:

(i) Throughout the greater part of the northern dialect area, when the final /s/ of a noun or adjective (occasionally a verb) comes into contact with the enclitic μου 'my', the /u/ drops and an [i] is inserted between the [s] and [m]. However, there are four possible outcomes, which may be studied by considering the forms taken by δικός μου 'my own':

[θkósim]	(Epirus, Lesbos, Samos)
[θkósum]	(N. Euboea)
[θkózim]	(Macedonia, Imbros)
[θkózum]	(Thessaly)

[1] For a detailed listing of cases see Papadopoulos (1927: 22 ff.). For Lesbian [ríx'in's] etc. see Kretschmer (1905: 107). He asserts that the velar is not palatalized in such cases, but my informants at Ayassos certainly had [č, x', y] in the third plural. I could find no stems in consonant + /n/ (e.g. for ρίχνω 'I throw', ψάχνω 'I seek' they had [ríxto], [pšázu]).

There are thus two points of variation. First the epenthetic [i] may undergo rounding before the following labial. For this we may compare the common rounding of /e/ to [o] before [m] as in [yomízo] 'I fill' from /γemízo/, and also the fact that when sporadic epenthesis affects a primary cluster the vowel typically selected is [i], unless [m] follows, in which case [u] is found. Thus /pníγo/ 'I drown' is occasionally found as [piníγo], /kapnós/ 'smoke' as [kapinós], while /tsakmáki/ 'lighter' appears as [t̑ˢakumáči] in Crete. Secondly the /s/ may go to [z]. We may account for this by supposing that in some dialects voice assimilation precedes, and in others follows, epenthesis:

(29*a*)	δikósmu
High vowel loss	δkósm
Voice assimilation	θkózm
Vowel epenthesis	**θkózim**

(29*b*)	δikósmu
High vowel loss	δkósm
Vowel epenthesis	δkósim
Voice assimilation	**θkósim**

Some dialects will now convert the final [im] to [um] by rounding. Other examples are [ufílusim] 'my friend' ὁ φίλος μου (Lesbos), [dzmánazum] 'of my mother' τῆς μάνας μου (Thessaly), [manaxózum] 'by myself' μοναχός μου (Thessaly). In Imbros the phenomenon apparently affected the word-medial [zm] of κόσμου 'world' (gen.), giving [kózim].

(ii) The third plural active verbal ending -ουν is replaced by [in] in Lesbos, Imbros and elsewhere in the area. The following are found in Ayassos (Lesbos):

φεύγουν	'they leave'	[févγ'in]
σμίγουν	'they meet'	[zmíyin]
βήχουν	'they cough'	[víx'in]
πλέκουν	'they knit'	[pléčin]
βάζουν	'they put'	[vázin]
θὰ πατήσουν	'they will step'	[θapatísin]
θέλουν	'they wish'	[θélin]
μπαίνουν	'they enter'	[bénin]
γράφουν	'they write'	[γráftin]

As was noted in 5·2 (see derivation (16)), while velar palatalization applies whenever its input conditions arise, dental palatalization does not follow high vowel loss. Thus while /s, z, n, l/ go to [š, ž, n′, l′] before primary /i/, epenthetic [i] does not palatalize them, although it does affect /k, x, γ/, as does softening ([plékin] > [plék′in] > [pléčin]). In certain dialects of Lesbos and Imbros this epenthesis is found in the second and third singular forms of verbs with a stem-final cluster of consonant + /n/: παίρνει 'he takes' > [périn′], ρίχνεις 'you throw' > [ríx′in′s].

(iii) In the dialect of Imbros epenthesis occurred before a final sonant in a cluster resulting from loss of final /i/ in nouns and adjectives. It is unclear from the only available account (Andriotis 1930) what the relation of epenthetic [i] to palatalization was, although primary /i/ palatalized all consonants (as in Thessaly). If we assume that, as in Lesbos, epenthetic [i] palatalized velars alone, then μαῦροι 'black', δάφνη 'laurel', τέχνη 'trade' would have developed thus:

(30)	mávri	δáfni	téxni
Palatalizations	mávr′i	δáfn′i	téxn′i
High vowel loss	mávr′	δáfn′	téxn′
Vowel epenthesis	**mávir′**	**δáfin′**	téxin′
Velar palatalization			**téx′in′**

In Lesbos this phenomenon appears to be limited to a small number of nouns in fricative + /n/ + /i/: /téxni/ > [téx′in′].

(*f*) *Buffer consonant epenthesis.* In the majority of northern dialects the secondary cluster [ml] converts to [mbl]; this goes by the general rule deleting initial nasals before a stop to [bl]. Thus we find the following northern forms for μουλάρι 'mule' and χαμόμηλο 'camomile':

(31)	mulári	xamómilo
High vowel loss	mlár	xamómlo
Raising		xamómlu
Buffer cons. epenthesis	mblár	**xamómblu**
Initial nasal deletion	**blár**	

In Thessaly and Macedonia [m], [n] and [l] (but not [r]) followed by a sibilant epenthesize a stop which agrees with the sibilant in voice and with the sonant in point of articulation. That is, [ms] > [mps], [ns] > [nts], [nz] > [ndz], [ls] > [lts], [lz] > [ldz]. In the case of [n′s] etc. it is not clear what degree of palatality, if any, attaches to the stop:[1]

[1] My own data for Velvendos and Thasos show palatal [l′], [n′] where an [i] has dropped but I can find no reference to this in the literature (Boundonas 1892, Tzartzanos 1909, Tombaidis 1967). I have the impression that [θélts] is sometimes heard, however, in which case we must posit palatality assimilation.

ἔλουσα	'I washed'	[éltsa]
ἔλουζα	'I was washing'	[éldza]
πουκάμισο	'shirt'	[pkámpsu]
τηγάνισα	'I fried'	[dγán'tsa]
τηγάνιζα	'I was frying'	[dγán'dza]
θέλεις	'you want'	[θél'ts]

As was pointed out earlier (see 4.7), when high vowel loss occurs, creating the clusters [mps], [nts], the rule of 'nasal deletion in clusters', which converts primary [mps] to [ps] (as in /élampse/ 'it shone' > [élapse]), has ceased to operate.

7.5 Secondary clusters: rules preceding high vowel loss

Having considered the rules which operate on both primary consonant clusters and those arising from the action of high vowel loss, we now review briefly the rules which affect only primary clusters, and which are therefore crucially ordered before high vowel loss. These are (*a*) postnasal voicing, (*b*) nasal assimilation, (*c*) degemination and (*d*) delateralization.

(*a*) *Postnasal voicing*. While stops are specified as voiced after nasals in primary clusters, this does not normally hold where an intervening vowel has been lost. Compare the derivations of μανιτάρι 'mushroom' and of πάντα 'always' in a typical northern dialect:

(32)	manitári	páNTa
Postnasal voicing		páNda
Nasal assimilation		**pánda**
Palatalization	man'itári	
High vowel loss	**man'tár**	

Compare also /aγénnitos/ 'unborn' > [ayén'tus], /vrómikos/ 'dirty' > [vrómkus], /mprómita/ 'prone' > [brómta], /fánika/ 'I appeared' > [fán'ka]. However in parts of Epirus postnasal voicing and nasal assimilation both affect at least the verbal formative -ηκ-. Thus /γínika/ 'I became' > [yíŋga], /fánika/ 'I appeared' > [fáŋga].

(*b*) *Nasal assimilation*. There is some evidence that a nasal may acquire the point of articulation of a following consonant with which high vowel loss has brought it into contact. Thus /anipsiós/ often goes via [an'pšós] to [ampšós] (see derivation (1) of this chapter), and [n′k], as we have just seen, may go to [ŋg]. However, complete nasal assimilation to a following continuant is never found. Thus /θa+kimiθó/ 'I shall sleep' goes to [θak′imθó], never to *[θak′iθθó], and /ániγa/ 'I was opening' yields [án′γa], never *[áγγa]. Similarly in dialects with [b, d, g] for /mp, nt, nk/ it is possible for high vowel loss to bring a nasal into contact with one of these voiced stops, but there is never any further nasal assimilation such as created the voiced stop in the first instance. This will be clear if we consider the form φαίνουνται 'they appear' in the dialect of Thrace:

(33)	fénuNTe
Postnasal voicing	fénuNde
Nasal assimilation	fénudde
Degemination	fénude
High vowel loss	fénde
Raising	**féndi**

While nasal assimilation operates before high vowel loss to convert [Nd] to [dd], it does not act on the [nd] which arises after high vowel loss. It is interesting to note that in a dialect of this type, which has nasal assimilation II and high vowel loss, it is possible to find at the phonetic level all three of [d], [nd], [nt] in intervocalic position, whereas no more than one of these is possible intervocalically in primary clusters, as in all Greek dialects. While in Thrace [d] will derive from /nt/, [nt] arises from, e.g., /nut/, and [nd] from /nunt/. Thus πέντε 'five' > [pédi], φαίν(ε)ται 'it appears' > [fénti], φαίνουνται 'they appear' > [féndi].[1]

(*c*) *Degemination.* Original geminate consonants have been simplified in all northern dialects. Those created by high vowel loss remain. Consider the northern forms θάλασσα 'sea' and μάσσησα 'I chewed':

(34)	θálassa	mássisa
Degemination	**θálasa**	másisa
High vowel loss		**mássa**

In dialects which do not convert [másisa] to [máysa] (see 3.6), we get a long sibilant similar to that heard in [θálassa] in 'geminating' dialects, and it is perhaps true of continuants in general that their pronunciation

[1] For syncope in φαίνεται see 7.2 (p. 191).

in primary geminate clusters in such dialects as lack a degemination rule is similar to that of secondary continuant geminate clusters in the north. Thus τὸ βουβάλι 'the buffalo' yields [tovvál'] in northern dialects, with a long [vv] similar to that of Dodecanesian [δévválli] δὲν βάλλει 'he does not put'. [nn] occurs commonly as a result of the loss of [u] in the third plural ending -ουν(ε): μπαίνουν 'they enter' becomes [bénn], μπαίνουνε [bénni]. As far as the stops are concerned, my limited observations suggest that when they occur geminate in northern dialects they are both released (while in geminating dialects we simply have a phonetically long stop, contrasting with a simple stop in the time which elapses between onset and release). Thus /ápu+pári/ 'whoever takes' is perhaps rather [áp.pár] in contrast to Cypriot [ap̄ári] 'horses'. Other examples are [pat.tá] 'slippers' from /patitá/, [turk'.k'i] 'Turkish' from /túrkiki/. Degemination does occur, however, in certain circumstances; thus the Thessalian for βουβάλι is reported as [vál'] and [péri] is found for /pipéri/ 'pepper' in Skiros. It may be that word-initial and word-final position are particularly vulnerable; μπαίνουν 'they enter', βάνουν 'they put' seem to become quite commonly [bén], [ván]. It may be noted, however, that these forms still remain distinct from their corresponding singulars μπαίνει, βάνει, 'he enters', 'he puts':

(35)	váni	vánun
Palatalization	ván'i	
High vowel loss	**ván'**	vánn
(*Final*) *degemination*		**ván**

An interesting point arises in connexion with expressions such as ὁ γαμπρός σου 'your brother-in-law'. In southern dialects outside the geminating group this is pronounced [oγambrósu] or [oγabrósu]; that is, degemination is applied in such dialects across word boundaries, but the final [u] prevents any loss of contrast between this and ὁ γαμπρός 'the brother-in-law'. In the north, where [u] is lost, it is apparently normal to conserve the contrast by restoring the geminate: [uγambróss].[1]

Another case in which degemination appears to be resisted in at least careful speech concerns second person singular punctual forms such as θὰ γράψῃς, 'you will write', θὰ κάτσῃς 'you will sit'. We would expect [θaγrápsis] to go by high vowel loss to [θaγrápss] and this by

[1] Contrast may also be maintained by extending to such constructions the epenthetic [i] found in [uγambrósim] ὁ γαμπρός μου, giving [uγambrósis] (Papadopoulos 1927: 21).

geminate reduction in clusters' to [θaγráps]. Now in many dialects this vill not result in any confusion with θὰ γράψῃ 'he will write', for ›alatalization will ensure that the latter remains distinct as [θaγrápš] ınd degemination of [θaγrápss] (< [θaγrápšs]?) might be expected. Fhat this is in fact the case is suggested by my observations on the point n Lesbos. In Ayassos, where /s/ is palatalized before /i/, we find θaγráps] 'you will write', [θaγrápš] 'he will write'; in Molivo in the ıorth of the island, in which [š] does not occur, we find [θaγrápss] versus θaγráps], although informants felt that this distinction might be lost in :areless speech. Epirot informants, who have [š] only for [sy], give a ›imilar account.

We found in our examination of velar palatalization (5.1) that the rule ›f degemination, in addition to removing the contrast between long and ›hort consonants, also eliminated that between [ts] and [t͡s], [tš] and [č] i.e. clusters and affricates). We have just seen that high vowel loss may 'estore the contrast between long and short consonants in general. Can t restore that between [ts] and [t͡s]? Apparently it can. In the dialect of ʟesbos the [ts] which arises by high vowel loss from the sequences tis], [θis], [δis], [ntis] is longer than the [t͡s] which reflects /ts/ (or in ›ome subdialects /k/ before front vowels).[1] Thus /rátsa/ 'race', /étsa/ so' are pronounced [rát͡sa], [ét͡sa], while for /pátisa/ 'I stepped', /méθisa/ I got drunk', /máδisa/ 'I plucked', /éntisa/ 'I dressed' we find [pátsa], métsa], [mátsa], [étsa] (this last forming a minimal pair with [ét͡sa]). To llustrate this point, let us take the common Lesbian forms of πάτησα I stepped', μάδησα 'I plucked', καπάκια 'lids', ράτσα 'race':

36)	pátisa	máδisa	kapákia	rátsa
ʒlide formation			kapákya	
ᴾalatalizations			kapák'ya	
ᴾostpalatal yod deletion			kapák'a	
Softening			kapáča	
Depalatalization			**kapát͡sa**	
Degemination				**rát͡sa**
Iigh vowel loss	**pátsa**	máδsa		
Voice assimilation		máθsa		
Manner dissimilation		**mátsa**		

Degemination here eliminates the distinction between the sequence

[1] I would imagine that all northern dialects contrast primary [t͡s] with secondary [ts], but I have no data on the subject, and I can find no reference to it in published studies.

/ts/ and the affricate arising from /k/ (while in N. Rhodes we find [kapátˢa]:[rátsa]). But it does not apply to the output of high vowel loss, thus ensuring that [pátsa], [mátsa] fail to rhyme with [rátˢa] by allowing them to retain a longer delay before the release of their stop elements. Primary /ps/ and /ks/, however, are not distinguishable from secondary clusters from /(N)pis/, /(N)kis/. Thus /δípsa/ 'thirst', /kolíNPisa/ 'I swam' rhyme as [δípsa], [kulípsa], and the [ks] of [áksa] from /ákusa/ 'I heard' sounds indistinguishable from that of [tˢítaksa] 'I looked' from /kítaksa/. This is precisely what one would expect, for [ps], [ks], in which the stop and fricative elements have different points of articulation, cannot constitute affricates and cannot therefore enter into oppositions of the type which set off an affricate [tˢ] against a cluster [ts].

(*d*) *Delateralization.* Delateralization does not affect secondary clusters. Thus ἔλουσα 'I washed' goes to [élsa] (or [éltsa]), never *[érsa].

Bibliography

Although there exists an excellent bibliography of books and articles on modern Greek written in languages other than Greek (see Swanson 1960), the considerable amount of work published in Greek itself has received no such attention. The following lists the main works consulted in the preparation of this book, but texts in dialect are included only where other published information is lacking.

The following abbreviations are used:

BNJ	*Byzantinisch-Neugriechische Jahrbücher* (Athens, Berlin 1920–)
BSLP	*Bulletin de la Société de Linguistique de Paris* (Paris 1869–)
Ἀρχ. Θρ. Θ.	Ἀρχεῖον τοῦ Θρᾳκικοῦ λαογραφικοῦ καὶ γλωσσικοῦ θησαυροῦ (Athens 1934–)
Ἐπ. Ἑτ. Β. Σ.	Ἐπετηρὶς Ἑταιρείας Βυζαντινῶν Σπουδῶν (Athens 1924–)
Λεξ. Ἀρχ.	Λεξικογραφικὸν Ἀρχεῖον τῆς μέσης καὶ νέας Ἑλληνικῆς (Athens 1914–)
Λεξ. Δελτ.	Λεξικογραφικὸν Δελτίον τῆς Ἀκαδημίας Ἀθηνῶν (Athens 1939–)

Alexandris, A. 1894. Περὶ τοῦ γλωσσικοῦ ἰδιώματος τῆς Κύμης. Athens.

Anagnostopoulos, G. P. 1915. Περὶ τοῦ δυναμικοῦ τονισμοῦ ἐν τῷ ἰδιώματι τοῦ Ζαγορίου. Thessaloniki.

1924. 'Περὶ τοῦ ρήματος ἐν τῇ ἐν Ἠπείρῳ λαλουμένῃ', Ἀθηνᾶ 36, 61–98.

1926. 'Περὶ τῆς ἐν Κρήτῃ ὁμιλουμένης καὶ ἰδίως περὶ τοῦ ἰδιώματος τῆς Ἁγίας Βαρβάρας καὶ περιχώρων', Ἀθηνᾶ 38, 139–93.

1930. 'Περὶ τοῦ ἰδιώματος τῆς Βουρμπιάνης καὶ τῶν περὶ αὐτὴν κωμῶν', *BNJ* 8, 448–61.

Andriotis, N. P. 1930. 'Περὶ τοῦ γλωσσικοῦ ἰδιώματος τῆς Ἴμβρου', Ἀθηνᾶ 42, 146–87.

1931. 'Περὶ τῆς ἀποβολῆς τῶν νόθων *i* καὶ *u* ἐν τῇ νέᾳ Ἑλληνικῇ', Ἀθηνᾶ 43, 171–85.

1933. 'Περὶ τῆς ἀρχῆς τῶν βορείων γλωσσικῶν ἰδιωμάτων τῆς νέας Ἑλληνικῆς', Ἐπ. Ἑτ. Β. Σ. 10, 340–52.

1939. 'De quelques faits phonétiques du dialecte moderne de Samothrace', Ἀρχ. Θρ. Θ. 6, 153–208.

1940. 'Πειραματικαὶ ἔρευναι περὶ τῆς φύσεως καὶ τῆς διαρκείας τῶν Νεοελληνικῶν φωνηέντων', Ἀθηνᾶ 50, 86–97.

1943. 'Zur vermeintlichen Nasalentwicklung im Neugriechischen', *BNJ* 17, 108–24.

1944. 'Τὰ ὅρια τῶν βορείων, ἡμιβορείων καὶ νοτίων Ἑλληνικῶν ἰδιωμάτων τῆς Θρᾴκης', Ἀρχ. Θρ. Θ. 10, 131–85.

1948. Τὸ γλωσσικὸ ἰδίωμα τῶν Φαράσων. Athens, Collection de l'Institut Français d'Athènes.

1961. Τὸ ἰδίωμα τοῦ Λιβισιοῦ τῆς Λυκίας. Athens, Κέντρο Μικρασιατικῶν Σπουδῶν.

1967. Ἐτυμολογικὸ λεξικὸ τῆς κοινῆς Νεοελληνικῆς (second edition). Thessaloniki, University of Thessaloniki.

Beaudouin, M. 1883. *Étude du dialecte chypriote moderne et médiéval*. Paris, Thorin.

Benardis, M. A. 1936. Ψήγματα Μεγαρικῶν. Megara.

Blanken, G. 1951. *Les Grecs de Cargèse* (*Corse*) I, *Partie linguistique*, Leiden, Sijthoff.

Bongas, E. 1964. Τὰ γλωσσικὰ ἰδιώματα τῆς Ἠπείρου (Βορείου, Κεντρικῆς καὶ Νοτίου) I. Ioannina.

Boundonas, E. 1892. Μελέτη περὶ τοῦ γλωσσικοῦ ἰδιώματος Βελβεντοῦ καὶ τῶν περιχώρων αὐτοῦ. Athens, N. G. Inglesis.

Boutouras, A. 1914. 'Über den irrationalen Nasal im Griechischen', *Glotta* 5, 170–90.

Chatzidakis, G. N. 1892. *Einleitung in die neugriechische Grammatik*. Leipzig, Breitkopf & Hartel.

1893. 'Περὶ τῆς Ἰκαρίας διαλέκτου', Εἰκοσιπενταετηρὶς Κ. Σ. Κόντου, 33–80 (reprinted in Μεσαιωνικὰ καὶ νέα Ἑλληνικά Β', 396–460 and translated as 'Ikarisches', *Indogermanische Forschungen* 2, 371–414).

1897. 'Zur Synizesis im Neugriechischen', *Kuhns Zeitschrift* 34, 108–25.

1905. Μεσαιωνικὰ καὶ νέα Ἑλληνικά, Α'. Athens.

1907. Μεσαιωνικὰ καὶ νέα Ἑλληνικά, Β'. Athens.

1912. Review of A. Boutouras, ''Ο ὑπολανθάνων νόμος τῆς ἐξασθενήσεως τοῦ ΟΥ εἰς Ι', Ἀθηνᾶ 24, 47–63.

1916. 'Περὶ τῆς Μεγαρικῆς διαλέκτου καὶ τῶν συγγενῶν αὐτῆς ἰδιωμάτων', Ἐπιστημονικὴ Ἐπετηρὶς Ἐθνικοῦ Πανεπιστημίου 12, 1–27 (his 'Zum neumegarischen Dialekt', *Indogermanische Forschungen* 36, 287–99, appears to be a translation of this item).

Dawkins, R. M. 1904. 'Notes from Carpathos, 8, The Dialect', *Annual of the British School at Athens* 10, 83–102.

1916. *Modern Greek in Asia Minor*. Cambridge.

1927. 'The Greek dialect of Cargese and its disappearance', *BNJ* 5, 371–9.

1940. 'The dialects of modern Greece', *Transactions of the Philological Society*, 1–38.

Deffner, M. 1871. *Neograeca*. Leipzig.

Dieterich, K. 1908. *Sprache und Volksüberlieferungen der Südlichen Sporaden*. Vienna, Holder.

Emellos, S. 1964. 'Γλωσσογεωγραφικά τινα ἐκ Νάξου', Ἀθηνᾶ 67, 33–46.

Foy, K. 1879. *Lautsystem der griechischen Vulgarsprache*. Leipzig, Teubner.

Georgakas, D. 1934. Θηραϊκὰ γλωσσικά Α', MS in archives of Ἱστορικὸν Λεξικόν, Athens.

1951. 'Dialektisches aus Rhodos. Ein Beitrag zu Lautlehre, Wortbildung, Flexion und Wortgeschichte', *Byzantinische Zeitschrift* 44, 143–57.

Georgiou, Ch. G. 1962. Τὸ γλωσσικὸ ἰδίωμα Γέρμα Καστορίας. Thessaloniki, Ἑταιρεία Μακεδονικῶν Σπουδῶν.

Giannoutsos, K. N. 1913. 'Συμβολὴ εἰς τὴν γραμματικὴν τοῦ Ζακυνθίου γλωσσικοῦ ἰδιώματος', Ἀθηνᾶ 25, 199–205.

Hamp, E. P. 1961. 'On so-called gemination in Greek', *Glotta* 39, 265–8.

Heisenberg, A. 1921. 'Die Liquida ρ im Dialekt von Samothrake', Ἀφιέρωμα εἰς Γ. Χατζιδάκιν. Athens.

Hoeg, C. 1925–6. *Les Sarakatsans*. Paris, Champion; Copenhagen.

Ἱστορικὸν Λεξικὸν τῆς Νέας Ἑλληνικῆς, edited by Academy of Athens, 1933– (has reached γάργαρος).

Kakridis, I. Th. 1930. 'Σημείωμα περὶ τσιτακισμοῦ', Ἑλληνικά 3, 261–2.

Kambouroglous, D. G. 1910. 'Στοιχεῖα Ἀθηναϊκοῦ γλωσσικοῦ ἰδιώματος', Δίπυλον 1, 16, 24, 32, 46–50.

Kanachis, A. Ph. 1915. 'Μεγαρικαὶ παραδόσεις καὶ ἱστορικαὶ διηγήσεις', Λαογραφία 5, 210–14.

Kapsomenos, S. G. 1939. ''Η λέξις φρέαρ εἰς τὴν μεταγενεστέραν καὶ νέαν Ἑλληνικήν', Λεξ. Δελτ. 1, 40–72.

Karanastasis, A. 1957. 'Τὸ ἰδίωμα τῆς Πάτμου', Δωδεκανησιακὸν Ἀρχεῖον 2, 206–17.

1958. 'Τὸ ἰδίωμα τῆς Ἀστυπαλαίας', Λεξ. Δελτ. 8, 59–144.

1963. ''Η φωνητικὴ τῶν ἰδιωμάτων τῆς νήσου Κῶ', Λεξ. Δελτ. 10.

Karatzas, S. 1940. 'Συμβολὴ εἰς τὴν Εὐβοϊκὴν διαλεκτολογίαν', Ἀφιέρωμα εἰς Κ. Ἄμαντον, 253–86. Athens.

1958. *L'origine des dialectes néo-grecs de l'Italie méridionale*. Paris, Collection de l'Inst. d'Études Byz. et Néo-helleniques de l'Univ. de Paris.

Kolia, A. 1933. 'Τὸ γλωσσικὸν ἰδίωμα τῆς Κέας', Ἀθηνᾶ 45, 262–85.

Kondosopoulos, N. G. 1959. 'Παρατηρήσεις εἰς τὴν διάλεκτον τῆς Δυτικῆς Κρήτης', Ἀθηνᾶ 63, 319–35.

1960. 'Περί τινων Κρητικῶν γλωσσικῶν φαινομένων', Ἀθηνᾶ 64, 209–20.

1958. 'Τὸ γλωσσικὸν ἰδίωμα τῆς Ἁλικαρνασσοῦ Μ. Ἀσίας', Ἀθηνᾶ 62, 248–319.

Kostakis, A. 1968. Τὸ γλωσσικὸ ἰδίωμα τῆς Σίλλης. Athens, Κέντρο Μικρασιατικῶν Σπουδῶν.

Koukoules, M. Ph. 1939. 'Περὶ ἀναπτύξεως ἐρρίνου ἐν τῇ νεωτέρᾳ Ἑλληνικῇ', Ἀθηνᾶ 49, 79–143.

Koukoules, Ph. 1908. Οἰνουντιακά. Chania.

1923. 'Γλωσσικὰ ἐκ Κύθνου', Λεξ. Ἀρχ. 6, 271–325.

Koutsilieris, A. 1963. ''Η ἐπένθεσις εἰς τὸ ἰδίωμα τῆς Μάνης', Λεξ. Δελτ. 9, 67–76.

Koutsoudas, A. 1962. *Verb morphology of modern Greek*. The Hague, Mouton.

Kretschmer, P. 1905. *Der heutige Lesbische dialekt, verglichen mit den übrigen nordgriechischen Mundarten*. Vienna, Holder.

Krumbacher, K. 1886. 'Ein irrationaler Spirant im Neugriechischen', *Sitzungsberichte der (philos.-philol. Klasse der) kon. bayerische Akademie der Wissenschaften* (1886), 359–444.

Kyriakidis, S. 1923. 'Γλωσσογεωγραφικὰ σημειώματα ἐκ δυτικῆς Θρᾴκης', Λεξ. Ἀρχ. 6, 362–87.

Lorendzatos, P. 1904. 'Ἀνάμειξις', Ἀθηνᾶ 16, 189–223.

Makrymichalos, S. I. 1961. Ἕνα πρόβλημα τῆς γραφομένης Νεοελληνικῆς. Athens (from Πρακτ. Ἀκαδημίας Ἀθηνῶν 35 (1960), 247–52).

Manesis, S. 1963. 'Τροπὴ τῶν συμφώνων ΤΣ καὶ ΤΖ εἰς Σ καὶ Ζ εἰς τὰ νότια ἰδιώματα τῆς νέας Ἑλληνικῆς', Λεξ. Δελτ. 10, 97–179.

Menardos, S. 1894. 'Φωνητικὴ τῆς διαλέκτου τῶν σημερινῶν Κυπρίων', Ἀθηνᾶ 6, 145–73.

Michailidis-Nouaros, M. 1936. Γλωσσικὰ καὶ λαογραφικὰ τῆς νήσου Κάσου. Athens, 'Phoni'.

1951. 'Περί τινων ἐνδιαφερόντων φαινομένων τοῦ γλωσσικοῦ ἰδιώματος τῆς Καρπάθου', Ἀθηνᾶ 55, 19–42.

Minotou, M. 1932. 'Παραμύθια ἀπὸ τὴ Ζάκυνθο', Λαογραφία 10, 381–448.

Mirambel, A. 1929. *Étude descriptive du parler maniote méridionale*. Paris, E. de Boccard.

1933. 'Le traitement du groupe nasale + occlusive dans les parlers néo-grecs et le problème de la classification', *BSLP* 34, 145–64.

1938. 'Notes de phonétique néo-hellénique. La contraction de *e* et de *i*', *BSLP* 39, 133–4.

1939*a*. 'Remarques de phonétique néo-grecque. La quantité vocalique', *BSLP* 40, 58–61.

1939*b*. 'Remarques de phonétique néo-grecque. Accent et diphthongaison', *BSLP* 40, 55–7.

1945. 'Le groupe *ts* en grec moderne', *BSLP* 42, 90–102.

1950. 'L'opposition de *ts* à *dz* en grec moderne', *BSLP* 46, 58–68.

1952. 'Du charactère des chuintantes dans certains parlers néo-helléniques', *BSLP* 48, 63–78.

1953*a*. 'Monosyllabes en grec moderne', *BSLP* 49, 52–66.

1953*b*. 'Les tendences actuelles de la dialectologie néo-hellénique', *Orbis* 2, 448–72.

Newton, B. E. 1967. 'The phonology of Cypriot Greek', *Lingua* 18, 384–411.

1968. 'Spontaneous gemination in Cypriot Greek', *Lingua* 20, 15–57.

1970. *Cypriot Greek: its phonology and inflections*. The Hague, Mouton.

Oikonomidis, D. V. 1952. 'Περὶ τοῦ γλωσσικοῦ ἰδιώματος Ἀπεράθου-Νάξου', Ἀθηνᾶ 56, 215–73.

Pandelidis, Ch. G. 1928. 'Προσθήκη καὶ ἀφαίρεσις τοῦ σ πρὸ συμφώνων ἐν τῇ ἀρχαίᾳ, μέσῃ καὶ νέᾳ Ἑλληνικῇ', *BNJ* 6, 401–31.

1929. Φωνητικὴ τῶν Νεοελληνικῶν ἰδιωμάτων Κύπρου Δωδεκανήσου καὶ Ἰκαρίας. Athens, P. D. Sakellarios.

Pangalos, G. E. 1955. Περὶ τοῦ γλωσσικοῦ ἰδιώματος τῆς Κρήτης, vol. 1. Athens, author.

Papachristodoulos, Ch. 1958. 'Μορφολογία τῶν Ροδίτικων ἰδιωμάτων', Δωδεκανησιακὸν 'Αρχεῖον 3, 9–106.
Papadopoulos, A. A. 1923. 'Περὶ τῶν γλωσσικῶν ἰδιωμάτων Ἄθω καὶ Χαλκιδικῆς', Λεξ. 'Αρχ. 6, 125–41.
1927. Γραμματικὴ τῶν βορείων ἰδιωμάτων τῆς νέας Ἑλληνικῆς γλώσσης. Athens, P. D. Sakellarios.
Patriarcheas, P. 1939. 'Περὶ ἐπενθέσεως ἐν τῇ Ἑλληνικῇ γλώσσῃ', 'Επετηρὶς Μεσαιωνικοῦ 'Αρχείου 1, 52.
Pernot, H. 1905. 'La dissimulation du Σ intervocalique dans les dialectes néo-grecs', *Revue des Études Grecs* 18, 253–76.
1907. *Phonétique des parlers de Chio*. Paris, author.
1912. 'Changement de *ts* en *k* à Delphes', *Revue de Phonétique* 2, 139–40.
1913. 'Phénomènes de contraction en grec moderne', *Revue de Phonétique* 3, 258–64.
Phavis, V. 1909. 'Γλωσσικαὶ ἐπιστάσεις ἀναφερόμεναι εἰς τὸ Σκύριον ἰδίωμα', Τεσσαρακονταετηρὶς Κ. Σ. Κόντου, 242–70. Athens.
1911. Γλωσσικαὶ ἐπισκέψεις ἀναφερόμεναι εἰς τὸ ἰδίωμα Αὐλωναρίου καὶ Κονιστρῶν. Athens.
1939. 'Μετάθεσις καὶ ἀντιμετάθεσις φθόγγων', Λεξ. Δελτ. 1, 89–142.
1948. 'Περὶ τοῦ λεγομένου ἀλόγου ἐνρίνου', 'Αθηνᾶ 52, 271–7.
1951. ''Ο δυναμικὸς τόνος τῆς βορείου Ἑλληνικῆς καὶ τὰ ἀποτελέσματα αὐτοῦ', 'Αθηνᾶ 55, 3–18.
Phoris, V. D. 1956.Τὸ ἀρσενικὸ ἄρθρο 'ι' στὰ βόρεια νεοελληνικὰ ἰδιώματα. Kozani, S. Theodosiadis.
1961. ''Η γραφὴ τῶν φθόγγων b, d, g τῆς νεοελληνικῆς', Παρνασσός (περίοδος δευτέρα) 3, 585–90.
Poulos, I. Ch. 1939. 'Γλωσσικὰ ἐκ Σίφνου', Λεξ. 'Αρχ. 1, 143–9.
Prombonas, I. 1963 ''Ο ροτακισμὸς καὶ ἡ ἰδιότυπος προφορὰ τοῦ φθόγγου λ εἰς τὸ γλωσσικὸν ἰδίωμα Φιλωτοῦ τῆς Νάξου', 'Επετηρὶς Ἑταιρείας Κυκλαδικῶν Μελετῶν 3, 504–32.
Psaltis, S. 1905. Θρᾳκικὰ ἢ μελέτη περὶ τοῦ γλωσσικοῦ ἰδιώματος τῆς πόλεως Σαράντα 'Εκκλησιῶν. Athens.
Sakellarios, A. 1890. Τὰ Κυπριακά, 1. Athens.
Salvanos, G. 1918. Μελέτη περὶ τοῦ γλωσσικοῦ ἰδιώματος τῶν ἐν Κερκύρᾳ 'Αργυράδων. Athens.
Seiler, H.-J. 1958. 'Das Problem der sogenannten Geminaten in den neugriechischen Dialekten mit besonderer Berücksichtigung einiger Dodekanes-Dialekte', *Glotta* 36, 209–34.
Settas, D. Ch. 1960. 'Γλῶσσα καὶ λαογραφία τῆς Εὐβοίας', 'Αρχεῖον Εὐβοϊκῶν Μελετῶν 7, 40–126.
Shipp, G. P. 1958. 'The phonology of modern Greek', *Glotta* 37, 233–60.
1963. 'Spirant+spirant in some dialects of modern Greek', *Glotta* 41, 147–56.
1965. 'ΙΟΥ=Υ in modern Greek', *Glotta* 43, 302–16.
Sigalas, A. 1949. 'Γλωσσικὰ ἰδιώματα καὶ ἐποικισμοὶ τῆς Νάξου', Ναξιακὸν 'Αρχεῖον 2, 192–216.

Skiadaresis, S. A. 1959. Κεφαλονίτικες Ἱστορίες, γραμμένες στὸ τοπικὸ γλωσσικὸ ἰδίωμα. Athens, Diphros.

Stamatelos, I. N. 1874. 'Φθογγογραφία τῆς ζώσης δημοτικῆς τῶν Ἑλλήνων γλώσσης', Ἑλληνικὸς Φιλολογικὸς Σύλλογος Κωνσταντινουπόλεως 8, 429–55.

Stavrianopoulos, N. 1948. 'Νεοελληνικὰ φωνητικά', Ἑλληνικὴ Δημιουργία 1, 719–21, 796–9.

Swanson, E. 1960. *Modern Greek Studies in the West*. New York, New York Public Library.

Thumb, A. 1891. 'Μελέτη περὶ τῆς σημερινῆς ἐν Αἰγίνῃ λαλουμένης διαλέκτου', Ἀθηνᾶ 3, 95–128.

1892. 'Der Dialekt von Amorgos', *Indogermanische Forschungen* 2, 64–125 (continued in 7, 1–37).

Tombaidis, D. E. 1967. Τὸ γλωσσικὸ ἰδίωμα τῆς Θάσου. Thessaloniki, University of Thessaloniki.

Triandaphyllidis, M. A. 1938. Νεοελληνικὴ Γραμματική. Ἱστορικὴ εἰσαγωγή. Athens, author.

(Ed.) 1941. Νεοελληνικὴ Γραμματική. Athens, Ὀργανισμὸς Ἐκδόσεως Σχολικῶν Βιβλίων.

Tsopanakis, A. G. 1940. *Essai sur la phonétique des parlers de Rhodes*. Athens, Texte und Forschungen zur Byzantinisch-Neugriechische Philologie.

1949. Τὸ ἰδίωμα τῆς Χάλκης. Rhodes, author.

1952. 'Τὸ Σιατιστικὸ ἰδίωμα', Μακεδονικά 2, 266–98.

Tzartzanos, A. 1909. Περὶ τῆς συγχρόνου Θεσσαλικῆς διαλέκτου. Athens.

1913. 'Περὶ τῶν ὁρίων τῆς ἀνομοιώσεως ἐν τῇ βορειοελληνικῇ', Ἀθηνᾶ 25, 65–77.

Vagiakakos, D. V. 1953. 'Συνίζησις καὶ ἐπένθεσις ἐν τῷ γλωσσικῷ ἰδιώματι τῆς Μέσα Μάνης', Λεξ. Δελτ. 6, 89–207.

Vogiatzidis, I. K. 1925. 'Κίμωλος, περὶ τῆς γλώσσης τῶν Κιμωλίων', Ἀθηνᾶ 37, 108–60.

Zevgolis, G. D. 1956. 'Γλωσσικὰ φαινόμενα ἀπὸ τὰ ἰδιώματα τῆς Νάξου', *Mélanges Merlier* 2, 7–25.

Index of Words

Page numbers in bold type indicate full derivations

General Index

Page numbers in bold type indicate main discussions